Voices of Change

Participatory Research in the
United States and Canada

Edited by
PETER PARK,
MARY BRYDON-MILLER,
BUDD HALL,
and TED JACKSON

Foreword by Paulo Freire

OISE Press

The Ontario Institute for Studies in Education

The Ontario Institute for Studies in Education has three prime functions: to conduct programs of graduate study in education, to undertake research in education, and to assist in the implementation of the findings of educational studies. The Institute is a college chartered by an Act of the Ontario Legislature in 1965. It is affiliated with the University of Toronto for graduate studies purposes.

The publications program of the Institute has been established to make available information and materials arising from studies in education, to foster the spirit of critical inquiry, and to provide a forum for the exchange of ideas about education. The opinions expressed should be viewed as those of the contributors.

©The Ontario Institute for Studies in Education 1993
252 Bloor Street West
Toronto, Ontario
M5S 1V6

Copyright Acknowledgment

The publisher, editors, and contributors are grateful for permission to use excerpts from the following:

J. Loxley, "The 'Great Northern' Plan," *Studies in Political Economy* 6:151–182 (1981).

Canadian Cataloguing in Publication Data

Main entry under title:

Voices of change

Includes bibliographical references and index.
ISBN 0–7744–0397–7

1. Social sciences—United States—Field work—
Case studies. 2. Social sciences—Canada—Field
work—Case studies. I. Park, Peter.

H62.5.C22V6 1993   300'.72071   C93–093233–1

ISBN: 0–7744–0397–7

1 2 3 4 5 MV 79 69 59 49 39

To dian marino
(1941–1993)

Founding member, Participatory Research Group
"for she is hearts, and wings, and bells"

Budd, Ted, Mary, and Peter

Contents

Foreword *by Paulo Freire*   ix

Acknowledgments   xi

Introduction
Budd Hall   xiii

1. What Is Participatory Research? A Theoretical and
   Methodological Perspective
   Peter Park   1

2. The Powerful, the Powerless, and the Experts:
   Knowledge Struggles in an Information Age
   John Gaventa   21

3. If You Can't Beat 'Em, Join 'Em: The Professionalization
   of Participatory Research
   Thomas W. Heaney   41

4. A Way of Working: Participatory Research and the
   Aboriginal Movement in Canada
   Ted Jackson   47

5. Putting Scientists in Their Place: Participatory Research
   in Environmental and Occupational Health
   Juliet Merrifield   65

Contents

6. The Appalachian Land Ownership Study: Research and Citizen Action in Appalachia

    Billy D. Horton   85

7. Participatory Research as Critical Theory: The North Bonneville, USA, Experience

    Donald E. Comstock and Russell Fox   103

8. Breaking Down Barriers: Accessibility Self-Advocacy in the Disabled Community

    Mary Brydon-Miller   125

9. Aboriginal Organizations in Canada: Integrating Participatory Research

    Marlene Brant Castellano   145

10. Challenges, Contradictions, and Celebrations: Attempting Participatory Research as a Doctoral Student

    Patricia Maguire   157

    Appendix: Contact Organizations   177

    Bibliography   179

    Index   193

    About the Editors and Contributors   201

Foreword

At a moment such as this in history, when people declare the impotence of action and the futility of values so insistently and with such certainty, when ideological discourse decrees freedom from ideology, the death of dreams, and of utopia, and when people justify adaptation to the world as it is, as opposed to the rebellious struggle to change it (through which we affirm ourselves and become creatures capable of decisiveness and rupture), it is appropriate and even necessary to celebrate the appearance of a book such as *Voices of Change*. The authors recognize the potential of women and men to know, to value, to establish limits, to choose, to imagine, to feel, to create, to decide, to formulate an action and direct it toward a goal, to refine and evaluate that action in order to humanize the world, reshaping or re-creating it. They recognize in the participatory research that they promote a politico-pedagogic instrument for moving women and men to such transformative action. The authors know very well that the silence and paralyzing fatalism in which millions of Marias and Pedros, Susans and Joes, and Fatimas and Mohammeds of the world find themselves as individuals and as social classes is not their fate or given destiny. Precisely because it is not destiny to wait for better days as they do—simply waiting expectantly, instead of expectantly struggling for better days—they can have hope and not the hopelessness of accommodation that fruitless waiting brings.

The authors of this book also know that participatory research is no enchanted magic wand that can be waved over the culture of silence, suddenly restoring the desperately needed voice that has been forbidden to rise and to be heard. They know very well that the silence is not a genetically or ontologically determined condition of these women and men but the expression of perverted social, economic, and political structures, which can be transformed. In the participatory research propounded here, the silenced are not just incidental to the curiosity of the researcher but are the masters of inquiry into the underlying causes of the events in their world. In this context research becomes a means of moving them beyond silence into a quest to proclaim the world.

This book deserves to be read.

Paulo Freire

Acknowledgments

The editors first want to pay tribute to all of the contributors to this book. The volume has been a long time in the making and we deeply appreciate the authors' patience, graciousness, and tenacity in staying with the project and seeing it through to the end. Thank you.

We would also like to thank Bronwyn Williams, whose help in copyediting a very rough manuscript was invaluable, and Christine Ransom, who took all of the various pieces and put them together on disk, beautifully. In addition, our thanks to Steve Rothanburg in Academic Computing and the staff of the New England College Library for their assistance in the final stages of production of the manuscript.

Several organizations have, in various ways, supported this project over the years as well. Among the most important of these are the International Council for Adult Education in Toronto; the Center for Community Education and Action in Northampton, Massachusetts; and New England College in Henniker, New Hampshire. The idea for the book was elaborated at a meeting on participatory research over a decade ago at the Highlander Research and Education Center in New Market, Tennessee; Highlander has, for all of us, been an important touchstone and inspiration.

We dedicate this book to the practitioners of participatory research in communities and workplaces, in popular organizations, and in universities and colleges throughout North America. Let us move forward together—acknowledging our diversity and deepening our solidarity.

Introduction

BUDD HALL ————————————————————

This book is a collection of articles which focus on the North American experience in participatory research. The authors have all been directly engaged in participatory research. Some of us have also been involved in theoretical elaboration and quite a few of us have been involved with creating or maintaining networks, centers, or other structures which support the work of many other organizations and individuals. I would submit that the fact that each of us has been engaged in practical, theoretical, and institutional aspects of the participatory research discourse gives our work its flavor.

The focus on the United States and Canada is deliberate and to some extent long overdue. As far as we know, the first uses of the term itself, *participatory research*, came from Tanzania in the early 1970s. And much of the early momentum behind participatory research came from groups in the dominated nations, who seized upon the ideas as part of the resistance to colonial or neocolonial research practices. There have been books on the African, Latin American, and Asian experience in participatory research (Kassam and Mustafa 1982; Tandon and Fernandes 1984; Vio Grossi et al. 1983), and some international collections (Hall et al. 1982), including a fine volume by Orlando Fals Borda and Anisur Rahman (1991). And the Bibliography in this book offers a great many other references.

We recognize that patterns of domination which produce violence, powerlessness, and poverty in the nations of the South are deeply present in both Canada and the United States. Advanced capitalist structures, racist institutions, and patriarchal patterning have created growing groups of diverse women and men who have fallen out of either the American, the Canadian, or the Quebecois(e) "dream." Deeply entrenched poverty; violence against women; toxic poisoning; homelessness; unemployment, par-

ticularly of young people of color; racism; ill health; and alcohol and substance abuse are "in your face" for all who have the courage to look.

We hope that this collection, which represents some of our ideas and an
incomplete record of some of our work over the past few years, will contribute to the larger discussions within and perhaps across community
groups, social movements, and universities. The experiences described in
this book are drawn from the work of women, First Nations, citizens of
Appalachia, rural activists in the state of Washington, disabled persons, and
health and environmental activists. We would like to contribute our discourse on participatory research in the United States and Canada to the
larger search for ways of working and ways of thinking which strengthen
democratic practice and the hope for genuinely transformative relationships.
We view our work as part of a larger discourse on emancipatory, liberatory,
or transformative practice, which includes such oppositional and resistance
interventions as critical pedagogy, popular education, integrative feminism,
antiracist or multicultural education, research as praxis, conjunctural analysis, integration movements of the differently abled, and Aboriginal science
or Native spirituality.

PARTICIPATORY RESEARCH

Participatory research has been expressed most generally as a process
which combines three activities: research, education, and action (Hall
1979b, 1981). The combination of these processes, which have commonly
been studied or examined as distinct and isolated practices, has generated
the most interest and debate in participatory research over the years. Various
authors have characterized the nature of participatory research as follows:

Participatory research attempts to present people as researchers themselves in pursuit
of answers to the questions of their daily struggle and survival. (Tandon 1988, 7)

[Participatory research] is a way for researchers and oppressed people to join in
solidarity to take collective action, both short and long term, for radical social
change. Locally determined and controlled action is a planned consequence of inquiry. (Maguire 1987, 29)

The final aims of this combination of liberating knowledge and political power
within a continuous process of life and work are: (1) to enable the oppressed groups
and classes to acquire sufficient creative and transforming leverage as expressed in
specific projects, acts and struggles; and (2) to produce and develop socio-political
thought processes with which popular bases can identify. (Fals Borda and Rahman
1991, 4)

Participatory research attempts to break down the distinction between the researchers and the researched, the subjects and objects of knowledge production by the
participation of the people-for-themselves in the process of gaining and creating
knowledge. In the process, research is seen not only as a process of creating knowl-

edge, but simultaneously, as education and development of consciousness, and of mobilization for action. (Gaventa 1988, 19)

An immediate objective . . . is to return to the people the legitimacy of the knowledge they are capable of producing through their own verification systems, as fully scientific, and the right to use this knowledge, but not be dictated by it—as a guide in their own action.(Rahman 1991, 15)

LINKS TO SOCIAL MOVEMENTS

Participatory research is most closely aligned to the natural processes of social movements. As groups begin to organize there is almost always a natural need to understand more about the situations which people are facing together. Some information can be obtained from sympathetic organizations and people who have access to what is needed, but very often groups have to dig in and pull the facts together themselves. These have been the settings where participatory research, over the years, has been most frequently found. In the 1990s we talk of alliances, coalitions, and working together more than we ever have. At the same time we also speak of building our alliances for change on authentic voices of people.

The International Council for Adult Education's Participatory Research Project of 1977, located in Toronto, Canada, was the means by which the initial sharing about methods and practices in North America occurred. The Toronto group played the role of the North American node of what eventually became a widespread and active international group, the Participatory Research Network. The principles which guided the work of the Toronto group meant that we would not participate in an international network without working from a rooted practice of our own in Canada or with others in the United States. We worked, to the best of our abilities, from within the context of what we then called "popular sectors". That meant establishing links with immigrant women workers in the factories, Latin Americans who had recently moved to Canada, First Nations' councils on Aboriginal issues, and literacy workers, and then sharing what we were learning with our colleagues in other parts of North America and, through the Participatory Research Network, the world. In Canada, one of the broadest-based coalitions which has used participatory research as a part of its day-to-day work is the Action-Canada Network, formerly called the Pro-Canada Network (Howlett 1989). Participatory research is also an important element in a bold experiment in citizen involvement in tax reform which is being undertaken by the 1992 New Democratic Party government in the Province of Ontario. Labor groups, peace and human rights groups, the homeless, and many other groups are taking an interest in how government income can be generated in a way which is fair.

In the United States, the work of the Highlander Center, among others, has led the way in the development and dissemination of information and

strategies for conducting participatory research projects among disempow-
ered groups there. A list of some current organizations and networks appears
at the end of this volume, which we hope may guide readers to the resources
and support they need to conduct such work in their own communities.

THE FEMINIST ADVANCE

We are deeply indebted to Patricia Maguire, one of the authors of this
collection, for her incisive, clear, and constructive revealing of what she has
called the "androcentric filter" in participatory research writing (Maguire
1987). Indeed, her book *Doing Participatory Research: A Feminist Approach* is the very best book on the subject that has yet been produced in
North America. Maguire has pointed out the distinct silence regarding gender and women in the participatory research discourse. The fact that so
many of the early writers were men undoubtedly influenced the discourse.

The earliest feminist influence in our work with the Participatory Research
Group was the work of Dorothy Smith. Dorothy and other women had
been active in Vancouver, British Columbia, in the Women's Research Project. Stories of the way in which she and others were working were important
contributions to our dialogue (Smith 1979, 1987).

It was not until the International Council for Adult Education conducted
a research project on women and adult education in 1980-81 (Gayfer and
Armstrong 1981) that I started to write about linkages between feminist
research and participatory research. I believe that we have much more to
do along these lines. Our framing of participatory research must explicitly
state that we are concerned with gender, class, race, ethnicity, sexual orientation, different abilities, relation to nature, and relation to other species.
Our early assumption that women were automatically included in terms
such as "the people" or "community" or the "oppressed" has rendered
them invisible in important ways.

Among the points which Maguire makes about feminist participatory
research are the following:

1. The critique is both of positivist and androcentric research paradigms.
2. Gender needs to be a central piece of the issues agenda.
3. Integrative feminism, which recognizes diversity, should be central to theoretical
   discussions on participatory research.
4. The role of gender needs to be taken into account in all phases of participatory
   research.
5. Feminist participatory research would give explicit attention to how women and
   men as groups benefit from a project.
6. Attention to gender-specific language use is critical.
7. Gender, culture, race, and class all figure into questions about the research team.

8. Gender should be a factor in considering evaluation.

9. Patriarchy is a system to be dismantled along with other systems of domination and oppression (Maguire 1987, 105-108).

The seminal work of Marja-Liisa Swantz (1982) during the 1960s and early 1970s in Tanzania was with women in coastal communities near Dar es Salaam. When she first started talking about research needing to benefit the community, what she had firmly in mind as the "community" were the many women with whom she had become friends and worked.

By contrast, the analytic frameworks which male researchers were using included "colonial-revolutionary," "oppressed-oppressor," "capitalist-socialist," "European (all mostly white expatriates)-Tanzanian," "rural-urban," and "bourgeois-peasant/workers."

THE QUESTION OF VOICE

Participatory research fundamentally is about the right to speak. It is about rural black women in southern co-ops talking about loans for planting. It is about Latinas in New York City building their own literacy curriculum. It is about citizens of Korean descent in the United States or Canada taking political action. It is about community groups in Ontario proposing tax reforms. It is about people of the First Nations researching land rights. It is about people in Quebec who do not read and write taking control of literacy programs. It is a process which supports the voices from the margins in speaking, analyzing, building alliances, and taking action.

The question of voice is disputed territory and one of the most important discussions many are now engaged in. It is not so simple. As bell hooks has said, "It is our responsibility collectively and individually to distinguish between mere speaking that is about self-aggrandizement, exploitation of the exotic 'other', and that coming to voice which is a gesture of resistance, an affirmation of struggle" (1988).

Participatory research argues for the articulation of points of view by the dominated or subordinated, whether from gender, race, ethnicity, or other structures of subordination. We believe that one's position in structures of subordination shapes one's ability to see the whole. We refer again to bell hooks:

Living as we did—on the edge—we developed a particular way of seeing reality. We looked both from the outside in and from the inside out. We focused our attention on the center as well as on the margin. We understood both. This mode of seeing reminded us of the existence of a whole universe, a main body made up of both margin and center. Our survival depended on an ongoing private acknowledgment that we were a necessary, vital part of that whole.

This sense of wholeness, impressed upon our consciousness by the structure of our daily lives, provided us an oppositional world view—a mode of seeing unknown to most of our oppressors, that sustained us, aided us in our struggle to transcend poverty and despair, strengthened our sense of self and our solidarity." (hooks 1984, ix)

PARTICIPATORY RESEARCH AS COUNTER-HEGEMONIC PRACTICE

Disturbed by the fact that the dissatisfaction of the working class in Italy produced fascism instead of a socialist transformation as in the Soviet Union after 1917, Antonio Gramsci undertook a lengthy study partially brought about by his own imprisonment. The translation of his work into English in the early 1970s allowed access to his complex and fascinating ideas (Gramsci 1971). Hegemony is one of the major concepts which helps us to understand our work. Gramsci noted that we are dominated by both coercion and consent. Laws exist which limit actions we can take in redressing structural imbalances, but in fact we most often "consent" to our own structures of domination. Dominated classes, genders, races, sexual orientations, or different ability groups internalize the views of what is "acceptable" resistance, "realistic" strategy, their own fault, or the natural order of things and thereby participate in the maintenance of hegemony.

But unlike orthodox Marxists, Gramsci saw a more dialectical relationship between consciousness and reality. While not accepting the idealist position that consciousness determines reality, Gramsci allowed that human agency does have a role and that the construction of counter-hegemonic patterns was what was needed. In the construction of counter-hegemonic ideas, there is a role for intellectuals, but new kinds of intellectuals, what he called "organic intellectuals," who are deeply rooted in and part of the class or other dominated structures that they come from. The knowledge produced in participatory research can be seen as part of the counter-hegemonic process.

CO-OPTATION AND THE ROLE OF THE UNIVERSITY

What is the role of the academy in participatory research? What has the academy done with participatory research? What is the status of the knowledge generated in a participatory research process? I have been very troubled by these questions over the years and cannot pretend to have a clear sense of the appropriate role for institutionalized university involvement in our work. Participatory research originated as a challenge to positivist research paradigms as carried out largely by university-based researchers. Our position has been that the center of the process needed to be in the margins, in the communities, with women, with people of color, and so forth. Our experience has been that it is very difficult to achieve this kind of process from a university base, hence the need for alternative structures such as networks and centers. But how do we reconcile this with the fact that most of the authors in this book have strong university affiliations, including myself?

I believe that many of us operate in situations of contradiction and self-conflict. Doubt may be one of our most identifiable common denominators. Doubt and humility may be one of the strongest contributions that our work collectively has to offer. If the research process is genuinely and organically situated in a community, workplace, or group which is experiencing domination, then we need not, I believe, be afraid that the knowledge which is being generated will be used for purposes that the community or group does not need or wish for. The difficulty arises because there are different uses of knowledge in the academy from those in community or workplace situations. According to the discourse of participatory research, knowledge generated—whether of localized application or larger theoretical value—is linked in some ways with shifts of power or structural changes. As we know, intentions do not always produce desired results, but those of us who have been working along these lines for a number of years share these assumptions. At a minimum we hope for a fuller understanding of the context and conditions within which we work or live.

Knowledge within the academy serves a variety of purposes. It is a commodity by which academics do far more than exchange ideas; it is the very means of exchange for the academic political economy. Tenure, promotion, peer recognition, research grants, and countless smaller codes of privilege are accorded through the adding up of articles, books, and papers in "refereed" journals and conferences. Academics in the marketplace of knowledge know that they must identify or become identified with streams of ideas which offer the possibility of publishing and dialogue within appropriate and recognized settings. Collaborative research or at least collaborative publishing is informally discouraged because of the difficulty in attributing authorship. Collaborative research with persons who are not academics by the standards of the academy is not common. And while academics in fact gain financially through accumulated publications of appropriate knowledge, community collaborators seldom benefit from such collaboration in financial terms. As can be seen, academics are under economic, job survival, or advancement pressures to produce in appropriate ways. And it is this structural pressure which plays havoc with academic engagement in the participatory research process. Is it not possible that in spite of one's personal history, in spite of ideological commitment, in spite of deep personal links with social movements or transformative processes, that the structural location of the academy as the preferred location for the organizing of knowledge will distort a participatory research process?

Does this mean that there is no role for university-based individuals to play in participatory research processes? I do not believe that. Patti Lather made a very comprehensive examination of the wide variety of postpositivist strategies with which university-based academics have been grappling (1986). I do, however, deeply believe that university or similarly accredited researchers are not necessary to a participatory research process. Participatory research ought to be a tool which social movements, activists, trade unionists, women on welfare, the homeless, or any similar groups use as part of a variety of strategies and methods for the conduct of their work. If they wish to invite a university-based group to become involved, they need to set up the conditions at the start and maintain control of the process if they wish to benefit as much as possible. My guess is that countless groups make use of processes which resemble participatory research every day without naming it or certainly without asking for outside validation of the knowledge which is produced.

Participatory research deserves to be taught in universities, and is increasingly being taught. The academic community deserves to discuss and challenge and be challenged by these and other ideas which raise questions of the role of knowledge and power. Adult educators, community workers, social workers, primary health care personnel, solidarity cooperators, cooperative movement workers, multicultural workers, teachers, and countless others who begin working after a university education deserve to study, read, and experience the ideas which make up participatory research.

Academics do not cease to become members of the community by going to work in a university. There are countless community issues, whether related to toxic dumping, homelessness, high dropout levels in local schools, or unfair taxation policies, which engage us all as citizens. Academics have some skills which can contribute to community action along with the skills of others in the community. Academics don't have to be "in charge" just because someone refers to a grass-roots knowledge-generating process as participatory research.

THE STRUCTURE OF THE BOOK

We begin with a theoretical overview by Peter Park which outlines an overall approach to understanding participatory research.

John Gaventa then explores knowledge, power, and the role of the expert. He shows us that citizens' groups and social movements need to be able to elaborate knowledge strategies for themselves which recognize the value of community-based research in order to counter the use of disempowering knowledge by "experts" that is often used by dominant structures.

Tom Heaney illustrates how the academic world appropriates concepts and ideas and often domesticates them.

The next two chapters of the book present overviews of the role of participatory research in two important movements, the movement toward self-determination and self-government among Aboriginal people of Canada and the environmental movement, particularly in the Appalachian region of the United States.

Ted Jackson writes of the extensive use of participatory research by the Aboriginal communities of Canada during the 1970s, 1980s, and 1990s.

Juliet Merrifield draws on her long involvement in the Appalachian environmental movement to describe the role of activist research in challenging the use of science by companies to try to bring citizens' groups in line.

In the subsequent chapters we present five case studies of participatory research in a variety of guises and settings.

Billy Horton writes from his involvement in the massive Appalachian Land Ownership Study, which involved citizens in six mountain states undertaking local courthouse research to determine who the absentee landlords of their mountains were and why they were paying so little tax. This case study has become one of the "classics" in the literature of participatory research.

Don Comstock and Russell Fox do two things: They link the intentions of participatory research with theoretical streams of thought outlined by the "Frankfurt School," particularly the work of Horkheimer and Adorno; and they use their involvement in the North Bonneville Hydroelectric Dam citizens' action to illustrate an approach to participatory research.

Mary Brydon-Miller describes her work with physically disabled people in her community in western Massachusetts and discusses the links between participatory research and the Independent Living Movement, an international self-advocacy movement of the disabled.

Marlene Brant Castellano describes the context for research and action within Aboriginal organizations in Canada. She illustrates participatory research principles in the experience of Inuit broadcasting in northern Canada.

In the final chapter Patricia Maguire describes in detail the struggles and joys of doing participatory research for a doctoral dissertation. Her project with a battered women's group shows how participatory research can begin to empower even the most disenfranchised, but she also warns us that these first steps are likely to be halting and that dependence and resistance continue to plague the process.

IN CLOSING

Our book does not try to smooth over differences. Disagreements and contradictions are visible and accepted. We are not attempting any kind of grand or totalizing theoretical magic. Our writing is varied in style and perspective, reflecting our different locations; but it comes from a shared vision of a world where justice is still to be struggled for, where the voices from the margins still need to be heard from more assertively, and where the creation of knowledge is an important site of resistance and struggle. Our work comes from the heart as well as the head. We are convinced that many of our readers will have similar experiences and ideas to share. We have benefited so much in the past from the dialogue and exchange of ideas of others. We hope that this book will open the discussion still further.

What Is Participatory Research? A Theoretical and Methodological Perspective

PETER PARK

Society evolves as a continual process of transformation in which people collectively inquire, evaluate, and take action to change their life circumstances. In postindustrial society, however, we are now witnessing a serious threat to this human right of mastery over our own fate. This threat is not new, but it is more systemic and more widespread than before the advent of the industrialized nation-state. Significant segments of society all over the globe are institutionally excluded from participating in the creation of their own world as thinking, feeling, and acting subjects.

Participatory research is emerging as a self-conscious way of empowering people to take effective action toward improving conditions in their lives. It is not new for people to raise questions about their conditions or to actively search for better ways of doing things for their own well-being and that of their community, but what we are proposing is to look at these actions as research that can be carried out as intellectual activity. Organized rational efforts with an explicitly liberatory goal are needed in order to counteract the disenfranchising features of modern society that are embedded in sociocultural structures.

But why call it research? Cast in the mold of research, the knowledge link between what is needed for a better life and what has to be done to attain it is made clearer; knowledge becomes a crucial element in enabling people once more to have a say in how they would like to see their world put together and run. Participatory research is a means of putting research capabilities in the hands of the deprived and disenfranchised people so that they can transform their lives for themselves.

I would like to present an overview of what participatory research aims to accomplish. In doing so, I will describe how a participatory research project is carried out in principle, articulating key moments in the process. Because this is a theoretical description concerned with identifying normative elements, no single project is expected to faithfully follow it in practice. It is at best a composite portrait. My purpose is not to give a step-by-step "how to" guide. Such an attempt would be unrewarding and futile anyway, since the nature of participatory research is interactive and dialectical. Nor is it to detail a model case study which would instruct by example. There are monographs and journal articles which describe concrete participatory research experiences (especially in the Third World, where participatory research has been most successfully used) and explain how it was done (Callaway 1981; Society for Participatory Research in Asia 1982; International Council for Adult Education (ICAE) 1988; Dubell et al. 1981). Other papers in this volume are also intended to provide examples that focus on the more developed parts of the world. What I plan to do, instead, is to have this literature as the backdrop and to articulate some basic features of participatory research in order to explain what it is.

GOALS

The explicit aim of participatory research is to bring about a more just society in which no groups or classes of people suffer from the deprivation of life's essentials, such as food, clothing, shelter, and health, and in which all enjoy basic human freedoms and dignity. The attainment of these goals—material well-being and sociopolitical entitlement—is indivisible. Participatory research chooses to work with the poor, who are, by definition, oppressed and powerless, but the aim is not to just alleviate or even eliminate their poverty while keeping them dependent and powerless. The solution it seeks is not one of paternalism, a kind of benevolent despotism that would provide while robbing its beneficiaries of their adulthood. Its aim is to help the downtrodden be self-reliant, self-assertive, and self-determinative, as well as self-sufficient.

Since much of the social injustice characteristic of modern society is structural in origin, participatory research acts as a catalytic intervention in social transformative processes. It assists organized activities of ordinary people who have little power and small means to come together and change the structural features of their social milieu in an effort to realize a fuller life and a more just society. In this process, individuals involved may often change by becoming more aware, more critical, more assertive, more creative, and more active. Participatory research aims to empower people, not only in the sense of being psychologically capacitated but also in the sense of being in-power politically to effect needed social change. This is a long-range objective which cannot be fully attained in one or two projects of a limited time span, but it is the horizon toward which the logic of participatory research pushes.

PRODUCING KNOWLEDGE

How does participatory research play this role? Participatory research provides a framework in which people seeking to overcome oppressive situations can come to understand the social forces in operation and gain strength in collective action. Its functions are both cognitive and transformative; it produces knowledge that is linked simultaneously with and intimately to social action. In participatory research, people who desire knowledge to bring about a more free and less oppressive world engage in the investigation of reality in order to get a better understanding of the problems and their root causes. The real investigator in this case is not the traditional researcher who, as a technical expert, relates to the "subjects" of research (questionnaire respondents, interviewees, participants in an experiment) only as objects of inquiry, the source of data. Rather it is the ordinary people with problems to solve who form a partnership with the researcher, for learning about the dimensions of oppression, the structural contradictions, and transformative potentials open to collective action. This is the "participatory" part of participatory research.

It is easy to see from this that participatory research work is profoundly educational. Education here is to be understood not in the sense of the didactic transmission of knowledge, characteristic of much of classroom teaching, but rather in the sense of learning by searching, or researching. The result of this kind of activity is living knowledge that gets translated directly into action, because it is created with this concrete appropriation in mind. From the point of view of pedagogic theory, participatory research captures the ideal of goal-oriented, experiential learning, and transformative pedagogy (Dewey 1963; Freire 1970c). This kind of learning, of course, also takes place in traditional research, but there only the researcher, the expert, learns, while the people who make the learning possible are left empty-handed.

The path from knowledge generation to knowledge utilization is direct in participatory research, since the same actors are involved in both activities. There is no middle-person scientist/researcher. In the traditional social science research model, especially of the "pure" type, knowledge that the researcher produces is deposited in the scientific storehouse from which, supposedly, policymakers, corporate executives, and other would-be social engineers draw requisite techniques for administering to, managing, and manipulating unwitting and pacified populations. Those who mete out these ministrations may have the welfare of the people in mind; they may even succeed in bestowing some benefits on their target populations. But this does not change the fact that the people so treated do not partake in the production of knowledge concerning their own lives and are thus left in a dependent position. Participatory research restructures this relationship between knowing and doing, and puts the people in charge of both the production and the utilization of knowledge.

WHAT KINDS OF KNOWLEDGE

We live in an era in which we tend to equate research with only one kind of knowledge, that which is associated with natural sciences. This ethos also permeates the methodological discussions of participatory research. In reporting and discussing participatory research projects, the emphasis is almost invariably on the technical dimension of the problem being addressed. Because the immediate problems are technological in nature, the solutions are also framed in narrowly technical terms. The aim in these projects is to produce appropriate technologies with the participation of their users. In these kinds of projects, people involved bring their indigenous knowledge to the problem, and collectively arrive at a new solution with the help of the facilitating researcher. The process is participatory and the knowledge produced is technical in nature.

The social and political significance of participatory research, however, does not lie only in the production of narrowly technical knowledge for the control of the physical and social realities. Theorists and practitioners of participatory research have used terms like *empowerment, critical consciousness, transformation, conscientization, dialogue, social action,* and similar terms, as well as *participation,* to characterize different aspects of participatory research. The discourse using this terminology clearly signals social and political, and even psychological, dimensions of participatory research that cannot be adequately accounted for within the context of producing control-oriented knowledge. Empowerment, for example, is an avowed goal of participatory research, but it does not result from technical knowledge alone. Empowerment is realized through the experience of engaging in collective social actions.

It is useful at this point to present a theory of knowledge that allows us to see the efficacy of participatory research more broadly than in terms of the natural science framework. Habermas's critical theory (Habermas 1972) postulates three kinds of knowledge underlying human conduct in society. I shall call these *instrumental, interactive*, and *critical* knowledge, somewhat departing from Habermas's terminology. According to this theory, each of these three kinds of knowledge goes into the human cognitive constitution, making it possible for social beings to relate to the world and one another, and to act as a group collectively. In this scheme, all three branches of knowledge should be called science, although this term has been appropriated by positivists, especially in the English-speaking countries, to refer exclusively to instrumental knowledge.

Instrumental Knowledge

Instrumental knowledge, the prototype of which is the natural sciences, has developed in the West since the Renaissance. It is useful for controlling the physical and social environment in the sense of both passively adapting to it and more actively manipulating it to bring about desired changes. Instrumental knowledge derives its ability to control external events from the structure of its explanatory theories, which are made up of a series of equations essentially expressing causal relationships (Habermas 1972; Fay 1975).

Natural sciences produce knowledge under the methodological dictate that strictly externalizes the object of inquiry and separates it from the investigating subject. (This is no longer strictly true in modern physics, in which the observer-event interaction is explicitly recognized. But social sciences, which are modeled after the nineteenth-century natural sciences, quixotically still insist on the researcher-researched dualism.) The claim to the value-neutral status, which apologists of natural sciences assert as an unreflected item of dogma, is largely based on this methodological posture. When applied to human affairs, as in its reincarnation in social sciences, this methodological stance takes on a decidedly antisocial character. For one thing, it entails a categorical distinction between the researcher and the researched, the one acting as active subject and the other as passive object that is acted upon. This is obviously an ethical issue, since it puts the scientists in the superordinate position vis-à-vis the lay people acting as informants. The ethical implication is even more serious when it comes to the application of such knowledge, which turns people into objects of control. Furthermore, on methodological grounds, it is questionable whether instrumental knowledge that is produced under antisocial conditions can fulfill its promise and be useful for control purposes of a social kind, even for the limited ends of adapting to existing external conditions. This is purely a question of validity, leaving aside the issue of manipulation. Knowledge produced by traditional social sciences ignores the fact that humans gain social knowledge through interaction as co-members of society, and it is therefore not likely to be valid in the instrumental sense of being practically useful. This undoubtedly is the reason why social sciences have been dismally unsuccessful in predicting and controlling social phenomena since their inauguration over a hundred and fifty years ago.

We should not dismiss the importance of instrumental social knowledge. We must have knowledge of how the social world is structured and operates and how people feel, think, behave, and relate to one another in order to create conditions for a good society. The research methods pursued by traditional social sciences, however, cannot accomplish this because they fail to recognize the special character of human knowledge (Winch 1958; Taylor 1987).

Interactive Knowledge

In living with other human beings we come to know them in an interactive sense. This knowledge does not derive from analysis of data about other human beings but from sharing a life-world together—speaking with one another and exchanging actions against the background of common experience, tradition, history, and culture.

Interactive knowledge makes human community possible. Without a common stock of knowledge of this kind, it is not possible to form social solidarity capable of mutual support and common action. Conversely, it is in community that we come to understand other human beings. It is by sharing, on a daily basis, mundane routines, lofty visions, joys, anguish, conflicts, accords, struggles, and successes, that we come to know one another as feeling beings. It is through talking to one another and doing things together that we get connected, and this connectedness gives us a kind of knowledge that is different from control-minded knowledge.

While instrumental knowledge requires separateness and externalization, interactive knowledge is predicated on connectedness and inclusion. Interactive knowledge is accomplished essentially through conversations in which we talk with personal feelings and listen with interest and supportiveness.

The women's movement that was grounded in the support groups of the 1960s attests to the power, as well as the insight, issued from collective activities in which sharing personal stories dominates the proceedings. From this experience emerges a feminist epistemology that shows the one-sidedness of instrumental knowledge of the masculine cast, and asserts the indispensability of the complementary interactive knowledge (Gergen 1988). This is the practical and theoretical contribution of the feminist movement to participatory research, which aims to practice a holistic science by embracing interactive knowledge beyond the instrumental.

Critical Knowledge

There is a kind of knowledge that comes from reflection and action, which makes it possible to deliberate questions of what is right and just. Although this kind of knowledge is an essential aspect of human life, today its pursuit is relegated to a status of secondary—perhaps trivial—importance in the intellectual order of things. In this positivistic age, scientific analysis is considered inapplicable to questions of values. As a consequence, research activities are thought to be appropriate only when directed at solving technical problems relating to practical ends that are set by others through a process not involving popular participation; rational investigation is not considered relevant when it is aimed at delving into the rationality of the ends themselves. For example, conventional social sciences can research the best ways of increasing participation in New England–style town meetings, but they are incapable of elucidating the rational grounds for democracy. This situation leaves in an intellectual and moral vacuum issues having to do with what social goals should be pursued. At the same time, ostensibly value-neutral social sciences tend to reify the status quo as the embodiment of the natural order of things. This has the effect of obscuring historically produced social forces that obstruct the realization of a righteous society. In these ways, the narrow view of science embodied in positivism acts as an ideology that prevents people from asking rational questions about oppressive forces standing in the way of asserting their rights to a materially and socially satisfactory life.

Critical investigation helps people to look at problems about the reality surrounding them in the light of what they wish to achieve as self-reliant and self-determining social beings. Research, in this case, has to do with questions concerning the life chances we are entitled to as members of a society, as well as with the comprehension of the social obstacles standing more immediately in the way of achieving these goals. Urgent social problems require uncovering the structural causes of social conditions that affect segments of a population, such as adult illiteracy, chronic poverty in rural areas, and pollution of air and water. They also require the raising of questions about public policy at all levels of society, such as environmental policy, defense research in biological warfare, tax processes, local zoning ordinances, and others which carry potential for affecting our lives now and at some future date. Discussions concerning these issues, if pursued with the seriousness that the task demands, should naturally lead to questions of what is right for the common good. At this point we reach the limits of technical advice proffered by experts, since these questions are no longer instrumental in nature. Such questions are also too fundamental to be left to experts in a free society and must be decided in a public forum with the full participation of the citizenry.

The reality, however, is that the present-day political economy of knowledge production and utilization results in the monopolization of expert knowledge by specialists (Hall 1982). Those who command expert knowledge also dominate any debate concerning issues of public interest because the noninitiated are unable to enter the scientized universe of discourse, as they lack the technical terminology and specialized language of argumentation (Habermas 1979a).

Critical examination means not only that people come to grasp the causes of their miseries, which can be dealt with instrumentally. But by reflecting on these causes as being historically rooted in human actions, they also come to realize that things do not have to remain the way they are and that they can engage in actions to transform the reality. Critique thus turns into will to action and action itself.

As action emerges from critical knowledge, so does knowledge issue from action. Critical consciousness is raised not by analyzing the problematic situation alone, but by engaging in actions in order to transform the situation. This is the meaning of *conscientization*, which Paulo Freire has helped popularize (Freire 1970a). It refers to the cycle of reflection-action-reflection through which both consciousness and conscience develop. The poor and the disenfranchised come to know the naked face of aggression that is directed at them by dominant forces through struggling against it. In the same way, warriors come to know their enemies fully only in combat. Reality is revealed to us in full clarity when we try to change it (Rahman 1982; Bronfenbrenner 1972).

THE RESEARCH PROCESS

Participatory research begins with a problem. The situations in which participatory research has been used include the following examples: peasants' struggles for land vis-à-vis the big landed interests and the state in the Philippines and in India (Callaway 1981; Society for Participatory Research in Asia 1982); women's efforts to free themselves from economic exploitation, sexual harassment, and domestic violence in India and the United States (Callaway 1981); immigrants' need to organize themselves for sociocultural solidarity and action in Canada and the United States (Callaway 1981; Park 1978); addressing the inequitable land ownership pattern producing rural poverty in the United States (Callaway 1981; ICAE 1981); safeguarding the rights of the pavement dwellers (squatters) and slum residents in India (Society for Promotion of Area Resource Centers 1988); dealing with the deplorable health conditions of the poor in Brazil (Equipe das Comunidades de Basee de Agentes da Diocese de Goias); and popular participation in the sociocultural transformations accompanying the revolution in Nicaragua (Fals Borda 1987).

The Researcher

In these instances, the sense of the problem arises from the people who are affected by it and whose interest demands that it be solved. And the problem addressed is social in nature and calls for a collective solution; otherwise, there is no participatory exigency. This sense of the problem may not always be externalized as a consensually derived and objectified target of attack in the community, although there may be suffering, a sense of malaise and frustration, and anger. For this reason, the situation characteristically requires outside intervention in the guise of a researcher, or a team of researchers, to help formulate an identifiable problem to be tackled.

The researcher participates in the struggle of the people. This is the other side of participation in this kind of work. He or she becomes a member of the research team with a specific role to play. The researcher works with the community to help turn its felt but unarticulated problem into an identifiable topic of collective investigation.

The Beginning

In practice the participatory research process of intervention is initiated by an external change agent, such as a community development agency, an extension service of a university, or a church group. A researcher or a team of researchers working with this intervenor enters the community to stimulate the community's interest in participating in the research activity. The members of the community are of course aware of the problems that are being addressed in this manner, since they experience these problems, such as toxic waste, inadequate housing, unemployment, drugs and crime in the neighborhood, and so forth. But it takes the initiative of individuals, or more typically community or development agencies concerned with the welfare of the community in question, to insert themselves for the purpose of mobilizing and organizing the community for investigation and action. It appeals to our democratic idealism to think that the oppressed can spontaneously get together to analyze their own situation in order to take effective collective actions to improve their lot. Perhaps they should do this as a moral and political imperative. But in reality this is not likely to happen, since their very powerlessness prevents them from organizing themselves or doing research. They usually require an organizing force that will act as the focal point around which they can rally and deal with their problem. This is the role that the researcher plays in participatory research.

The researcher who undertakes participatory research must know the community personally as well as scientifically before starting the participatory research work. This means that he or she must learn everything that can be found out about the community and its members both historically and sociologically through available records, interviews, observation, and participation in the life of the community (Freire 1970c; Freire 1982). In the ideal situation, the researcher already lives in the community and partakes in its affairs. This preliminary phase then takes place naturally and with ease. But more typically, the researcher is not an established member of the community or even known in the community. For this reason, he or she needs to be introduced and become accepted as a participatory researcher. It is also during this phase that the researcher explains the purpose of the project and begins to identify and solicit help from key individuals who would play an active role in the execution of the project. The organizational aspect of participatory research actually begins at this moment.

People's Participation

The most obvious aspect of participatory research that distinguishes it from the more traditional research mode is the practice of the people in the community taking part in the research process as active members. This means that, to begin with, the community decides how to formulate the problem to be investigated, what information should be sought, what methods should be used, what concrete procedures should be taken, how the data should be analyzed, what to do with the findings, and what action should be taken. In this process, the researcher essentially acts as a discussion organizer and facilitator and as a technical resource person.

At the beginning of a project, the researcher, together with the collaborating organization, contacts members of the community and activates their interest in the problem to be dealt with by action-driven research and helps to organize community meetings where the relevant research issues will be discussed. This initial organizing phase of the project can require considerable time and effort. Its success will depend on how acutely the problem is felt by the community and how motivated its members are to do something about it. There are situations where the community is fed up with its miseries and is ready to do something about them, in which case the researcher's role as an organizer is secondary to that of a facilitator. On the other hand, to the extent that the problem is submerged under noncritical consciousness, for example fatalistic resignation, and the people are not used to speaking out and taking actions to better their lot, it will be harder for the researcher to find and mobilize interested people to join the project.

This situation will demand interpersonal and political skills of the researcher as an organizer. Although typically the researcher is part of a team that includes the sponsoring social change agents as well as other researchers, it is well to recognize the community organizing efforts that he or she must engage in. This pre-data gathering phase of participatory research has its analogue in traditional field research, in which the researcher establishes rapport with the community for cooperation in the research process. But of course its purpose is different in that participatory research puts community members in the role of active researchers, not merely acquiescing providers of information.

Once community members begin to get together to discuss their collective problem, the researcher participates in these meetings to help formulate the problem in a manner conducive to investigation, making use of the community knowledge that he or she developed earlier. From this point on, the researcher acts more as a resource person than an organizer, this latter function being better carried out by community people with organizational skills and resources. It is an objective of participatory research to provide the catalyst for bringing forth leadership potential in the community in this manner.

Problem Formulation

One of the first tasks of research is to define the problem to be investigated, by defining its scope and sorting out the dimensions to be explored. The first thing that the group may wish to investigate is the magnitude and the contours of a problem. For example, how many and who in the community are suffering from inadequate health care and how does the consequent suffering manifest itself?

It might appear that people suffering from poverty and its accompanying ills should be able to readily identify their problems and discuss them in order to deal with them. In reality, however, there are factors which make it difficult for oppressed people to discuss their problems in public. For one thing, they may not be used to speaking in public. In some cases they may be intimidated from speaking out about their suffering by fear of offending the powerful who are implicated. They may even feel ashamed to admit their problems, feeling somehow responsible for their conditions. They may even deny their suffering, sweeping it under the rug out of a sense of fatalism. Even if they feel their deprivation and oppression acutely, they may not be able to delineate and tag what lies at the core of their problems, not knowing where to begin the process of naming the problem complex.

Research Design and Methods

The next step in the research operation is for community participants in the project to decide on the design of research having to do with how data are to be gathered and eventually analyzed. Here the researcher plays an important role of presenting to the group methodological options that can be considered within the available personnel and material resources of the community and explaining their logic, efficacy, and limitations. The extent to which the problem is to be elaborated will inform the decision-making process at this stage. But, conversely, the methodological shortcomings and limited accessibility to available techniques will also shape the contours of the problem to be investigated.

This aspect of participatory research serves to demystify research methodology and put it in the hands of the people so that they can use it as a tool of empowerment. This is a long-range goal of participatory research toward which the researcher moves the process by sharing his or her knowledge and skills with the groups. In this capacity, he or she works essentially as a workshop facilitator. To the extent that the researcher is successful in this, the capacity to investigate community problems scientifically becomes a permanent feature of the community that can be used over and over again without having to rely on experts.

Logically, the next step in the research process should be to map out the data to be gathered and to work out the mechanics of achieving this goal.

It should then proceed to the actual business of gathering data, which is then analyzed and reported. In every step the community people are to be involved actively. In reality, however, questions having to do with data analysis arise early in the game. What and how data are to be gathered are questions that cannot be answered independently of how they are to be analyzed in the end. And the mode of analysis, in turn, depends on the purpose which the resulting findings will serve. For example, if statistical analysis of quantitative data is to be performed, then information relying solely on group discussions will not be very useful. For this reason, the methodological discussion at the beginning stages of participatory research should attend to the question of analysis as well.

Participatory research, in theory, draws upon all available social science research methods. However, because participatory research insists that the people with a problem carry out the investigation themselves, it eschews certain techniques that dictate the separation of the subject from the object of research, as researcher and researched. This means that certain social research techniques, such as social psychological experimentation where the experimental "subjects" are kept ignorant of the purpose of the study, are excluded on principle. Even techniques such as interviews and questionnaires may be modified to allow greater interaction between the questioner and the questioned. Methods that are beyond the technical and material re-sources of the people involved in the research are, of course, also excluded. Field observation, archival and library research, and historical investigation using documents and personal history, as well as questionnaires and inter-views, have been used in participatory research. But the last two, especially interviews, are probably the most widely relied upon, although it must be understood that these operations are used as a vehicle of dialogue.

Dialogue

If there is any one methodological feature that distinguishes participatory research from other social research, it is dialogue. Through dialogue people come together and participate in all crucial aspects of investigation and collective action. This cannot be achieved through the exercise of merely answering questions in a conventional questionnaire or a formalized inter-view, because these techniques do not allow the respondent to speak in a full voice. Problems facing the poor and the powerless must be understood in the hearts and the guts as well as in the heads, and the people with the problems must talk to each other as whole persons with feelings and com-mitment as well as facts. As a tool of research, dialogue produces not just factual knowledge but also interpersonal and critical knowledge, which defines humans as autonomous social beings. This is an essential reason for the people's participation in research. It is not just so they can reveal private facts that are hidden from others but really so they may know themselves better as individuals and as a community.

Data Gathering and Analysis

Aside from dialogues, which by definition are participatory, ordinary people in participatory research engage in activities that, in conventional research, are traditionally reserved for technically trained personnel. These include making up questionnaires and interview schedules, and actually collecting data using these instruments.

The purpose of the formalized procedures for data gathering in traditional quantitative research is to convert the responses into measures of variables. Accordingly, the researchers operate under the dictate of reliability, which requires as an ideal that the data-gathering instrument, consisting of the questions and the questioner, be standardized across all respondents. Under this standardization requirement, the questioner is instructed to administer the questions under uniform conditions, to keep social distance from the respondent, to avoid ad hoc amplifications on the data gathering instrument, and so forth. In participatory research, by contrast, the assumption is that validity of data depends on the subjects fully empathizing with the purpose of the study, thoroughly understanding the intent of the questions, and wanting to give the needed information the best way they know how. For this reason, in administering a questionnaire or giving an interview, the indigenous investigators are expected to explain to the respondents the nature of the data being collected to the best of their understanding.

This task requires training, at least to the extent of helping inexperienced people feel comfortable with and competent in the role of asking questions for information. In participatory research, everybody connected with the project is informed of the intent and the logic of the questions, and is in a position to share this knowledge with others. Nevertheless, they will require, if not training in the art of interviewing, a collective orientation to make sure that the objective of the questions involved is apprehended and correctly conveyed to the respondents and that the essence of the answers received is accurately interpreted and recorded. This need is especially great in the case of interviews with open-ended questions.

In participatory research data are analyzed with the intention of discovering the dimensions of the problem under investigation and of coming up with a guide to collective action. For this purpose, both quantitative and qualitative approaches can be used. In either case, the participation of the people whose problem is being addressed is of critical importance in participatory research, and this consideration limits the type of analysis possible.

Simple descriptive statistics such as the mean, the median, percentages, and ratios often eloquently depict the phenomenon under investigation.

These measures are within easy grasp of ordinary people and are often used in participatory research. Also, simple two-way tabulations, capable of telling powerful stories of association that point to possible causal relationships, are useful and appropriate. People with modest facility in simple arithmetic can participate in the calculation of these measures to good effect. Statistical techniques more complicated than these in logic and technical skills, if needed, will require the assistance of outside experts for both execution and interpretation and do not fit well with the exigencies of participatory research. Even if there are members of the research team who are capable of carrying out these kinds of analysis, care should be taken not to create specialist roles whose functions are to carry out operations which the rank and file cannot fully understand. This kind of division of labor tends to re-create relationships of dependence and powerlessness.

Qualitative data require different analytical approaches, which are in some ways more capable of uncovering the depth and the nuances of the problem than quantitative methods. In qualitative analysis, data are not abstracted into summary statistics, but allowed to speak for themselves as a manifestation of different aspects of the problem. They reveal the connections inherent in the stories that people tell, not through statistical manipulation, but through the pattern of events that cohere. The resulting insights are indispensable complements to what numbers depict.

Qualitative research techniques, however, are not well systematized as standard operational procedures. The reason for this is probably that what transpires in qualitative data analysis is holistic, defying categorical treatment. A more holistic approach is also closely allied to the way people come to understand a situation in everyday life on the basis of what they hear, see, and share. The solitary qualitative researcher in the social science tradition—the ethnographer, the participant observer—follows this path in arriving at his or her findings. The skills involved are more those of an art than of a method. The same thing is true in participatory research, except that people as a community arrive at insights which are both interactive and critical, as well as instrumental.

Utilization of Results

To the extent that participatory research is a form of interactive and critical action in itself, it is artificial to separate the utilization from the generation of knowledge. In the instrumental dimension, however, it does make sense to speak of utilizing the results of research as in conventional social research.

Facts emerging from the investigation of a problem can be useful in organizing community actions to be taken, shaping social policies, and implementing social change measures. The research process reaches a kind of crystallization point when the findings of the investigation are brought together in a systematic fashion at the end. This helps reveal the extent and the depth of the problem by turning individual miseries into a social mosaic, thereby helping to discern the pattern of social causation.

Identifying concrete measures to be taken is also a result of the findings, whether they be installing appropriate technologies or engaging in political processes to influence social policies. It is, however, misleading to think of research as always leading stepwise to practical applications. Often in participatory research, what is investigated is not a theory to be applied but rather the ways of implementing a practical idea, such as installing a fuel-saving stove for communal use (Swantz and Vainio-Mattila 1988), starting a women's cooperative (Cheong 1981), or establishing squatters' rights and eventually securing housing for pavement dwellers (Society for Promotion of Area Resource Centers 1988). In these instances, action takes place concurrently with research activities, illustrating how knowledge and practice are not easily separated and also how the former issues from the latter. And, the resulting knowledge does not merely improve the technical capability of the participants but often leads to the formation of collaborative ventures and political alliances that help strengthen an awareness of the political necessity of the struggle.

Most important, the assembled findings of the investigation serve as topics of collective reflection achieved through dialogue. The products of participatory research not only provide people with the technical ammunition for improving their material conditions and for engaging in political struggles, but also supply the grist for their reflection mill. This is true in traditional social science research, and it is even more so in participatory research. One purpose of participatory research is to provide space for the oppressed to use their intellectual power to be critical and innovative in order to fashion a world free of domination and exploitation. To this end, they must exercise, in dialogue with one another, their collective ability to draw causal inferences for strategic actions and to contemplate the social ramifications that ensue. It is also necessary for the oppressed to see the larger picture of structural contradictions which cause their economic miseries and social dislocations. Through this theoretically broadened view they can come to understand the plight of other socially marginalized groups as stemming from the same structural source. This understanding paves the way for horizontal coalitions with other communities and groups in struggle and highlights the necessity for linking one participatory research effort with another. Because participatory research is a continuous educational process, it does not end with the completion of one project. When successful, it lives on in the radicalized critical consciousness and the renewed emancipatory practices of each participant.

THE QUESTION OF VALIDITY

The question often raised about participatory research has to do with objectivity and validity. It is asked: How can the results of participatory research be objective, since the whole enterprise is motivated by the political goals of helping the poor and the powerless? Even worse for objectivity, doesn't the involvement of the beneficiary of research in the investigative process seriously compromise the results? Implied in these questions is the presumption that knowledge that is not objective is not valid and therefore not worthwhile. This presumption, however, stems from the epistemological prejudice of positivism, which narrowly equates valid knowledge with what natural sciences produce. According to the criteria of these sciences, especially as interpreted in social research, the procedures followed in participatory research are at odds with the canons of good methodological practice. How are we then to claim that participatory research leads to valid knowledge?

First, we must examine the concept of objectivity. Natural sciences are thought to be the epitome of objective knowledge because they are capable of depicting the reality that exists out there independently of us, the observer-knowers (Popper 1972). This idealistic view of science is a difficult one to maintain in the light of historical (Kuhn 1962) and philosophical (Feyerabend 1975) arguments brought against it in recent years. It appears more reasonable to think of the sciences as creating, rather than discovering, knowledge that gives us different ways of relating to natural and social environments. From this perspective, natural sciences produce knowledge that is effective in dealing with the physical world.

In the epistemological framework of this paper, instrumental knowledge is only one of the three cognitive forms contributing to human life, the other two being interactive and critical. The question of validity, then, must be dealt with in terms of this conceptual framework. Each knowledge form has its own criteria of validity, so that one form of knowledge cannot be judged in terms of the validity standards of another (Habermas 1979b; Held 1980). The validity of instrumental knowledge is demonstrated, in the final analysis, in being put to technical applications which improve the ability to control the physical environment with new physical, chemical, and biological inventions. For interactive knowledge the claim to validity is to be redeemed in producing communal relations that are characterized by understanding in the broad sense of empathy and connectedness. And finally, critical knowledge validates itself in creating a vehicle of transformation and in overcoming obstacles to emancipation—both internally and with respect to the external world.

In participatory research, then, the question of validity cannot be raised and answered only in terms of instrumental knowledge, as is often done, ignoring the other forms of knowledge. Even if we are to restrict ourselves to this one dimension alone for the moment, much of the criticism of participatory research procedures from the point of view of the traditional social science methodology misses the mark. The gist of the criticism is that not maintaining a proper distance between the researcher and the researched, as is the policy in participatory research, seriously compromises the objectivity of the data, thus destroying its validity. This charge, however, derives from a misguided emulation of natural science methodology which has maintained the separation of the subject and the object in controlled experiments. The arguments concerning this shortsighted methodological stance in social sciences are overwhelmingly on the side of the practice prevalent in participatory research (Polyani 1958; Winch 1958; Geertz 1983; Taylor 1987).

The fact that participatory research proceeds as a holistic activity, not compartmentalizing the instrumental, interactive, and critical dimensions, makes it difficult to deal with validity issues on all fronts. Important beginnings are being made in the discussion of alternative research paradigms (Lather 1986; Reason and Rowan 1981; Heron 1985), but more explicit linkages need to be made between the methodological question of validity and theories of knowledge. Although I will not be able to develop it here, one fruitful direction this effort can take is in the appropriation of Habermas's theory of communicative action, which informs the epistemological framework presented in this paper (Habermas 1979b; Kemp 1985). Regardless of the particular theory utilized, the actual process of establishing the validity of participatory research must also be participatory, taking the form of participatory evaluation (Fernandes and Tandon 1981).

RECOVERING POPULAR KNOWLEDGE

Participatory research produces people's knowledge in the sense that it creates new ways of doing things for the participants. However, this process is not one of acquiring externally generated information and know-how through training and transmission, but more that of recovering people's practical skills, communal sentiments, ancient lores, and collective wisdom that live on but are submerged. Under the onslaught of the capitalist political economy, people are uprooted from their cultural moorings and are made dependent on the market economy as unconnected individuals. The traditional sources of human strength and capacity are taken away and replaced with incapacitation and helplessness. As a consequence, people feel invalidated and useless, thus becoming more deeply dependent on the debilitating system. Participatory research provides the means for people to regain their ability to think for themselves and to innovate, as well as to remember their history and to revive their culture for the re-creation of the authentic life.

Innovations and Reinventions

In dealing with practical communal problems, such as installing fuel-saving stoves or starting a cooperative, participatory research helps people to exercise their ingenuity and to come up with technical solutions that are meaningful and appropriate for their specific circumstances. In this process, they also reach into the storehouse of now-devalued traditional ways which at one time sustained the people as a community capable of providing much of their daily needs. For example, the peasants of the Third World, many of whom have been absorbed into plantation and agribusiness economies destructive of subsistence farming, can turn to their collective memory and bring back the old ways of living off the land without relying on harmful chemicals and expensive and wasteful machinery. The point is not to go back to the past but to bring back suppressed traditional knowledge that can be reused for creating a self-sufficient life. What is created is people's knowledge, consisting of innovations and reinventions that free them from dependence on external experts and thus make them more self-reliant.

Collective Life and the Will to Be Free

For the reinforcement of community and the reconstitution of the will to be free, participatory research is especially crucial in digging up the necessary cognitive layers that are buried under technical consciousness and commodity relationships, and returning them to the people. The reason is that in these layers lie submerged structures of atrophied community relations and critical consciousness which cannot be redeemed except by deliberate practice.

In this context participatory research is as much a process of recovery as of discovery. In the less-developed rural communities of the world, people live the traditions which are kept alive in daily routines, rituals, festivities, story telling, small talk, singing, dancing, and playing (Fals Borda, *Cono- cimiento*). The intervention of participatory research is useful in counteracting the invading industrial culture that devalues and suppresses the traditional ways of the community life as ignorance, backwardness, superstition, and inefficiency.

From this point of view, the participatory research work in the less-developed areas of the world is made easier in comparison with industrialized urban settings, because in the former the destruction of the indigenous communal practices is less advanced. By contrast, in industrialized urban areas, as in the cities of North America, the destruction of the communal way of life is more complete, which makes it difficult to recover what might be called "people's interactive knowledge," that forms the basis for communal unity. This is one of the reasons why participatory research has been more successful in the Third World than in developed countries. And for the same reason, within industrialized countries, participatory research is more easily carried out in settings where the vestiges of shared culture and common ties are relatively strong, for example, among Native populations, in rural areas, among women, and in labor unions. Where there is little shared life, participatory research must first create a community base before it can do collective investigation, not to speak of action and reflection. This is of course a difficult and time-consuming task.

Industrial civilization, ushered in by capitalism, has been assaulting people's capacity to fashion their own future just as effectively as it has uprooted indigenous community structures. But old ways die hard, and capitalism's onslaught has been met with resistance from popular quarters, notably peasants and workers (Thompson 1966), as well as indigenous peoples. The war on human adulthood continues relentlessly with material and ideological weapons that kill, maim, and take prisoners of critical consciousness. Pockets of resistance, however, persist in the lingering memories and practices of the people. Participatory research connects with this capacity to envision a freer world lying dormant in the oppressed consciousness of subjugated people, with the objective of giving it the potential for liberatory action.

Traces of a once-authentic life that was tradition-bound but self-determined live on in the collective memory of the people sharing a common history (Fals Borda, *Conocimiento*). They remember through lore handed down and stories told and retold of the time when the land was theirs to roam on or cultivate, when they could feed themselves with what they produced with their own hands, when they did not have to sell their labor on the block, when families were not pulled asunder by migratory labor, when they were able to feel free and think for themselves, when they had an organic way of life and self-esteem. They also remember people's struggles to resist the expropriation of their right to the land and the exploitation of their labor, to preserve their way of life, and to remain free to pursue their dreams. Heroic deeds of native leaders, peasants, and workers fighting against outside invaders, landowners, and factory bosses live again in oral histories told in the intimacy of close encounters and in the pages of written history. These are tales of common people and their families and communities pitted against ruthless wielders of power who are bent on forcing them into the political-economic order built on material deprivation and spiritual degradation of the masses. These are not always romantic tales of victory for the weak, for the conflict has been an unevenly matched warfare. But no matter; there are lessons to be learned in witnessing the unbroken spirit of freedom rising up over and over again, defeating the gloom of defeat itself. Participatory research provides opportunities for people to learn these lessons through oral and written histories that they themselves tell and collect.

We urgently need to recover people's wisdom and turn it into a potent force for emancipating the rest of humanity. This task needs to be done with the participation of the people themselves. Saving the world from technological and spiritual destruction depends on transforming it into a human sphere of life where community and critical consciousness thrive.

2

The Powerful, the Powerless, and the Experts: Knowledge Struggles in an Information Age

JOHN GAVENTA ————————————————

I have a friend, an activist, worker, and former coal miner who knows and loves the Appalachian mountains as well as anyone in my acquaintance. Over the last two decades, he has become his own self-taught "expert" on the ravages that strip-mining have gouged into the countryside. A "mountain man," he has spent hours walking the hills, observing the destruction of wildlife, streams, and natural soil cover. Though he does not have a college education, he has studied the laws and scientific literature on mining, and the economics and history of mining, so that he can educate others and struggle against the technology which has taken jobs, destroyed farms, and endangered his way of life. His knowledge derives from vast experience and self-education, though it lacks the credentials that a degree or a government office might bring.

One day, this friend asked the appropriate government inspector to file a complaint against what appeared to be a clear violation of the law. Though weak and gutted by special interests, the law clearly says that muck and debris from strip mines shall not be deposited directly into streams. My friend had discovered a major slide of silt running from a mine into a nearby stream on the mountain above his home, endangering the aquatic life and increasing the likelihood of flooding.

The government inspector possessed a knowledge very different from that of my friend. A recent product of a state university, he was now a certified geologist. A junior post in a state regulatory agency helped to ordain his knowledge as "official." His knowledge of the countryside was not personal and firsthand, but acquired through maps and textbooks based, one supposes, on science. Unlike my friend, his was the knowledge of expertise, not of experience.

He accompanied my friend to inspect the mine on the basis of this expertise—as required by law. My friend showed him the silt oozing into the water. As also provided for by the law, he exercised his right as a citizen by asking the inspector to file a complaint against the responsible mining company. The expert official studied the situation. He drew out his maps and documents. And then he said, "I'm sorry, I cannot take action. According to my map, there is no stream there."

The example is perhaps an extreme one, but it suggests, I believe, key themes of power facing relatively powerless groups in the United States today. By definitional fiat, the official had rendered the citizen's complaint a nonissue. Technical, expert knowledge had predominated over the knowledge derived from experience, common sense, and citizenship. Corporate exploitation had been protected by the state, buttressed by the power to define what constituted valid knowledge.

The incident raises many questions pursued by the growing literature on participatory research. Who has the right to define knowledge? How does the control of knowledge affect power relations? What is the relation of "popular" knowledge to "official" knowledge? How do relatively powerless groups empower themselves through research and information?

This chapter addresses several of these questions. The first part of the chapter will look at the growth of the "knowledge society," suggesting that the change in the political economy of the United States has had a major impact upon power relations. The second part will then examine strategies by which relatively powerless groups in our society can mobilize information and knowledge resources, as one part of their broader strategies for empowerment.

THE POLITICAL ECONOMY OF THE KNOWLEDGE SOCIETY

In recent years a number of social theorists have proclaimed the emergence of a new era, calling it the "postindustrial society," the "knowledge society," the technotronic society," or a variety of other labels. To witness the change in a firsthand way, one need only compare the advertisements in leading commercial magazines between, say, the 1940s and the 1980s. Where once glossy photos of heavy industry and machines heralded developments of the times, now the slogans of "the age of information" shape our notions of progress. As one university president observed in the early 1960s, "Knowledge has never in history been so central to the conduct of the entire society.... The knowledge industry may serve as a focal point for national growth" (Kerr quoted in Machlup 1980, xxi) in the second half of the century.

Economists have concurred. In what many academics regard as a pioneering work, Machlup, a Princeton economist, wrote in 1962 that 29 percent of the gross national product (for 1958) consisted of knowledge-producing industries—education, research and development, media and communications, and information machinery (1962). In a 1980 update he suggested that given the projected growth rates of these knowledge industries, the share of knowledge production in total activity would soon reach 50 percent (1980).

One of the sociologists to develop the idea of the knowledge society most extensively, and perhaps most controversially, was Daniel Bell, in his book *The Coming of Post-Industrial Society*. Bell describes the move from preindustrial society, where the ownership of land is the key resource, to industrial society, to postindustrial society:

Industrial society is the coordination of machines and men for the production of goods. Post-industrial society is organized around knowledge, for the purpose of social control, and the direction of innovation and change, and this in turn will give rise to new social relationships and new structures which have to be managed politically. (Bell 1974, 20)

From the grass-roots perspective, the macro-theoretical question of whether, in fact, a postindustrial society has superseded the industrial society is not the crucial question. For the rural Appalachian in the example given earlier, the power relations of the agrarian society, based on the ownership of land, are important. So are those of the industrial society, based on the ownership of industry, and so are those of the postindustrial society, based on the ownership and control of knowledge. How these factors interact to strengthen the power of others, increasing his powerlessness, and how to forge a unified response to each face of oppression, are more important questions than which of these faces is the theoretically correct one.

On the whole, while economists have documented the growth of a knowledge industry, and sociologists have described the knowledge society, political scientists have ignored important questions these changes pose for power relations and for social movements: In the conflicts in the knowledge society, who wins, who loses, and why? What are the implications of a changing economic and social order on the relatively powerless? Whose knowledge is growing and for whose benefit? Who are the have-nots in the knowledge society, and how do they organize against the new elements of oppression the knowledge society brings?

In examining these issues, we shall look first at various characteristics of the knowledge society, including (1) the transmission and communication of existing knowledge; (2) the production of new knowledge; (3) the role of the knowledge elite; and (4) the ideology that the society contributes.

The Consumption and Communication of Knowledge

To consume the knowledge produced by others is the role that the marketplace assigns to the masses of the knowledge society. Advertisements for home computers, videotapes, videodiscs, and data banks use the slogan "putting information at your fingertips" to imply the availability of knowledge to virtually everyone. The explosion in the field of information and communications is irrefutable. But if we look more closely, the knowledge explosion works to put information in the hands of some more than others. As the economists say, there are "dramatic imperfections in information markets."

The imperfections are seen perhaps most clearly in the relations of the First World, where the knowledge industries are primarily based, to the Third World. A growing number of writers refer to such "data dependency," observing, for instance, that "information handling capacity already offers industrialized countries and firms considerable economic and political leverage in North-South interaction. Information vital to developing countries is frequently concentrated in the capitals of the North" (O'Brien and Helleiner 1983, 1). These inequities have led to calls for a new international information order, in which data-dependent nations have the right and the capacity to create and transmit knowledge for themselves (see Smith, A. 1980).

Similar information inequalities exist within the First World as well. Herb Schiller, in his book *Who Knows: Information in the Age of the Fortune 500*, observes that "in the global shift of economic and informational activity now proceeding *the center of the system, no less than the periphery, experience deepening inequalities....* It requires little imagination to guess who benefits from the new information technology in corporate-dominated America, where a few hundred businesses control more than three-fifths of the national economy" (1981, 18). In brief, several trends may be seen:

1. *The Commodification of Public Knowledge.* Many data banks and information sources once available to the public in libraries and government offices now are becoming commodities to be sold and transmitted in the information marketplace. As Schiller writes, "The process of information generation is under commercial siege and private interests have encroached substantially on what once were nonprofit activities producing a wide range of information" (1981, 56).

2. *The Use of Computers.* While the computer industry offers promises of a computer in virtually every household, the fact is that those who can most easily afford the hardware and software required will benefit the most. Corporate America is dominating the use of computers to process and transmit knowledge, and to strengthen its own networks.

3. *The Growth of Corporate Message Making.* Much has been written in the social sciences about the extent to which the media control or shape the nature of information that is transmitted, as well as about the rising concentration of corporate ownership of media industries. The communications revolution offers the opportunities of new types of communication: corporate or private video that links the industry directly to the worker or

consumer. In Britain, for example, corporate video has become a major tool for companies in labor disputes.

All of these trends help to strengthen already-existing gaps between the "knowledge haves" and the "knowledge have-nots." They increase the difficulties that the powerless have in obtaining information that is useful to their interests, while strengthening the capacities of the powerful to mobilize the knowledge which they need to prevail in any given conflict.

While it may benefit some more than others, the electronic revolution also offers new possibilities of decentralized and grass-roots use of information technology. Already a number of community groups, unions, minorities, and other disenfranchised segments of society are using computers, video, cable, and other tools in creative and empowering ways (see Community Careers Resource Center 1985; Heaney 1982). They have also called upon and used the tradition of freedom of information, a uniquely important asset in our society, to resist the privatization of information into corporate and dominant hands.

Such strategies are and will continue to be important ones for the information have-nots to pursue. However, even if the inequalities in the consumption and transmission of knowledge are altered, the have-nots are still affected by a perhaps more important set of questions—"Who produces knowledge?" and "For whose interests?"

The Production of Knowledge

The production and application of new knowledge, or research and development, is itself a major industry, amounting to over $150 billion a year across the globe, and employing more than three million scientists and engineers. As in the information machinery or communications industry, the overwhelming proportion of this industry is found in the developed countries, which accounted in 1973 for 97 percent of the formal global research and development capacity (Norman 1979, 5).

Among the Western nations, the knowledge production industry is greatest in the United States, whose research and development outlay in 1979 of $56 billion was greater than that of Japan, Germany, France, the United Kingdom, Italy, Canada, and the Netherlands combined (Organization for Economic Cooperation and Development [OECD] 1984, 21). As a Worldwatch Institute study has shown, in 1979 the United States spent "almost $200 for every person in the country on R and D. In contrast Latin American countries spent less than $5 per person and poorer countries of Africa and Asia spent less than $1 per person" (Norman 1979, 10-11).

Who are these knowledge producers? Who benefits from their knowledge? Within the United States, about two-thirds of this research and development in 1979 was performed by private enterprise (mostly in the area of applied research). The corporate researchers include some of the largest multinationals in the world, in the fields of automobile manufacturing, aerospace, chemicals, and communications. The $2 billion annual R and D budget of General Motors alone is greater than that of most countries, including Sweden, Australia, Belgium, Yugoslavia, and Norway (OECD 1984).

If the corporations are at the center of applied research, the universities gain their central role in the knowledge industry as the producers of "basic knowledge," as well as the training ground for the industry's qualified personnel. The fact that the university serves the interests of the state and of industry may be seen from the amount of money invested in it. What is produced is determined in large part, in fact, by a complex system of contracts with purchasers—government, industry, foundations, and so forth (see Nelkin 1983). In the past, the largest amount of money available to universities has come from government; increasingly, with the federal cutbacks, the universities are becoming more and more dependent upon private interests. And, while there is an apparent multiplicity of colleges and universities, which might imply a pluralism of research production, there is, in fact, a great deal of concentration in the industry: According to Bell, "Of the 2,500 colleges and universities in the country, one hundred carry out more than 93 percent of the research. And, within this circle, twenty-one universities carried out 54 percent of all university research, and ten universities carried out 38 percent of university research" (1974, 20).

While an enormous sum is thus spent for "new knowledge," it is not, as one might suspect, aimed at meeting the needs of the poor and disenfranchised. Over half of the research and development expenditures in the United States are financed by the taxpayer, through the federal government. In 1984, an estimated 70 percent of these research and development funds were spent upon the "external challenge" (Bell 1974), primarily defense and space (National Science Foundation 1984).[1] The preponderance of expenditures on military and space means not only that money is not available for attempting to solve domestic needs—health, poverty, environment, transportation, and housing—but also that knowledge that is produced for external challenges has domestic and potentially destructive applications. For instance, today the Pentagon is among the chief funders of robotics research, which takes "human factors" out of defense production as well as jobs out of the rest of the economy! (See Schlesinger, Gaventa, and Merrifield 1983, 157-186.)

Where knowledge is produced about the problems of the powerless, it is more often than not produced by the powerful in the interest of maintaining the status quo, rather than by the powerless in the interest of change. In a frank critique of the role of sociology made before the 1968 convention of the American Sociological Association, Martin Nicholaus described this view:

The corporate rulers of this society would not be spending as much money as they do for knowledge, if knowledge did not confer power.... That knowledge that confers power moves along a one way chain, taking knowledge from the people, giving knowledge to the rulers. . . . Sociology has worked to create and increase the unequal distribution of knowledge. It has worked to make the power structure relatively more powerful and knowledgeable, and thereby to make the subject population more impotent and ignorant. (Reynolds and Reynolds 1970, 277)

The producers of knowledge are the universities, industries that are linked to and supported by large corporations and government. Rarely seen are institutions that produce the knowledge to serve the interests of the poor and powerless. Of research and development of new knowledge, for instance, only 4 percent is done by nonprofit institutions (OECD 1984, 80), many of which are think tanks for the powerful. A much smaller proportion of the research is done for, or done by, or is even available to, the have-nots in the country who most need the power that knowledge can bring.

The Knowledge Elite

The power of the knowledge industry is derived not simply from what knowledge is produced and for whom, but also from the growth of new elites who people the knowledge production process. "The central point about the last third of the twentieth century . . . ," writes Bell, "is that it will require more societal guidance, more expertise" (1974, 263). Indeed, the growth in the number of those who may be called experts has been enormous. Between 1964 and 1975 the "professional and technical" job category grew at a rate twice the average to 132 million, "making it the second largest of the eight occupational divisions in the U.S., exceeded only by semi-skilled workers." Within this, the growth rate of natural and social scientists and of engineers has been triple that of the average labor force rate (Bell 1974, 21).

One's place among the knowledge elite is not determined simply by one's occupation: One is certified, determined by society to be an expert, usually by other experts, either through the granting of degrees or through other rewards. In this sense, the club is a closed one, open to membership only by invitation of existing members. Once in the club, one encounters other social controls, which influence what type of knowledge is produced and for whom—organization by departments and disciplines, peer pressure, economic and career incentives (McRae 1971, 9). Much of what this knowledge elite produces is transmitted through journals, meetings, and networks available only to those certified as part of the system, and is written in language designed to separate them further from the common person.

A crude analogy is, nevertheless, important. In a feudal society, the key resource is the land, and those who control it, the landlords, are the key political actors. In an industrial society, power derives from the ownership and control of factories, where the boss is the mediator between the capitalists and the workers. And in an information society, as we have seen, knowledge, in addition to land and industry, becomes a product to be owned as capital. Within that economic structure, the expert, the specialist of knowledge, becomes the power broker, much as the landlord or boss in other political economies.

What are the mechanisms of the power of expertise? First, there is the power to withhold knowledge from those whose well-being is affected by it. Recent history is replete with examples in which the withholding of knowledge served as an exercise of power, allowing those who "know" to cause those who do not to take actions they otherwise might not have taken. For instance, government doctors who failed to reveal to federal employees the potential impact of radiation exposure in the development and testing of the atomic bomb caused those employees to take risks (increased possibility of cancer) which they might not otherwise have taken.

Where issues do begin to emerge, the expert may possess the power to define them. Increasingly in social conflicts the power struggle is not simply one of who prevails in the resolution of an issue but also in who prevails in measuring its very existence. Vast bodies of technical regulations exist whose application becomes the responsibility of the political technician. Thus, in the earlier example, the geologist defined away an environmental problem perceived and understood by everyday experience, because his official measurement denied that the problem existed. In this fashion, what constitutes even the definition of a political problem is decided *for* the people by the experts who study them, not by the people themselves.

The institutionalization of expertise in politics leads to another phenomenon of power as well. Expertise increases as knowledge is divided into specialties and subspecialties, each organized into disciplines. Little attention is given to the cumulative or interactive effects of related problems, or to the problem which consists of the sum of the various parts. The powerless, on the other hand, experience problems differently—powerlessness itself is the sum experience of a number of components of a problem—economic, social, political, and psychological. Each component of the problem merely reinforces the other. However, the domination of expertise and technique in political decisions works to exclude consideration of the sum and breaks political questions into the problems of the minute.

Laws, internal organizations of regulatory bodies, political jurisdictions— all reflect these subdivisions of knowledge by science. Take, for instance, the case of a worker who is employed in a chemical plant, lives in a nearby community, eats and drinks the food and water from the land, and is dying of cancer. To gain a response from the system for action on the cause of the cancer, he or she will have to subdivide the problem into that derived from work, governed by the Occupational Safety and Health Administration or the Department of Labor; that derived from air pollution, governed by the Air Quality Control Board; that derived from the water, governed by the Water Quality Control Board; that derived from toxins in the food, regulated by the Department of Agriculture; that derived from eating wildlife obtained through hunting, regulated by the specialists in the Department of Fisheries and Wildlife; that derived from the consumption of other foods, regulated by the Consumer Protection Agency; and that derived from the interactive effects of them all—regulated by no one. Unless a problem can be broken down into discrete parts for entry through the array of specialized gateways into the system, the problem may not find entry at all. It will simply be a personal problem, not one for the polity.

Underlying all of these elements of the power of expertise is the expert's lack of any accountability to the nonexperts affected by his or her knowledge. Knowledge production, then, is accountable not to the public interest, not to the needs of the powerless who may be affected by it, but to an ideology which serves to justify the superiority of the expert—the ideology of science and objectivity.

The Ideology of the Knowledge Society

One of the claims often put forth about the knowledge society is that decisions based upon the expertise of science, embodied in the actions of experts and scientists, would transcend politics as we know it. According to Bell, an earlier technocratic theory might posit that "in such a technocratic society, politics would disappear, since all problems would be decided by an expert. One would obey the competence of a superior just as one obeys the instructions of a doctor or an orchestra conductor or a ship's captain" (1974, 263).

This notion has at its roots a modern-day faith in science as *the* road to truth, and in scientists and experts as those who embody and institutionalize it. A number of writers describe the trend. Fals Borda and others refer to science as the modern-day fetish of the Western world (Dubell et al. 1981, 13-40). Habermas has termed such dominance of science "scientism," meaning "science's belief in itself: that is, the conviction that we can no longer understand science as one form of possible knowledge, but rather must identify knowledge with science" (Bottomore 1984, 57). The claim to truth gives rise to hierarchies of knowledge which reinforce and legitimate the economic and social hierarchies we have seen earlier: If science is superior knowledge, then presumably those who are paid or credentialed to possess it are, in some sense, superior to those who are not.

The claim to the superiority of science lies in its related claim to objectivity. There are many critiques of the philosophy of positivism, but here we concentrate on its practice. In practice, objectivity is translated in scientific method to mean a sharp bifurcation between expertise, based on the study of a problem, and experience, the subjective living of that problem. Scientists produce by objectifying others, making them data, who, as the objects of another's inquiry, are denied the position of subjects who can act, create, and observe for themselves. The bifurcation is a rigid one: The experts may study the powerless, but must not experience the problems they face, or identify with them, for fear of losing their objectivity. On the other hand, the nonexperts may experience a problem, and through that experience gain valuable knowledge and insights, but when it comes to political debates, their knowledge is given little weight because it is not scientific. The practice of science gives rise to other divisions, too, each of which has political impact—between those who speak on the basis of facts and those who speak from mere values, between thinkers and practitioners, between the researchers and the researched, students and the studied, minds and masses.

The belief in the new authority of expertise is inculcated in many ways—by the media, in the schools, through socialization at home. Inequalities in past societies have been legitimated similarly. Peasants were taught to believe that the landlord really had their interests at heart. Workers in the early days of industrialization were taught to believe in the benevolence of the corporation. (One coal miner once described this to me in saying about the company town, "The miners worked for a song—and they sung it themselves.") Today this ideology manifests itself in the deference of the people to the expert, and ultimately to a belief in their own ignorance and the subordination of their own knowledge to that of expertise. It involves the mystification of dominant knowledge, and the subjugation of common knowledge.

Despite the realities, the ideology of the knowledge society is a potent one, with profound consequences for participatory democracy: A knowledge system which subordinates common sense also subordinates common people.

STRATEGIES FOR KNOWLEDGE STRUGGLES

The previous section has described the establishment of the control of knowledge in the hands of the few, in a manner that exercises power over the lives of the many. Inequalities abound—in access to information, in the production and definition of legitimate knowledge, in the domination of expertise over common knowledge in decision making. The point, however, is not only to document and describe these inequalities, but also to analyze the strategies by which they may be overcome.

In so doing, we shall distinguish between those strategies which are, in essence, reforms from within the knowledge structure, and those from without—by those workers, community groups, minorities, and others who need information and knowledge for action, but who at the same time are affected by those who control the dominant knowledge production system.

Reforming the Knowledge System

From within the knowledge production system, there are many who seek to change the nature and content of the knowledge produced. Vast quantities of material are written calling for knowledge that is more critical, for experts and scholars who are more committed to social struggles, for the production of information that serves certain interests as opposed to others. Given the analysis of the previous pages about the impact upon power relations of what knowledge *is* produced, we must accept the importance of these struggles. Those persons within the knowledge industry who espouse them often face severe sanctions—loss of credibility, funding, tenure, jobs, prestige, and so forth. However, to the extent that these struggles attempt to change the *content* of knowledge, without altering the process *for* whom and *by* whom it is produced, they are inevitably limited. The mere substitution of one set of social diagnoses and prescriptions for another does not make them more democratic, or more accountable to those who remain the objects of another's theory.

Rather than start with such strategies for reform from within the knowledge system, we can perhaps more usefully step outside it to ask, how do those groups who are dominated by "official" knowledge organize themselves to deal with such domination? In so doing, we do not mean to imply that the control of knowledge is the only, or even the most fundamental, issue these groups must face. We agree with Rahman that:

the dominant view of social transformation has been preoccupied with the need for changing existing oppressive structures of relations in material production. But . . . by now, in most polarized countries, the gap between those who have social power over the process of knowledge generation—and those who have not—has reached dimensions no less formidable than the gap in access to means of physical production. . . . For improving the possibilities of liberation, therefore, these two gaps should be attacked, wherever feasible, simultaneously. (1982)

Too often, the response of the powerless to their own domination is one which accepts the paradigms of the dominant knowledge system itself. In particular, groups tend to accept the divorce made by positivist science between the minds and masses, the experts and the experience, and to respond in either of two ways, through blind action, or through faith in experience.

Blind Action

One response is to reject the necessity of strategies perceived to bear any of the characteristics of the dominant knowledge system. Liberation from oppression by dominant knowledge takes the form of rejection of the importance of knowledge altogether, for example anti-intellectualism and anti-theory. Emphasis is placed on the direct and physical action of the masses, but not on the actions inspired and directed by the minds of the masses; on organizing the people under the direction of others, not on developing the research and education necessary for the people to define their own actions. In the name of rejecting dominant knowledge, this approach rejects the necessities of the development, systematization, and analysis by the people of their own knowledge. It leads to "blind action," and thus to an unwitting acceptance of the role of the masses as unthinking objects—precisely what those who claim to monopolize their minds would prescribe.

Faith in Expertise

While this first approach accepts the mind-masses polarization by glori-fying the actions of the masses, the other accepts it by maintaining a naive faith in the "minds," the experts. The people's own knowledge is depre-ciated, even by the people themselves, who have internalized the degradation of their own experiences. Lawyers, scientists, and other experts are perceived as having more knowledge, and are looked to by the people for directives, for answers as to what to do.

The faith in the expert to solve the problems of others is today eroding among many sectors of the population. The "best and the brightest" have brought the "worst and the darkest" of many of the problems they face—Three Mile Island, nuclear threats, chemical hazards, and degrading social programs.

Nevertheless, though the faith may be eroding, the dependency upon the experts for waging tactical battle has not, for the political structure still ascribes higher value to the experts' authority than to the people's knowl-edge. Thus, even though they may distrust the dominant science, groups turn to the mobilization of scientists, or their own hired experts, as their strategy for action. Against the corporate and governmental experts, the powerless must array their own, for without doing so, they feel that their collective voice will go unheard.

In some cases, groups may turn to those experts within the knowledge system who are themselves trying to reform it, such as those involved in the "science for the people" movements. At such times, the needs of the popular groups for the assistance of the expert may match the expert's sympathies.

While often a tactical necessity, this "hired gun" strategy to overcoming knowledge domination is fraught with peril, and in the long run is extremely limited for altering the power of the powerless group. In the first place, no matter how sympathetic in fighting the external problem, the expert may come to dominate the internal operations of the group, either because he or she believes in his or her superior knowledge, or because members of the group are still affected by the "expert faith," or simply because the group spends its energies in mobilizing funds to pay the experts.

If this approach is limited because it still maintains the internal dependencies of the group upon the expert, it is limited by broader aspects of the knowledge system as well. First, in general, the strategy is a losing proposition for the relatively powerless group, because the powerful, virtually by definition, have the ability to hire more experts and put more resources at their disposal. Moreover, the strategy is limited because the dominant side also "chooses the weapons"; that is, those who define what is appropriate knowledge, a valid model, a scientific fact, and so on will be able to define what sorts of knowledge are allowed as legitimate discourse for the battle. Finally, the knowledge structure "makes the ammunition"; that is, it has the ability to produce the data, facts, and statistics to suit the chosen model of discourse in vast quantities, and the various specifications required to engage the counter-expert most effectively.

Research with the People

In order to escape the dependencies within the "hired gun" or researcher-client approach, many unions, community groups, and public interest groups have attempted to develop their own knowledge-production and information-gathering capacities. In so doing, they often assign the tasks to persons within the organization who have professional backgrounds, or they may join forces with those who have left the knowledge industry to do research *with the people*. Such an approach draws heavily upon traditions of action research, activist research, and militant observation that have been developed by reformers within the universities (see Darcy de Oliveira and Darcy de Oliveira 1982, 41-62; Stavenhagen 1971, 333-344). It also may draw upon the tradition of tactical research, or power structure research, that emerged from community organizing in the 1960s (Greever).

Such a tradition of research with the people goes a long way toward narrowing the knowledge gap, in that it relates the production of knowledge to the process of action and to the actual experiences of the powerless group. Ideally, there is some accountability between researcher and researched: The researcher begins with questions that the powerless group has posed, and the information is provided back to him or her in a usable and understandable form.

At the same time, the research-with-the-people approach still has its limits. To the extent that the research still remains in the hands of the researcher, a real transfer of ownership of knowledge may not have occurred. The dichotomy between those who produce knowledge and those who are most affected by it still exists, though the element of the superiority of the researcher may have been reduced. Moreover, in empirical fact, the approach is usually dependent upon the initiation of the outside, committed researcher, and is dependent upon the researcher's presence. Eventually, the researcher may decide to leave, taking the skills, experience, and newly acquired knowledge along with him or her.

To overcome this later dependency, the de Oliveiras write, "We must prepare for the moment when the presence of the researcher—who came from the outside—is no longer necessary." The group must gain control of the research process, meaning "that they have succeeded in appropriating to themselves the knowledge and science which the researcher brought. Acquisition by the group of methodological tools, which were once the monopoly of the researcher, prevents the repetition of the dependence relationship vis-à-vis those who 'have knowledge' and allows the group to develop, autonomously, its movement of action and reflection" (Darcy de Oliveira and Darcy de Oliveira 1982, 58). The transferral of such knowledge and tools, however, is still dependent upon the prior presence of the researcher, and what is transferred is limited to the tools and methods which professional research has created. For these reasons, we must examine a further form of overcoming knowledge domination, research *by the people* themselves.

The Participatory Research Movement

In an essay on research and education, Paulo Freire wrote, "If I perceive the reality as the dialectical relationship between subject and object, then I have to use methods for investigation which involve the people of the area being studied as researchers; they should take part in the investigation themselves and not serve as the passive objects of the study" (Hall et al. 1982, 29). With Freire's theme in mind, participatory research attempts to break down the distinction between the researchers and the researched, the subjects and objects of knowledge production, by the participation of the people-for-themselves in the process of gaining and creating knowledge. In the process, research is seen not only as a process of creating knowledge, but simultaneously as education and development of consciousness, and of mobilization for action.

Participatory research may be seen:

- in areas, or by groups, where dominant knowledge has been a force for control but in which there is little access to sympathetic expertise. This includes rural areas like Appalachia, and oppressed groups whose interests are not well represented within the knowledge elite, such as minorities, women, workers, and the poor. Lacking the capacity to rely on counter-experts for solutions to their problems, they must create knowledge and wage knowledge struggles for themselves.
- conducted by groups concerned with education of the people. Such groups may not be part of the formal adult education networks, which have often become highly professionalized and career-oriented, but consists of community groups, labor unions, and minorities involved in concrete, grass roots-based action.

• growing out of a concern with participation by the people in decisions that affect their lives, a theme that has been part of the New Left, civil rights, community-organizing, and environmental movements of the 1960s and 1970s.

Three strategies of participatory research have emerged which are particularly important in the North American context.

Research by the People: The Reappropriation of Knowledge

Unlike many Third World countries where information centers are almost entirely out of the reach of relatively powerless groups, in North America, the center of the information industry, there is potentially a vast storehouse of knowledge about people's lives. While abundant, such information is often beyond ready access to those affected by it.

The approach draws heavily upon the investigative research tradition in the United States, and upon the public interest research movement, championed by Ralph Nader. However, this approach popularizes not only information possessed by the knowledge elite, but also the process of obtaining it. It insists that those who are directly affected by a problem have the right to acquire information about it for themselves.

There are numerous examples of this approach:

1. *Community Power Structure Research:* In many cases, citizens have learned to research their own power structures through gaining access to courthouse records about property transactions, tax rates, housing codes, and land and mineral ownership; and to government records about company finance, military industries, and so on. Popular manuals and training programs have taught groups to develop these skills for themselves (Greever).

2. *Corporate Research:* Vast quantities of information exist in the public sector about corporations that affect workers and communities in the United States and abroad. Other data exist in the hands of federal and state agencies that are supposed to regulate corporate behavior. While much of such research may be done for grass-roots groups by sympathetic professionals, a number of good manuals exist on how workers and communities may obtain information themselves (Food and Beverage Trades Deptartment, AFL-CIO 1984).

3. *Right-to-Know Movements:* Workers, community groups, and professionals in a number of states and towns have launched campaigns claiming the public's right to know the contents of toxic chemicals which are used at work or which affect their communities. Such information, it is argued, should not be the sole province of either the corporation or of the medical and scientific professions (see Nelkin and Brown 1984, 17-22).

Many of these battles have at their heart the claim to public access to information produced by the knowledge system. Compared to citizens' research in other countries, groups are vastly aided by the Freedom of Information Act (FOIA), which provides citizens access to an array of government documents which may be thought to affect their or the public's interests. Many states have passed similar legislation. The effective use by groups of the FOIA, and the popularization of it, have caused the powers that be, especially in the Reagan and Bush administrations, to attempt to weaken the legislation, and to invoke such arguments as "national security" to keep the information from the public.

In our work at the Highlander Center, we have found that this process of people gaining control over knowledge and skills normally considered to be the monopoly of the experts is an empowering one, which produces much more than just the information in question. The participatory process of confronting the knowledge holders provides an experience which can help to develop consciousness of how the power structure actually works. People may discover for themselves dominant knowledge or interpretations of reality which do *not* conform to their own experience, in which case they must ask, "Why not?" Or the process of popular investigation may reveal previously hidden information that does confirm through "official" knowledge what the people have suspected from their own experience. When the former occurs, people may continue to question and to pursue the contradictions. When the latter is the case, the fusion of the official knowledge with that of popular experience gives validity to the people's claims and may unleash new movement.

Once people begin to see themselves as researchers—that is, able to investigate reality for themselves—they will develop other popular and indigenous ways of gaining information from the power structure (what we have come to call "guerrilla research"). Coal miners needing data on their employer have discovered a great deal of useful data by monitoring garbage cans at the corporate headquarters. Alliances may develop within the plant among the secretaries in the manager's office and the workers. Workers on the production line may steal labels off barrels of chemicals and take them home to look them up in medical textbooks, or sneak them to laboratory workers who run tests on the sly in the company labs to discover what the real impact on their health might be. Workers and grass-roots activists have learned to use their own water-sampling kits, or video cameras, or computers to get and compile information they need. Because those experiencing the problem also become the ones researching it, they will have a variety of approaches and information sources based in the community open to them which may not be available to the outside professional.

When people are so armed with the information, several things may happen. First, the process of confronting the experts and gaining an understanding of their tools and their knowledge may serve to demystify the myth of expertise itself. People may learn that the "scientific" foundation upon which regulations are made, and through which their own experiences are discounted, is not so solid, that it is subject to fallibility, conflicting viewpoints, misinterpretation, and plain falsification. With this also comes a renewed examination of their own "popular knowledge," which, since the first days of schooling, they have been taught to depreciate. Attitudes of dependency begin to move toward ones of self-reliance.

Second, those who participate in the unmasking of dominant knowledge and the exposure of the power structure have the experience themselves; they "own" the knowledge they have gained and can reflect upon it. Finally, the process becomes a resource for analyzing the dominant ideas, or it may help to clarify strategies through identifying the Achilles' heels of the system where action should begin.

While the process of the reappropriation of dominant knowledge by those who are affected by it is empowering as a strategy, by itself it is limited. While participatory, it is still based upon gaining access to and control over knowledge that has already been codified by others. It is an access to a paradigm which the people had little part in creating. A further strategy evolves as the powerless develop, create, and systematize their own knowledge, and begin to define their own science.

Research by the People: Developing the People's Science

The intellectual roots for the people's science concept are developed quite forcefully in the participatory research literature, most clearly by Orlando Fals Borda: "We regard popular science—folklore, popular knowledge, or popular wisdom—to be the empirical or common sense–knowledge belonging to the people at the grassroots and constituting part of their cultural heritage." It "remains outside the formal scientific structure built by the intellectual minority of the dominant system because it involves a breach of the rules, and hence its subversive potential" (1982, 26). The ideas also draw upon the European Gramscian tradition, which considers the capacity of every person to be an intellectual, and to develop a popular, organic knowledge which converts spontaneous common sense into "good sense."

Much of the writing about popular knowledge places great value on that knowledge which grows directly from nature, from a peasant-based culture, and pits it against the dominant knowledge of the industrialized world. The knowledge of folk medicine, or peasant technology, or means of survival— all are examples of useful knowledge whose validity has been suppressed by Western science and Western technology. The book by Robert Chambers, *Rural Development: Putting the Last First* (1983), describes and documents many instances in which the knowledge of "primitive," preindustrialized peoples proved more useful and appropriate to them than did that of the modernizational agents. Such knowledge, it is argued by Fals Borda, must be recovered through oral histories and other research, and must be systematized and preserved to provide a power to resist Western industrialization and to chart a more authentic future.

Given the emphasis on people's knowledge as peasant knowledge, some writers in the participatory research debate have asked, "Is it a concept useful for participatory research within the industrialized and even postindustrialized Western world?" We must answer "Yes." The experiences of the people of Appalachia, African-Americans, Native Americans, ethnic minorities, and others demonstrate the existence of cultures whose knowledge has not been fully absorbed by the dominant knowledge structures.

What, though, of the oppressed groups in our society who can lay no claim to a "folk" or "peasant" past, who are in some sense a product themselves of the industrial world and of Western science? Do they possess a popular knowledge? Again, we argue "Yes." It must be remembered that Gramsci's ideas, which are often used in reference to the notion of popular knowledge, grew not out of the context of a peasant economy versus an industrialized one, but out of his experiences with the Italian workers' struggle, in which the value of the workers' own knowledge was diminished by the hegemony of the ruling class. Within the Western world, popular knowledge is constantly being created in the daily experiences of work and community life. The legitimacy of such knowledge, too, is constantly being devalued and suppressed by the dominant science.

Within industrial and postindustrial societies, as within peasant societies, popular production and recovery of the common person's knowledge is also a means of gaining strength. There are many examples:

- Popular planning of new communities and workplaces draws upon people's knowledge, and visions for the future (Wainwright and Elliott 1982). One of the most significant examples of such planning was that of the Lucas Aerospace workers in Britain, who, when faced with closure of their plant, developed their own ideas for new, socially useful products to manufacture.
- People's health surveys have allowed people to systematize their own experiences with environmental and occupational problems. This has been seen, for instance, in Rocky Flats, Colorado, leading to a campaign against nuclear poisoning, and in Love Canal, leading to a campaign to clean up toxic waste dumps (see Gibbs 1982, 66-69, 79-82; Levine 1982). In both cases the "discovery" of devastating health problems came from "housewife researchers," who were led by their own experiences to document and analyze the health experiences of others in the community.

As in the case of reclaiming knowledge from the dominant system, this process of popular production of the people's knowledge has a number of effects upon its participants. In seeing themselves capable of producing and defining their own reality they may become activated to change it; a greater consciousness and clearer analysis of the political context and of their situation may develop; and the new knowledge can become a resource for challenging the hegemony of the dominant ideas.

However, this approach also has its limitations. To the extent that it relies upon the people's experience as the basis of knowledge, how does it develop knowledge within the people that may be in their interest to know but is outside of their experience? What about the situation in which *neither* the dominant knowledge production system *nor* the people's own knowledge has the information to respond to the potential impact of a new technological development, such as the introduction of a new chemical in the workplace? Are there not circumstances, even for the oppressed, in which there is a need for a science which is democratic, but which does not require all of the people to become scientists in order to control and benefit from it? Is *direct* participation in all aspects of the knowledge production system the only form of its popular control? Is there not some need for a division of labor, which recognizes that it is more useful for certain persons to act as researchers and others to act as controllers of their own destiny in other ways?

Research by the People: Popular Control of Knowledge Production

Obviously, to clone the expert in every person, or even in every oppressed group, is not the only response to expert domination. Alternatives would include forms of democratic participation and control in defining the problems to be studied, in setting the research priorities, and in determining the ends to which the results are to be used. They would recognize the importance of the production of scientific knowledge by scientists as one type of knowledge production that is not inherently superior to others. Such strategies would insist, as some have proposed, on having laypersons involved in deciding about the production of knowledge if not actually doing it, for example, through the development of popularly controlled research centers.

In actual practice, examples of this approach are less developed in North America than are the emerging approaches for popular reappropriation of knowledge or for developing the people's science. Elements of the approach are found in some research groups in Denmark and Sweden, where "reference groups" of those who are affected by research are involved with professional researchers in carrying out projects. In one such project, the Utopia Project, members of the Typographical Workers Union work side by side with professional researchers to analyze the impact of new technology upon their workplaces (Utopia Project Team). Other elements of this strategy develop as relatively powerless groups demand a voice in the allocation of public research funds, as was found in the Appalachian Land Ownership Study (see Gaventa and Horton 1981, 32).

IMPLICATIONS: TOWARD A KNOWLEDGE DEMOCRACY

In recent years there has been much debate about the need for an economic democracy, which suggests that the control and concentration of economic production in the hands of a few must be altered if we are to realize a real political democracy. The concentration of dominating knowledge in the hands of the few, allied with the power to proclaim it "official," is also producing new debates about what constitutes genuine democracy in a knowledge society. In their conservative neo-elitist forms, the arguments are for greater government by expertise, and against the "irrationality" of participation by the masses in the knowledge production system. In their liberal form, these arguments are for greater access and more equal opportunity for all members of the public to the benefits of the existing knowledge system and paradigms. But in their most radical form, these arguments recognize that it is not enough simply to democratize access to existing information. Rather, fundamental questions must be raised about what knowledge is produced, by whom, for whose interests, and toward what ends. Such arguments begin to demand the creation of a new paradigm and organization of science—one that is not only for the people, but is created with them and by them as well.

Genuine popular participation in the production of knowledge has implications, of course, not only for the realization of classical notions of democracy but also for the body of knowledge that will be produced. By altering who controls knowledge and what knowledge is produced, such participation may also change the very definition of what constitutes knowledge. For example, given a chance to participate in the production of knowledge about products, not simply in the production of productions, the Lucas workers chose to develop plans that met basic social needs, not that served as instruments of war. Given the opportunity to define the reasons for poverty through self-analysis, the participants in the Appalachian Land Ownership Study gave a very different set of reasons than had been developed by the mainstream social scientists. The vision and view of the world that is produced by the many in their interests will be vastly different than that produced by the few. The believer in democracy must also have faith that this participatory knowledge of tomorrow will be more humane, rational, and liberating than the dominating knowledge of today.

NOTE

1. Based on report by National Science Foundation, *Federal Funds for Research and Development*, Surveys of Science Resource Series, 1984, vol. 32, p. 170. "External challenge" is the phrase used by Bell, *The Coming of Post-Industrial Society*, in a similar measurement. It includes research and development funds allocated to the Department of Defense, NASA, and a portion of the funds to the Nuclear Regulatory Commission.

3

If You Can't Beat 'Em, Join 'Em: The Professionalization of Participatory Research

THOMAS W. HEANEY ⸺⸺⸺⸺⸺⸺⸺⸺

The origins of research as a human activity have been lost in our distant emergence from a prehistoric swamp. Undoubtedly, survival of the species set an endless agenda for creating new knowledge. Today's experience of "knowledge as commodity" is probably not a useful guide to our past (Hall 1979a). For example, it is most unlikely that one of our ancestors held a patent on fire or the wheel; knowledge which was useful was, by its nature, common knowledge, being a reflection of shared activity. Each person was free to improve upon such knowledge and, happily, did so. We do not know when knowledge production became a specialized task for "experts." It probably occurred when someone recognized that considerable advantages accrued to those who could interpret the stars or master the lore of wild beasts.

Despite these vested interests of priests and huntsmen, our survival suggests two aspects of early research. First, much early research must have been participatory—each person contributing what he or she could to the store of what was known. And second, discovery must have been closely linked with dissemination—the group coming to know in dialogue and passing on accumulated knowledge to the next generation.

Of course, by the time early historians first began scratching and painting on the walls of caves, appropriations of secret knowledge had fairly well established the prestige and power of religious leaders. Not to be outdone, tribal chiefs, kings, and subsequently national governments developed their own secrets, sometimes linked to divine revelation, and almost always related to the emerging science of war. With the writing of history, knowledge became power, or rather an expression of power and a tool for maintaining it. History, and later, science, were frequently used not

merely to understand, but to legitimize historically shaped political relationships and institutions.

Because the given orthodoxy at any point in history explained why things
were the way they were, action to change the status quo could only be an
attack on the "natural" order of things (Foucault 1970). To challenge existing social relationships and institutions was (and is) first a challenge for
the mind. That is, before changing the world, much of what had been
assumed to be legitimate knowledge had to be re-created.

While the growing store of accepted knowledge has been determined more
by power than insight, nonetheless it has also been impossible to suppress
the questioning spirit of humankind. "Experts" in the art of questioning
from Plato to the Scholastics, whose research often represented a threat to
the powerful, as often lacked institutional support. They worked collabo-
ratively through dialogue. Truth seeking was a participatory task; their
discoveries were linked to dissemination.

But by the thirteenth century, the interests of a new institution overcame,
and in some cases co-opted, the creative energies of thoughtful individuals.
These institutions—universities, as they came to be called—were newcomers
to the knowledge competition. Of course, the knowledge by which day-to-
day life was guided and governments governed had little to do with the
university; quite the reverse, in fact. Useful knowledge grew inductively
from the work people did (i.e., from what they were allowed to do by bishop
and monarch) and was transmitted by apprenticeship. Innovations were
sometimes made by a sole inventor or discoverer; but often they were made
by several persons working independently at about the same time. Many
would suggest, by way of explanation, that discoveries occurred when "their
time had come," but it is also likely that the work of preparing ground for
the growth of innovations is not confined to the efforts of a few maverick
inventors. Creativity requires a frame of reference, the building of which
demands the collaboration of all.

In 1977, when Budd Hall spoke about "breaking the monopoly" of the
university, he pointed to centuries of expansionist claims by academic institutions, exacerbated by a relatively recent and peculiarly American issue
in the history of research (1977). Knowledge under the control of the university had been largely academic. That is, it didn't affect the price of cheese
or beer. But in the 1920s, Harvard created the first "vocational" doctorate,
the Ed.D. (Brubacher and Rudy 1958), and with it asserted the university's
monopolistic hold on the production and legitimation of useful knowledge.
Henceforth, in rapid succession, postsecondary institutions began to claim
proprietary rights over practical knowledge in relation to almost every
known human enterprise.

Universities did not act alone. Their silent partners were government
(especially the military) and business interests (especially those represented
by the largest corporate foundations—Carnegie, Ford, and Rockefeller),

who set the research agenda, shaped standards for the legitimation of knowledge and skill, and discredited knowledge produced outside the lockstep rituals of academe (Smith, David 1974). Predictably, the result has been monopolistic control of research and the knowledge it produces which parallels, and eventually supplants, more overt economic and political controls (Apple 1982; Harris 1979).

In most instances, professional researchers and faculty have been unwitting accomplices. The rigors of academic discipline and the diversion of mental energy into narrowly defined and discrete fields of expertise keep broader social consequences of research from view. Academic life is given to maintaining a system over which faculty exercise little control, but of which they (we) are in some tangible ways beneficiaries—at least in terms of prestige, if not genuine power and wealth. The absence or neglect of methodologies for critically analyzing social and political issues within discrete academic disciplines has clearly sterilized most research, insuring its role as eunuch in the court of world power and multinational corporations. As a result, official knowledge and those who produce it pose little threat to those others who use it to wield power.

Of course, there are critical voices raised in most disciplines, clearly a minority, but nonetheless vocal. In fact, those who promote alternatives, such as "participatory research," are usually employed by universities. As in most self-contained systems, the university has shown a resilient ability to incorporate its critics, who add spice to an otherwise bland curriculum. Paulo Freire, for example, came to the attention of his English readers through the kind offices of Harvard University, which brought him to the United States in 1969. Now, Freire's writings are commonly included in the required bibliographies of graduate programs in adult education, despite his singularly devastating critique of both the methods and content of learning in still-dominant institutions of adult education (Freire 1970c). Freire himself has joined a university faculty in his native Brazil, where his books, once banned by the military government, are now used to guide the training of the Brazilian military.

Something similar has begun to happen with participatory research, especially in relation to the study of adult education. At first participatory research was either ignored or roundly condemned (Griffith and Cristarella 1979). But for the past several years it has not only been favorably discussed at respectable conferences; it has become the subject of academic courses in graduate degree programs. And at least one university is proposing to establish a "center" for participatory research. While these developments might seem to give cause for rejoicing, it is nonetheless inconceivable that colleges and universities, for centuries having been the exclusive arbiters of truth, would now forsake their privileges and commit themselves to so self-destructive a task. However well-intentioned and zealous the efforts of individual faculty who have brought participatory research into the academic arena, one can only question by what compromises such researchers are likely to survive.

The answer lies in the naming of the thing. The decision to designate as "research" the production of knowledge by those of us who seek social and political change was already a decision to link the intellectual work of activists with the more widely respected, albeit impractical, work of professors. The coinage of the term *participatory research* was an attempt to legitimize the products of our activity as worthy of the same honors bestowed upon "real" university faculty. Most of us are at least university graduates. Having been weaned from our alma mater, many of us work with and on behalf of those for whom the university holds no promise, for whom academically produced knowledge is a tissue of irrelevant, partial truths behind which the blemishes of an oppressive world remain hidden.

In a sense, the creation of the term *participatory research* has been hype— an attempt to gain leverage in a struggle for limited funds and resources. Perhaps parity between "participatory researchers" and their more tradition-bound academic counterparts could also be gained, with consequent invitations to present papers at research conferences and, of course, to publish articles such as this.

The hype has worked. But unfortunately, embedded within the growing recognition of participatory research as "legitimate" research is an inevitable contradiction. To barter with the coin of an institution is to bank on that institution's prosperity and good health. By reappropriating the word *research* to describe our activity, we seek legitimacy in terms native to the university and thereby bank on the very institution which is the object of our critique. Having made our work acceptable in academic terms, we see that work now being incorporated into academic curricula. Our papers have become required readings for professional researchers who are expected to master the theory and methods of participatory research. It is not difficult to imagine the day when Third World governments and community organizations will hire only professional participatory researchers trained and certified by graduate institutions. Already, some academically based participatory researchers have called for more rigorous standards and sophisticated methodology (Swantz 1981), reasserting the university's preemptive control over what counts for knowledge.

Unfortunately too, both faculty and students are likely to be inextricably caught in this web of contradiction when they attempt to do participatory research in the context of doctoral work or the search for tenure. There are two overarching criteria for university-based research which have little to do with epistemology, hermeneutics, or methodological concerns. Both are political and structurally linked to the time frame of the academic calendar.

The criteria are political in that they both determine and are determined by relations of power only partially related to research itself. These criteria are used to select and promote the brightest and the best in terms defined by government policy, professional associations, alleged experts, and, increasingly, employers. The gambit by which a degree or tenure is gained requires, above all, the art of compromise and a rigorous capacity for linear vision. Participants in the selection process are reduced to individual competitors in a game watched over by referees—the latter having proved their skill by surviving internecine struggles in the same self-defining process. The game is governed by the clock: tenure within a set number of years, doctoral defense before the depletion of available assets. All in all, they are criteria which have subordinated public and socially useful knowledge to the more highly valued rigors of diplomatic inquiry, disciplined work habits, and knowing a great deal about very little.

The consequences of this for participatory research are obvious, even to the novice researcher. First, in order to win the game over all other competitors, the researcher must have *control* over the research project from start to finish. Timing is critical. A doctoral student working on a dissertation cannot afford the luxury of working *with* a community on the community's timetable and with the possibility that the project will be called off or take on a different set of goals—in fact, become a different project. Financial considerations and doctoral committees conspire to impose rigid controls on the student's proposal, research, and its allowable conclusions, all of which not only inhibits community participation in the project, but effectively prohibits community control over the outcomes.

Second, the conclusions of university-based research must be *attributable to an individual* (or a small group of individuals). Whether the prize is tenure or academic grades, the contest is competitive and the winner must be identifiable. Participatory research, on the other hand, diffuses responsibility for its outcomes and makes recognition of an individual's contribution difficult and frequently impossible. Those attempting to do participatory research while meeting the requirements of academic review or doctoral committees face predictable frustrations—and anger which, hopefully, they do not direct toward the community which fails to dance to the university's tune. Such researchers will risk separating themselves from the community, grandstanding, laying claim to the project, and drawing their own conclusions as though they were the conclusions of the community with which they have been working.

Control and *attributability* are central to the political and structural limitations of university research. As a result, participatory research can be discussed, analyzed, studied, criticized, attacked, and even lauded within the university, but its practice cannot be genuinely legitimized there. The legitimacy of participatory research can only be determined by groups engaged in its practice. The criteria here are more tangible than in the rarified atmosphere of professional research. Participatory research is credible and legitimate when the action to which it leads brings about better conditions for life. Period.

University faculty—as individuals—can become involved in the struggles of oppressed groups, can participate in and contribute to the ongoing efforts of such groups to create new understandings of their world, can collaborate in planning strategies for change and in implementing those strategies. They can, by reason of their expertise, contribute knowledge and skill to these tasks in a special way. They can even use the weight of their credentials and the credibility of their institutions to legitimize knowledge produced by others in order to rectify political imbalances maintained, in part, by assumptions of "legitimate knowledge." But these faculty, by reason of their expertise and credentials, can assume no special or guiding role as "participatory researchers." To claim a special role for the "expert" in participatory research is simply to be deceived by our own hype and make mockery of the underlying critique upon which it is based.

In fact, university-sponsored participatory research threatens to overshadow the grass-roots production of knowledge, reaching as it does into areas previously ignored by the university. Our mandarin power ceded by captive students in the lecture hall too easily expands beyond the university campus to encourage the community's dependence on assumed special knowledge and skill. Clients and communities led by professors are always at risk of losing control, as with the practice of law, where a dispute quickly becomes submerged in the incomprehensible "legalese" of litigation.

Attempts to "legitimize" knowledge produced by those who would use it to redress injustice or right inequities can go too far. The proclamation that such knowledge production is "research" was a political act. It reappropriated a term which had been limited in its use to the work of those who followed a narrow and historically defined set of rules. Having "legitimized" the research, there are those who would now "professionalize" the researcher, who would impose *new* rules to limit and circumscribe what counts for knowledge among those doing participatory research. And as self-styled legislature and judiciary, the university is ready to take over, laying claims to fruits for which it did not toil.

Despite newfound acceptance, participatory research is more than theory or method. It is above all a critique—built on a critical analysis of assumptions underlying knowledge derived from historically shaped and politically beholden institutions. Beyond articulating this critique, the role of academics in participatory research will always mirror the ambivalence of our trained incapacities. The reason participatory research has always existed—millennia before it was named—is that the intellectual efforts of experts throughout the ages have seldom influenced the distribution of power or eliminated oppression. On the contrary, since its inception the university has been a major element in the system by which official knowledge is promulgated and the given order maintained. Participatory research is simply a contradiction of that system.

4

A Way of Working: Participatory Research and the Aboriginal Movement in Canada

TED JACKSON _____

The purpose of this chapter is to summarize and critique the experience since 1970 of Canada's Aboriginal[1] movement in using participatory research—people's research for action—in order to achieve its self-defined goals and objectives. Participatory research—an approach which calls for collective analysis and collective action by rank-and-file members of communities and workplaces—has become a focus of interest and a mode of operation for a growing number of activists and academics internationally. Advocates of this approach are especially concerned with participatory research which is conducted within, and under the auspices of, social movements of all types, including the trade union movement, the women's movement, peasant movements in the Third World, the antinuclear movement, and indigenous people's movements.

Concern with the relationship between participatory research and social movements is more than purely methodological. It is true that certain methods for carrying out participatory research may be applied with effectiveness across a wide range of movements, and therefore frequent and frank exchanges among those who do participatory research in unions, women's organizations, and so on must be promoted. However, the concern is also strategic. Understanding participatory research experiences, particularly at the local level of social movements, may yield valuable information regarding the potential bases of new political alliances across the movement. Of course, the precise nature of cross-movement alliances will be determined by the specific conditions existing in a given social formation, at a particular historical moment.

The fundamental problem before us is how to use experience as a basis not only for predicting, but also for collectively directing, our future. An attempt is made in the following pages to modestly contribute to such prediction and direction by analyzing one particular social movement—the Aboriginal movement of Canada. It will become clear to the reader that class and class conflict are indispensable analytic categories in understanding, in a substantive way, a twenty-year period of rich and varied experience in the conduct of participatory research by Aboriginal peoples in Canada. It will also become evident that the interests of the Native working class, in the workplace, have been seriously neglected in this experience.

THE ABORIGINAL MOVEMENT: CLEAVAGES AND COMMON BONDS

The Aboriginal movement is a complex social movement in today's Canada, and few people, including many of its own leaders, claim to fully understand its potential as a force for progressive social change. From the outset it must be pointed out that to speak without qualification of "the Aboriginal movement in Canada" is to risk serious oversimplification. In organizational terms there in fact exists a cluster of several Aboriginal "sub-movements."

The most important of these sub-movements include: treaty and status Indians, Metis and non-status Indians, the Inuit, Aboriginal women, and urban Aboriginal people. Each sub-movement employs a system of local, regional and supra-regional organizations and relates to the Canadian state, under legislation, in different ways. The most prominent of these different relationships is that treaty and status Indians and the Inuit are serviced by the Department of Indian and Northern Development (DIAND) and other federal agencies, while the remaining sub-movements are serviced by provincial ministries as well as some federal agencies, excluding DIAND. It is well-known (Price 1978) that these legislated cleavages have assisted the state in exerting social control over Aboriginal protest activities in Canada.

Furthermore, in periods of economic recession and cutbacks in social spending and the legitimation activities of the state, the Aboriginal movement has been deeply fragmented by the process of competing for limited government funds both within and across federal and provincial levels. Moreover, there are wide variations in terms of the power bases of various Aboriginal groups. For example, those with clear Aboriginal claim to their traditional lands, or those with ownership of lands rich in energy resources, move from points of greater political and economic strength (when world energy prices are favorable) than those groups who do not possess these advantages. Sources of additional fragmentation have included differences among Aboriginal peoples in terms of tribal affiliation, religion, language, region, and political partisanship.

Having identified and recognized these major sources of cleavage, it is nevertheless possible, and useful, to speak of an Aboriginal movement per se. It is possible, first and foremost, because Aboriginal peoples in all parts of Canada share what Vachon (1979) calls a common heritage of traditional political culture. He identifies six original characteristics of Aboriginal political culture regarding the question of political self-determination: (1) ontodetermination ("freedom-that-comes-from-being," collaborating with all beings); (2) responsibility toward the Earth, duty of thanksgiving, harmonization, and guardianship in a nonproprietary type of usage; (3) a communitarian, consensual, and confederative dimension; (4) originality of Aboriginal political notions; (5) nonviolent, nonassertive, long-term resistance; and (6) a spiritual dimension: "spirits" and the Spirit.

It is possible, and useful as well, to speak of the Aboriginal movement per se in relation to the cumulative impact of the broad range of Aboriginal sub-movements upon the non-Aboriginal, dominant society at large. As a result of the *totality* of the political lobbying and public awareness campaigns of these groupings, certain reforms relating to economic and social provisions for Aboriginal persons have been effected.

PARTICIPATORY RESEARCH AS A TOOL OF THE ABORIGINAL MOVEMENT

Whatever else may constitute the common ground of the sub-movements within the Aboriginal movement, few other social movements have in recent years so thoroughly adopted participatory research as a tool to attain their goals as has the Aboriginal movement in all of its manifestations.

One early antecedent was the community self-survey, a methodology which had grown out of the short-lived but potent community development program of Indian Affairs in the mid-1960s (CENTRAD 1973; Ponting and Gibbons 1980). However, it was usually incorporated into band training activities within a liberal, capitalist framework which did little to challenge, in a fundamental way, existing Aboriginal/non-Aboriginal social relations.

It is not surprising that strong interest in Aboriginal-defined and Aboriginal-controlled research approaches coincided with the politicization of Aboriginal organizations in response to the federal government's assimilationist white paper of 1969 (see Weaver 1981). Aboriginal leaders began to see that research activities could assist in the movement toward political strength and, ultimately, political self-determination.

The struggle around the white paper stimulated many Aboriginal organizations to assert, once and for all, Aboriginal claim to their traditional lands. By the early 1970s, comprehensive land use and occupancy studies were underway across Canada. These studies, funded by the state, were placed under the explicit direction and operational control of the Aboriginal organizations. They involved the use of maps and oral history and focused in particular on traditional land use activities such as hunting, trapping, and fishing. Many of the northern land use studies, such as those in the Northwest Territories, were completed by the mid- to late 1970s.

By the late 1970s, however, Aboriginal organizations at all levels had begun to refine and extend the practice of community-controlled research. In many parts of the country Aboriginal-initiated and directed research into social problems such as water and sanitation, health, housing, and social services was initiated at the community level. Innovative research methods involving, for example, the use of study trips, community research committees, drawings, and photographs were explored in these efforts. Greater attention was paid to resisting and circumventing the social control of the state through funding mechanisms. Aboriginal participatory research began to focus on women as a group with special social requirements in Aboriginal communities, and assessment of Aboriginal community needs was undertaken, not only in rural, but also in urban settings.

By the end of the 1970s, participatory research also began to be used by Aboriginal communities to identify alternative economic strategies. Across the country, many Aboriginal groups shifted their focus from primarily political to economic issues as well, particularly with the problem of creating a base of wealth independent of the state. While interest in participatory research for the development of alternative economic strategies was strong, this phase in the use of research as a tool by the Aboriginal movement had only just begun by the onset of the 1980s.

A DECADE OF EXPERIENCE: ACHIEVEMENTS AND DEFICIENCIES

Experience in participatory research by Aboriginal people in Canada during the 1970s was rich in achievement, in both methodological and political terms. There were also major differences in the practice of participatory research by the Aboriginal movement during this period which merit reflection and review.

The methodological achievements of the land use studies were impressive indeed. Nahanni's (1977) account of the Dene land use and occupancy study emphasized the use of songs, dances, and legends in understanding the Dene relationship to the land. Oral history with elders and with hunters, trappers, and fishermen, and detailed, layered land use maps including Dene place names provided data upon which the Dene argument of Aboriginal title was made. Similar methodological approaches were employed in the eastern Arctic by the Inuit (Brice-Bennett 1977), in British Columbia (Nazko-Kluskus Study Team 1974) and in northern Ontario (Sieciechowicz 1977). Most of these studies took place in the mid-1970s.

Common to most of these studies was an additional methodological element: The land use findings frequently were "fed into" political hearings involving land and resources by the Aboriginal organizations. In the case of the Dene, it was the Mackenzie Valley pipeline inquiry (Jackson 1978). The Nazko-Kluskus and the Nishnawbe-Aski of northern Ontario also employed their land use data in hearings on the land and environment in their regions (Jackson 1977).

One of the most important methodological achievements of the land use studies, however, was the clarity with which they established the role of the outside, professional, non-Aboriginal researcher in the research enterprise (see Lockhart 1982). As Nahanni noted:

...our community leaders and community people expressed their dislike of the invasion of their privacy by outsiders who didn't speak their language. We know from past experiences that government research by white researchers never improved our lives. Usually white researchers spy on us, the things we do, how we do them, when we do them, and so on. After all these things are written in their jargon, they go away and neither they nor their reports are ever seen again. We have observed this and the Brotherhood resolved to try its best to see that, in future, research involves the Dene from beginning to end. (1977, 23)

In terms of political achievements, the case of the land use studies is more complex, and nowhere is this complexity more apparent than in the Northwest Territories and the Yukon. Great gains were made in the 1970s, by virtue of the evidence collected by the land use research, in the political leverage of Aboriginal organizations north of sixty degrees north latitude. Presently Aboriginal claims by the Council for Yukon Indians, the Dene Nation, Inuit Tapirisat of Canada, and the Committee for Original People's Entitlement (the Inuit of the western Arctic) call for large amounts of land and money in compensation for the use by non-Aboriginal Canadian society of unsurrendered indigenous land. These claims may also spur the development of special provinces of the Dene and the Inuit in the Northwest Territories. Along the way, Aboriginal organizations, using in part land use data, were also primarily responsible for soundly defeating some initiatives of U.S.-based multinational capital, much as they were in the Dene victory in stopping the proposed Mackenzie Valley natural gas pipeline in the 1970s. Such political achievements should not be taken lightly.

The Canadian state, however, moved to minimize the impact of Aboriginal claims in the North. First, the passing by the federal government of the Canada Lands legislation (Bill C-48) permitted exploration and extraction activities by resource corporations on Aboriginal lands *before* land claims were settled. The federal National Energy Program provided incentives for the Canadianization of capital in the oil and gas industry, but at the same time provided incentives for immediate corporate activity on all Canada lands.

As part of a seemingly coordinated strategy, the federal government opened the 1980s with a new, very hard-line stance on negotiations over

Aboriginal claims. Consequently, the political pressure and the political onus again shifted onto Aboriginal peoples. An organization such as the Council for Yukon Indians not only had to negotiate its claim against the twin backdrops of the Canada Lands Act and the National Energy Program, but also had to contend with a pipeline under construction by Canadian capital, literally through its own "front yard." Northern Aboriginal organizations, whose political power was enhanced by participatory research into land use, were forced to lower their hopes for the land claims process. The state once again muted their political achievements.

While the land use studies covered many communities and related expressly to relationships with land and natural resources, the needs assessment studies, whose onset can be traced to the late 1970s, were concerned with services: water and sanitation, health, housing, and social services. For the most part these studies were concerned with specific communities or small groups of communities. However, the needs assessment studies built upon the methodological base established by the land use studies. Several cases are instructive.

One of the most extensive of these needs assessment efforts was the environmental assessment of water and sanitation alternatives undertaken by the Big Trout Lake Band Council from 1977 through the early 1980s. In response to a federal initiative to build a $2 million sewer line in the community, which would service only a small minority of non-Aboriginal residents, the band council carried out its own technical study, which recommended trucked water and sewage systems, based on the principle of democratized servicing rather than "technical apartheid." The Big Trout Lake effort employed a variety of participatory research methods, including local research committees, community seminars, study trips, local training, and popular research reports in Cree syllabics, and placed continued emphasis upon the control of all knowledge produced by the research in the hands of the band for its political use. The project, which received international attention, was also significant because of its demonstration of the power of local or indigenous knowledge in combination with "scientific" or official knowledge and because of its particular technical findings. The state has resisted the band's democratized technical solution, but the band persisted, and by the mid-1980s, DIAND funded a trucked water and waste system that serviced all houses in the community. This process of research and action had taken a decade (see Jackson 1980; Jackson and McKay 1982).

The late 1970s also saw considerable organizational energy, on the part of Aboriginal groups in the south, channeled into the issue of health. In one such instance, the health steering committee of the Union of Ontario Indians was engaged in a process of participatory health policy production and planning. Community health representatives, band council members, and citizens at large sat on the committee, which was developed following the report of a national royal commission into Indian and Inuit health consultation structures (Berger 1980). The Union's committee collectively investigated community-controlled health clinics, health training and nutrition education, and many other questions.

In 1979, one of the first comprehensive approaches to social service needs assessment in the *urban* Aboriginal community was initiated by the Native Canadian Centre in Toronto. This one-year study employed "network" sampling methods in order to identify the dispersed Aboriginal population in Toronto. Open-ended interviews sought information from respondents regarding their personal background and their needs in terms of employment, housing, education, child care, family services, and recreation. The results were analyzed by computer and then produced in popular report format. Public meetings and "coffee gatherings" at the homes of respondents provided forums for staff to present the results and obtain feedback and action recommendations from the persons interviewed, who were mainly women. Lack of funds prevented a second phase of the research project from being carried out, but several of the recommendations have been acted upon by the Centre (Bobiwash and Malloch 1980).

These few examples are presented for illustrative purposes. Similar studies, using participatory research methods to assess community needs, were conducted by Aboriginal organizations across the country throughout the late 1970s. The major methodological achievements of such studies were rooted in the technical nature of the problems under study and their technical solution through a participatory, investigative process. Sophisticated quantitative measures and, in some cases, computers, were employed in these studies. Whereas the early participatory research advocates had rejected survey methods and promoted qualitative data almost exclusively, the Aboriginal movement in Canada now had begun to employ more traditional social science methods in combination with other qualitative, participatory methods, and with all of these methods firmly under Aboriginal direction.

The political achievements of the needs assessment studies are much more difficult to ascertain. Taken on its own, each individual experience shows that participatory research for Aboriginal needs assessment puts new, accurate technical information in the hands of the Aboriginal organizations. They could use this new information to improve state policy and services in their communities, and many did so with some success.

One political lesson seems clear, however. New and accurate technical information is not enough to change the policies and services of the state. In many instances in the needs assessment studies (the Big Trout Lake effort is a case in point), the state was able to resist change through its control over research dollars, bureaucratic delays, and other measures. Rational arguments based upon better information—the people's information—are necessary, but not sufficient, to trigger real change.

Closer to the central contradictions of capitalism are questions related to economic organizations, production, and distribution. This was the third and most recent phase in Aboriginal participatory research and it remained the least developed in the 1970s. One experience from the Yukon serves as an example.

In the spring of 1981, the Council for Yukon Indians (CYI) recommended a comprehensive training plan for the Yukon Indian People (including both status and non-status). In order to assess the needs of Aboriginal residents in twelve communities, several levels of participation were needed: a co-ordinated training committee within CYI representing all Council departments; a mobile participatory research team to link the committee with the communities; local Indian education authorities to take responsibility for convening meetings on training needs and programs in relation to employment development; and local-level resource people to learn training techniques. Although repeated efforts to obtain funds for implementing this plan met with reluctance on the part of the federal government, CYI decided to go ahead with the plan in a partial way and devoted its own staff resources to work on the mobile team (Council for Yukon Indians 1981a).

In this example, participatory research served as a method of generating popular knowledge on possible options with respect to economic strategies, and CYI was clear on the application and importance of this method. However, the political organization was still left with conflicts to resolve among factions promoting different strategies within the Council.

What, in summary, can be said of the experience in Aboriginal participatory research in the 1970s? The richness of this particular decade, both methodologically and politically, is striking. Yet some critical observations are necessary.

One major problem was the fragmented nature of the experience. Certainly, such fragmentation was paralleled by and originated in the fragmented nature of the movement itself. But with minimal effort, some very exciting exchanges about participatory research theory and practice could have taken place, to the ultimate gain of many parties. However, this did not occur. At the root was, probably, competition for limited research funds among Aboriginal sub-movements and groups within the various sub-movements. In this sense again, the state—ubiquitous and infinitely creative in those years—exerted social control through social spending (see Loney 1977).

Strategies were needed to circumvent this problem. Workshops on participatory research by Aboriginal peoples could have stimulated exchanges and unified efforts. Handbooks on how to do participatory research in relation to Aboriginal culture could have been valuable in addressing the fragmentation problem and would at the same time have recruited new advocates of participatory research. Seminars on such increasingly important areas as participatory evaluation and the popularization of corporate research could also have improved methodological and political results while also helping to create a sense of solidarity and common struggle among activists. There are many other strategies that could have been tried as well.

There is, however, a problem of another order in this decade of experience in participatory research by Aboriginal peoples, and it turns on the question of who, within the Aboriginal movement, was in control of the participatory research process. A closer look at the examples cited in the foregoing pages indicates that, almost without exception, Aboriginal participatory research efforts were under the direction of middle-class Aboriginal leaders. This in itself is hardly a surprising finding. Non-Aboriginal researchers and leaders are usually middle-class. However, in terms of understanding the relationship between participatory research and the Aboriginal movement in Canada as a social movement, this problem was a serious and very complex one.

ABORIGINAL LEADERSHIP AND THE NEW MIDDLE CLASS

To be more specific, most participatory research undertaken by Aboriginal organizations during the 1970s was initiated and directed by Aboriginal members of the *new* middle class. In Canada the new middle class, or new *petite bourgeoisie*, is dominated in terms of occupational categories by managers, administrators, professionals, and technicians. Canada's pattern of capitalist development, particularly since the Second World War, has elaborated this class and the classifications within it. A major feature of this pattern of development was the rapid growth during the period 1945-75 of the state apparatus in Canada, providing employment for hundreds of thousands of members of the new middle class.

Although this process had been an ongoing one for nearly forty years, studies of the effects of land claims settlements threw the problem into bold relief. In Alaska, a new Aboriginal business class emerged to run the regional corporations created by the Settlement Act. Struggles for control over these large corporations ensued, "the educated, professional management group being challenged by less well-educated Native Villagers and urban blue-collar workers" (Hanrahan and Gruenstein, cited in Council for Yukon Indians 1981b). The new business class had won almost total control of the regional economic organizations, while the village corporations remained undercapitalized and subservient to non-villager class interests.

At the same time, a study of the impact of the James Bay and Northern Quebec Agreement found that a new group of Cree bureaucrats trained to implement the agreement constituted a differentiated class which was beginning to reproduce itself exclusively.

Their mastery of what the study termed "the technical idiom" permitted the new middle class in the Aboriginal movement to use participatory research to achieve its goals. The class locations of both these Aboriginal initiators of participatory research and the consultants whom they engaged for technical assistance were similar, if not identical. Class representation in the key positions in the participatory research process was dominated by the new middle class both in terms of Aboriginal and non-Aboriginal participants. Representation of other classes, particularly the working class, was minimal. Members of the new middle class, working on behalf of the Aboriginal movement through participatory research, related to agents of the state—the funder of the research—who were, in turn, members of the same class. These members of the new middle class, it must be stressed, owed their existence to the post-war growth of the Canadian state. To act against the ultimate interests of the state was to endanger the relatively privileged class position they continued to occupy. For this reason, Aboriginal leaders who advocated participatory research were unlikely to push the research process—in methodological, political, or financial terms—to a point where it endangered their membership in the new middle class or the "symbiotic" relationship between this class and the successful operation of the state apparatus.

CONTRADICTORY CLASS LOCATIONS

The problem of the new Aboriginal middle class is indeed a complex one. Wright (1979) has developed the notion of contradictory class locations. For Wright, class relations in advanced capitalist society must be understood in terms of three processes: control of labor power, control of the physical means of production, and control of investment. The popular class positions within each of these processes are represented by the bourgeoisie and the proletariat. However, certain occupations are located in contradictory positions between the bourgeoisie and the proletariat:

Three clusters of divisions within the social division of labour can be characterized as occupying contradictory locations within class relations...: 1. *managers and supervisors* occupy a contradictory location between the bourgeoisie and the proletariat; 2. certain categories of *semi-autonomous employees* who retain relatively high levels of control over their immediate labour process occupy a contradictory position between the proletariat and the petty bourgeoisie; 3. *small employers* occupy a contradictory location between bourgeoisie and the petty bourgeoisie. (Wright 1979, 63)

The category of "managers" includes technocrats as well as top and middle managers, while the category of "supervisors" includes bottom managers, foremen, and line supervisors. Although the analysis developed by Wright refers to relations of production, he argues that the concept of contradictory class locations may also be applied to nonproductive sectors, such as the apparatus of the state.

Loxley has pointed out, with reference to Manitoba, that elected Aboriginal officials and state and band employees together occupy a contradictory class location:

They own no means of production and are not policy makers. Yet they hold positions of authority within the ideological apparatus and exercise powers of hiring, funding and sometimes of coercion. They are subject to contradictory pressures from the state on the one hand, from whom they receive their finances, and from the native communities on the other, whose interests they supposedly serve. At the community level the latter pressures often outweigh the former giving rise to quite radical leaders, but the complete dependence of even elected officials (such as Chiefs) on state finances places severe limitations on the independence of their actions. (1981, 162-163)

At the onset of the 1980s, this same group of leaders and employees in the Aboriginal movement increasingly began to feel the impact of severe cutbacks in social, or legitimation, spending by the Canadian state in response to pressures from capital. Recessive economic conditions thwarted the class aspirations of some of these leaders, and they were radicalized.

We should, therefore, expect that those who push participatory research to the limit will be, in Wright's terminology, the semiautonomous workers and bottom-level managers. Higher-level managers, technocrats, and employers are less likely to act against their class interests—they have more to lose. This raises the even more complex question of the Aboriginal working class.

THE QUESTION OF THE ABORIGINAL WORKING CLASS

The general "question" of the Aboriginal working class is actually several equally challenging specific questions. One of these is the fundamental problem of how to define the Aboriginal working class, particularly with regard to the Aboriginal persons who are permanently unemployed, of whom there are tens of thousands in Canada. A second question is: How has the Aboriginal working class related to the trade union movement historically and what is the potential for organizing Aboriginal workers in the future? Third, what data are available to understand the particular needs of women within the Aboriginal working class? Fourth, what workplace issues are currently the focus of struggle by Aboriginal workers? Finally, what is the potential for worker ownership and worker self-management in Aboriginal enterprises? Answers to these questions give some direction to perhaps the most basic question of all: How can participatory research be used to further the interests of the Aboriginal working class?

If there is any doubt that Aboriginal organizations, almost universally, have ignored the interests of the Aboriginal working class, the case of the Dene—one of the most progressive and ideologically consistent organizations in the 1970s—offers especially insightful lessons. In a critique of Dene plans for self-government, Daniels wrote:

Before someone builds a boat they normally know what they want to use the boat for. If they know the "function" or purpose then it is relatively easy to decide if the boat should take the "form" (shape or design) of a kayak, canoe, barge, speedboat, oil tanker or skiff. Similarly, if the Dene decide first the function or purpose of their government then the form will follow logically. For example, if the Dene want a government to create a few rich people and leave the rest on welfare then they can choose one type of government. If on the other hand, they want a government that will keep the Dene more or less equal and help create work for everyone (whether traditional bush work or modern wage work or a combination) then they will choose a very different form of government. Yet it is just such an issue—the type of class structure that the Dene Nation expects or wants to develop—that Dene Government proposals have ignored or treated very vaguely. Instead, the proposals have all gone at it backwards like looking through a boat catalogue to see what you want to do out there on the water. (1982, 2)

Daniels put the case that the Dene plans have failed to pay attention to the needs of a growing Dene working class:

Right now it looks like most of the plans for the future Dene Nation have Dene people outside, above or below the working class—anywhere but *inside* the working class. (1982, 7)

Although his analysis was directed to the Dene situation, it could have been applied to the great majority of Aboriginal organizations. The neglect of the Aboriginal working class, or the class question generally, is an almost universal characteristic of Aboriginal groups throughout the movement.

With regard to defining the Aboriginal working class, John Loxley of the University of Manitoba provides a beginning. With reference to northern Manitoba, he wrote in 1981: "It appears that the majority (perhaps 55 percent with dependents) are members of the proletariat albeit frequently occupying positions in what Marx called the stagnant form of relative surplus population." He continued, "Beneath these is a much smaller but nevertheless large and growing group of native people (25 percent) who really are permanently unemployed as far as the formal labour market is concerned."

In urbanized areas, however, there exists a well-defined Aboriginal proletariat. Aboriginal persons in southern Ontario, for example, are employed as wage laborers in textile operations and as high steel workers in building construction, to name only two examples. Furthermore, many Aboriginal persons are employed as secretaries and clerks in white-collar, working-class occupations in both Aboriginal organizations and non-Aboriginal organizations in the cities of the nation. The ranks of this urban working class grew with the migration of Aboriginal people to urban areas in the 1960s and 1970s. Migration patterns stabilized in the 1980s.

The relationship between the Aboriginal working class and organized labor has been mediated by the leadership of the Aboriginal movement, which belongs to the new middle class, and is fundamentally antiunion.

Close relations between Aboriginal leadership and the state have embedded a capitalist managerial ideology in Aboriginal organizations. This has not, however, prevented leaders of the Aboriginal movement from making alliances with organized labor to oppose, for example, environmentally damaging capitalist initiatives. But it *has* meant that Aboriginal workplaces have been slow to organize.

Nevertheless, by the onset of the 1980s, the tide began to turn. Aboriginal workers began to organize to fight for their rights as *workers* as distinct from their rights as Aboriginal persons. One successful case involved the 1980 certification of an Ontario Public Service Employees Union (OPSEU) local at the central office of the Ontario Metis and Non-Status Indian Association in Toronto, though OMNSIA leaders claimed the union restricted the association's effectiveness in bettering the economic conditions of Aboriginal people in Ontario. A major problem was that the provincial government chronically underfunded the association, and financial pressures on the organization were therefore very real. Relations with the state, in this respect, have structured a situation where the interests of Aboriginal office workers are pitted against the interests of Aboriginal leaders and communities—a not-so-subtle variation on the long-used, divide-and-conquer approach of the state.

Tobias explored the political economy of Aboriginal women with special attention to the role of Aboriginal women workers in Ontario. She found

that Native women in Ontario are concentrated in "feminized" occupations; that a large proportion are unemployed; that employment is on a part-time, temporary or seasonal basis and that for women on Reserves a principal source of employment is government grants. Furthermore, a large proportion of women and/or members of their family units receive social assistance. The only comparative figures... indicate that Native women as a group may be unemployed or under-employed more than men and receive a lower income from employment.

Native women are not represented at the leadership and decision-making level of Native organizations, almost the only area open for professional employment for Native women and men, especially in urban areas.... In short, Native women as a group are virtually invisible and very oppressed. (1980, 16)

And finally, what are some of the workplace issues currently facing Aboriginal workers and around which organizing can proceed? Among the most important, of course, are wage levels and job security. However, other issues of importance, with reference to white-collar workplaces in particular, relate to health and safety provisions and automation. In the larger Aboriginal organizations, workers are being displaced by technological change. What provisions for retraining or a redivision of labor within the workplace will be made? What provisions, as well, are there for the participation of

Aboriginal workers in workplace decisions generally? This issue may be reconceptualized as *Aboriginal worker self-management* and raises some fundamental questions about the structure and functions of Aboriginal political and economic organizations in general.

Aboriginal worker self-management is not the same proposition as Aboriginal economic self-determination as advocated by certain groups. In many instances, the development of an Aboriginal managerial class has been seen as a prerequisite for Aboriginal economic self-determination. However, worker self-management in Aboriginal enterprises is a class question rather than a question of nationality or race. It proposes that *workers,* rather than professional managers, manage the enterprise. There are many possible arrangements for worker ownership and worker governance of enterprises, as Zwerdling (1980) and others have shown.

The struggle for control of the Aboriginal workplace will continue. Models of worker control, such as the Mondragon network of successful worker cooperatives (industrial, service, and financial) in Spain, may prove to be useful guides in this regard. Participatory research, for its part, may be found to be very useful in identifying appropriate worker self-management structures in the Aboriginal context. Some promising methodological directions are suggested in Levin (1981), Brown and Tandon (Reason and Rowan 1981) and elsewhere in this book.

The overall point of this discussion on the Aboriginal working class is that participatory research efforts in the 1970s did not address the needs of Aboriginal workers directly or thoroughly. Aboriginal workers should consider adopting for their own use, and for their own class interests, the methods of participatory research which have worked for other class groupings within the Aboriginal movement. The use of participatory research in identifying the Aboriginal working class, in developing Aboriginal workers' organizations, and in addressing the workplace needs of Aboriginal workers is possible, desirable, and timely. It is understandable why such uses of participatory research were not effected in the past, but continued neglect is inexcusable.

CURRENT TRENDS

As 1991 came to a close, the Aboriginal movement was poised to launch its largest and most ambitious participatory research project ever. Appointed earlier in the year by the federal government, the Royal Commission on Aboriginal Peoples was preparing to hold hearings across the country on issues of fundamental concern to Aboriginal groups, including: the possible dismantling of the Department of Indian Affairs and Northern Development, the rapid settlement of land claims, appropriate forms of enabling legislation for self-government, and strategies for sustainable economic growth in Aboriginal communities. With a three-year mandate and a large research budget, the commission held the potential to become an important agent of change. Most important of all, four of the seven members of the commission, including its cochairs, were strong, credible Aboriginal leaders.

In spite of a sustained, mean-spirited, and capricious attack by the government on the budgets of public programs in support of Aboriginal communities and organizations (see *The Moment* 1987; Angus 1991), and in spite of two tough recessions (1981-82 and 1989-91) that had Aboriginal (and non-Aboriginal) communities reeling, the Aboriginal movement lobbied hard for its rights under amendments to the Canadian constitution in the early 1980s, worked ceaselessly to establish new economic, social, and educational institutions to support its objectives, and joined in an almost never-ending series of coalitions to resist the neoconservative onslaught against jobs, human rights, and social services that characterized the 1980s in Canada.

The summer of 1990 was the turning point, however, in relations between Aboriginal peoples and non-Aboriginal Canadians. First, an Aboriginal legislator in Manitoba named Elijah Harper quietly voted against a new constitutional amendment to protect Quebec's special status as a cultural entity, thus killing the amendment (known as the "Meech Lake Accord"), and drawing the outrage of many mainstream politicians. But, in Harper's view, the amendment was not worth supporting. Elijah Harper became an instant folk hero among his people.

Later that summer, a series of blockades by heavily armed Mohawks and traditionalists from reserves around Montreal resulted in the shooting death of one police officer and a protracted and tense standoff between a small group of warriors and several hundred soldiers of the Canadian army. Further bloodshed was avoided and the standoff was defused peacefully, but not before millions of Canadians had been exposed to almost a full month of television images of Mohawks and soldiers standing nose to nose over barbed wire. Canadians, who smugly pride themselves in having created a kinder, gentler nation than that of their neighbors to the south, were shocked. Aboriginal issues became visceral and visible; Aboriginal rights were now on the public agenda in a big way.

These were some of the events that shaped the backdrop against which the Aboriginal movement proceeded to expand and refine its use of participatory research from 1981 onward. It was in the 1980s that participatory research truly became the movement's *way of working*.

Early in the decade, after considerable pressure from and dialogue with the movement, the Social Sciences and Humanities Research Council of Canada, an authoritative national funding body for scholarly research, issued a statement supporting community-based and community-directed research in Aboriginal communities. The council urged non-Aboriginal researchers to take their ethical and cultural direction from Aboriginal communities and to produce knowledge of use to these constituencies and to

academic institutions. At the same time, professionals of all kinds (anthro-
pologists, sociologists, educators, economists, business consultants) began
to discuss more systematically appropriate roles for themselves in relation
to Aboriginal political objectives.

A special 1982 issue of the *Canadian Journal of Native Studies* highlighted
the role of professionals from outside the Aboriginal community in contributing "knowledge of the functioning of institutions of the larger society
as they impinge on native concerns while community members provide
expertise in defining the issues and in culturally and behaviorally appropriate
ways of addressing them. Together both groups search for methods of
linking resources to communities to solve development issues" (Jackson et
al. 1982, 5).

The 1980s also saw a consolidation and refinement of some of the methods
of participatory research used by Aboriginal groups. For example, efforts
by faculty and students at the Department of Native Studies at Trent University resulted in the production of a set of guidelines for doing participatory oral history research in Aboriginal communities, as well as a field-
oriented undergraduate course in this technique (Conchelos 1985).

Participatory research methods were also used to develop comprehensive
plans for sustainable resource use on Aboriginal lands. For instance, in the
mid-1980s, the community of Old Crow in the northern Yukon produced
a socioeconomic plan based on sustainable use of renewable resources such
as water, wood, fish, fur, caribou, and waterfowl, as well as the promotion
of tourism to complement the traditional economy.

Pam Colorado of the University of Calgary has broadened the debate
concerning these issues by discussing traditional Aboriginal science in contemporary terms and linking it to participatory research, in order to
strengthen traditional Aboriginal science, restore integrity to the practice of
Aboriginal science, and to generally promote peace, understanding, and
environmental responsibility among Aboriginal and non-Aboriginal peoples
alike. In Colorado's view, participatory research can act as a "flow-through"
mechanism for scientific findings from both the Aboriginal and non-Aboriginal worlds. Participatory research itself contains many important parallels to Aboriginal science, including its commitment to qualitative data,
local participation, the learning process, the value of fun in research work,
and the role of professionals in facilitation and group building, among other
things. However, Colorado notes that participatory research as it heretofore
has been practiced must break through its own, self-imposed barriers: "The
word 'participate' usually refers to a group of people, but what about the
groups of different parts of our senses and functions within our mind? To
what extent is participatory research willing to participate in feeling, passion
and values?" (Colorado 1988, 64).

Another characteristic of the 1980s was the extensive use of participatory research to promote Aboriginal economic development. At the beginning of the decade, a continuing education course of Native economic development and small business management at Trent University offered a key module on participatory research linked to fieldwork in students' home communities. This course served as a pilot project for two later programs at the university (undergraduate) and community college levels, both of which placed great emphasis on community-based research (see Theilheimer 1990). In the Kayahna Tribal Area in northern Ontario, economic development workers promoted "human-centred community-based development" that relied heavily on "consensus planning." This is usually done by means of a community survey, group discussion, the use of the radio station, and other means necessary to acquire a good understanding of the proposed organizations, such as the Kayahna Area Trappers Association, which regularly produced popular research tools to spur discussion and action (e.g., Chervin and Norman 1982).

Overall, it can be concluded that during the 1980s participatory research became, in every respect, the *way of working* of the Aboriginal movement in Canada. Yet the theory and practice of Aboriginal participatory research remain underdeveloped. Theoretical analysis remains partial, fragmented, and uncoordinated. The wide range of institutes, study groups, departments, lobbies, and firms interested in participatory research have leaned even further toward practice and techniques. Theory has taken a back seat, and this may have been inevitable, perhaps even desirable. But it is now necessary to return to theory. The raw material available promises some fascinating and productive theoretical debates ahead.

In terms of practice, we are still confronted by a body of experience that has been and remains in the control of the middle class. There is also the gender issue. The "gender issue" is simply that Aboriginal women continue to constitute the most aggrieved and oppressed constituency within Aboriginal communities.

Aboriginal participatory research continues to be held hostage to government funding. This issue has also been with us for twenty years. Aboriginal communities and organizations must redouble their efforts to create an independent economic base. This means creating business enterprises, financial institutions, and economic plans that retain and manage economic surplus under Aboriginal control for Aboriginal objectives.

These problems notwithstanding, participatory research will continue to be a source of hope and pride and practical advantage to the Aboriginal movement in Canada. On the eve of the launching of the Royal Commission on Aboriginal Peoples, the possibility for further Aboriginal gains is very real. Sustained pressure will be required to maintain the integrity and forward motion of the commission's work, but this pressure is very likely to be forthcoming. What isn't clear at this point is how the commission will address the perennial problems faced by such exercises, particularly class and gender biases and the politics of funding. The struggle to address these problems continues.

NOTES

The original version of this paper benefited from the insights of my students at Trent University, in Peterborough, Canada, during 1981-82, particularly Michael Chervin, Shelley Bressette, and Daintry Norman, as well as those of my colleagues Don McCaskill, Marlene Brant Castellano, Greg Conchelos, and Budd Hall. In the 1980s, my work in support of Aboriginal participatory research was heavily influenced by Jennifer Mauro, Lynne Dee Sproule, Jane Henson, and Scott Clark, and by Gerry McKay and Grace Hudson, leaders and activists from Big Trout Lake.

1. In Canada, Native Canadians refer to themselves as *Aboriginal peoples*, *First Nations*, or *First Peoples*. The terms *Aboriginal peoples* and *Aboriginal movement* are used in this paper because these terms are central to the current political, economic, and social activism of Native Canadians today.

5

Putting Scientists in Their Place: Participatory Research in Environmental and Occupational Health

JULIET MERRIFIELD ─────────────────────────────

Many community and workplace activists have come into head-on collision with the scientific establishment in recent years over threats to people's health from toxic chemicals in the environment and workplaces. These conflicts have cast doubts on some of the most deeply embedded values of science itself, including the central concept of objectivity. This chapter reviews some of the issues of control over the production and use of scientific knowledge which have emerged from struggles over the past decade in the southeastern United States.

SCIENCE AND SCIENTISTS

Around the world, the years since the early 1970s have seen a remarkable growth in community and workplace activism on health issues. In the United States, the black-lung movement of disabled coal miners in the early 1970s led to precedent-setting legislation on coal mine health and safety, which was the precursor of a new wave of legislation to regulate workplace and environmental health hazards. Unions have become involved in health and safety issues, and coalitions of workers and professionals have formed to work for cleaner and healthier workplaces. More and more communities across the country have organized around environmental health hazards of toxic wastes and air and water pollution.

The reasons for this period of activism have yet to be fully analyzed. We might point to the period of stable economic growth and relative prosperity which enabled unions to look beyond purely economic issues in the workplace. The environmental movement of the 1970s, while having little to do with people's health and more to do with saving trees and wildlife, did begin to develop a public consciousness in this area. The federal legislation which was developed, in part as an attempt to contain and deflect union and community organizing, opened up avenues for public participation which had not been there before.

But perhaps most important of all, the second half of the 1970s and first half of the 1980s was a period in which the cancer scare grew. People who had been exposed to new chemical hazards during the period of greatest growth of the petrochemical industry, in the early 1950s, began to develop symptoms of cancer and other long-latency diseases. Mass media were filled with reports of research into cancer's causes, which heightened public awareness of environmental and occupational health hazards.

Science itself changed, and continues to do so, in this period of public awareness and involvement in toxic chemical threats to health. Epidemiologists, immunologists, neurologists, and others are being pushed to the frontiers of their fields, as they try to understand and document subtle changes in body chemistry and function following exposures to particular substances. The fact that science does not now have answers to the many questions that the public is asking contributes to a sense that science has failed.

The new awareness of and activism concerning environmental and occupational health problems have brought many people into confrontation with the scientific establishment and its values for the first time. Often, science itself, or at least applied science and technology, has come to be seen as the cause of the problem rather than as the neutral and benevolent source of knowledge to *solve* problems. The particular causes of the confrontations between activists and science are many and varied, but most stem from the relationship of scientists and scientific knowledge to the power holders of our society.

Of course, part of the mythology of science is that it is politically neutral, value-free, and "above" politics. In practice our science has come to be seen by many as inextricably intertwined with the power relationships of late-twentieth-century capitalism. In the context of the political economy of twentieth-century Western science, we can look at some examples of how community and worker activists have experienced problems in dealing with the scientific establishment and scientific knowledge about environmental and occupational health problems. The areas of dispute range from the validity of people's own knowledge versus that of scientists, and the way that subjects are selected for study with little regard to issues of pressing concern to the communities at risk, to problems with gaining access to scientific knowledge, and the way that science is used to buttress political power and keep people quiescent.

CONFRONTING ESTABLISHED SCIENCE

During our work at the Highlander Center during the past decade, we have seen many examples of communities and workers trying to deal with toxic chemical problems, and the problems that established science has caused them. A few are described here. These are not special or unusual cases. The kinds of problems they represent will be familiar to most people who have themselves been involved in such issues.

Experimental Knowledge Is Dismissed as Subjective and Irrelevant: Bumpass Cove

Science usually dismisses knowledge derived from experience as biased and subjective. It may be a subject matter for study, in such "soft" scientific subjects as anthropology. In the "hard" sciences it is normally regarded as irrelevant. But people living with a problem may know more about it than scientists who are far away and have not studied the issue. Community residents may be the first to know that something is wrong, but the last to have their story accepted by scientists and officials. An example is that of Bumpass Cove, a small rural community in upper east Tennessee.

An old mining valley, where the last remaining mine shut down in 1961, Bumpass Cove is in a fairly remote, mountainous area of the state. Springs and the creek running through the valley, or wells, provide drinking water to the residents. The creek flows into the Nolichucky River, on which many people used to fish. Downstream that river supplies drinking water to the small towns of Jonesborough and Greenville. Bumpass Cove residents have either been unemployed, living off the land, since the mines closed down, or have traveled long distances to work in factories.

Residents were relieved when in 1972 the Bumpass Cove Environmental Control and Mineral Company announced plans to resume mining and to backfill the mined areas with a household garbage landfill. The mining was never undertaken, but the landfill meant a few jobs for valley residents— working in the company office, or driving the trucks which brought the garbage to the site. And household garbage seemed harmless enough to everyone.

In fact, a feasibility study conducted for the Tennessee Department of Public Health before the landfill opened showed how unsuitable the area was for waste disposal. The water table was only fifty to one hundred feet below the surface, and there were numerous open shafts, pits, and boreholes which connected the surface directly to the water table. The study recommended that no hazardous waste be stored there. But the report, which did not become public knowledge for years, did not stop the landfill operators.

Soon after the landfill began operations, people in the valley began to notice strange things happening. Trucks would come into the landfill at night, without lights. One time a barrel rolled off a truck onto the side of the creek, and all the vegetation around it was killed off. An incinerator started to emit noxious smoke and fumes. As it turned out, the incinerator was unlicensed, but the neighbors did not know that. Some of the people who lived beside the only road up the cove began to suffer new illnesses.

One woman's daughter began to suffer from serious asthma attacks, especially when she was playing outside in the yard beside the road where the trucks came through.

Most people ignored what was happening: There were jobs at stake, and they could not believe that the government would allow any serious threats to their health. But one man, Hobart Storey, who had spent his life roaming and hunting the hills around the cove, began to notice changes among the wildlife. He would find animals dead for no apparent reason, birds disappearing. He began to write letters to the Tennessee Department of Public Health, asking what was going on with the landfill, and requesting that they investigate. His handwritten letters were filed, but were not acted upon.

Hobart Storey was ignored not only by the officials, but also by his fellow residents. The more he talked about the problems he saw, the more people dismissed him as a "crazy old man." Surely the Department of Public Health would not allow dangerous materials to be placed in their community. But slowly the evidence began to gather. One man died of a raging fever after hunting in the hills and drinking from a spring there. Doctors would not go public, but privately said they thought the death was from poisoning. Hobart and another community resident used a home movie camera to document the trucks bringing barrels into the landfill and the barrels left split open on the hillside. But still most people in the community could not believe in the seriousness of the problems the landfill was causing.

It took a crisis to precipitate action. One Saturday night in the spring of 1979 there was a flood which washed barrels out of the landfill into the creek and downstream into the Nolichucky River. Next morning when people attended church in the cove, the fumes were so strong that some passed out. The local Red Cross ordered the evacuation of the community, and people were finally mobilized.

Monday morning saw most of the community out on the road blocking the way of the landfill trucks. When the trucks later tried to bypass the blockade via a dirt road, that road was strewn with nails. The county government cooperated by putting a weight limit on a bridge, which effectively excluded the landfill trucks. No trucks reached the landfill, and the company, three months later, finally closed the landfill.

It was much later that scientists from the state health department admitted what Hobart Storey had known all along: that hazardous chemicals had been placed in the landfill, although it was licensed only for domestic garbage, and that they had already begun leaching out of the landfill into groundwater and the creek. How a group of citizens from Bumpass Cove educated themselves about the chemicals that were in the landfill and their effects on human health, and challenged the state health department inspectors on their own ground, is described later in this chapter.

The lessons of cases like Bumpass Cove, and the more famous Love Canal, are that people who must live with toxic chemicals may recognize their effects long before scientists ever get around to studying them, and that they do so through observing changes in phenomena well-known to them—it may be their children's health, as in Love Canal, or it may be wildlife and natural phenomena, as in Bumpass Cove. They may not know these phenomena in the same way that scientists do, or use the same concepts and language to describe them. But they do know them. Scientists must learn to acknowledge this.

The Bumpass Cove example also shows that the prevailing myth of science as the domain only of those trained for it may discourage many people, persuading them that what they know is not valid, that only the experts "really" know. And the notion that it is politically neutral may persuade people that scientists would not allow bad things to happen to them. Our deference to the experts may continue to allow science to be used to buttress political power, and to disempower ordinary people.

Problems Are Selected for Scientific Study with Little Regard to the Interests of Powerless People: Oak Ridge Mercury

How can a community full of scientists with Ph.D.s, with research projects on many forms of pollution, toxic wastes, and health hazards, nevertheless allow in its own midst the highest level known in the United States of pollution by mercury, a hazardous substance—and then refuse to study it? It happened in Oak Ridge, Tennessee, home of World War II's Manhattan Project and birthplace of the atomic bomb, and it speaks volumes about the selection of subjects for scientific study (Schlesinger et al. 1983; various issues of *Appalachian Journal* and *Knoxville News-Sentinel* 1983-86).

Subjects are selected for study by scientists with a good deal of influence from government and industry, and with little comparable pressure to include issues of importance for powerless people. The government and the industrial contractor that runs Oak Ridge Operations (the bomb manufacturing and uranium enrichment plants and research laboratories) for the government had considerable interest in *not* researching the problem. The community most at risk was the still-segregated black community of Scarbro, which could have little influence on the selection of scientific studies in its hometown. Scientists who did become concerned about the level of pollution around them were strongly discouraged from pursuing their ideas, even to the extent of losing their jobs.

It was years after the 1950s mercury contamination had taken place, in 1983, and then only through the efforts of a crusading local newspaper, the *Appalachian Observer*, that the extent to which the production of nuclear weapons had affected the environment of Oak Ridge began to be made public. The Department of Energy then revealed that in the years up to 1977 it had lost an estimated 2.4 million pounds of mercury used in extracting lithium, a vital ingredient in atomic bomb manufacture.

Mercury has been known since days of the "mad hatters" in the eighteenth century as a very hazardous substance, causing damage to the nervous system. In 1953, soon after Oak Ridge began using mercury in massive quantities, the people of Minimata, Japan, began suffering the first symptoms of their chronic nervous system disease, caused by methyl mercury contamination of the fish they ate. Mercury is converted into the methylated form by the action of bacteria once it is released into the environment.

In the 1950s, Oak Ridge scientists were sufficiently aware of the potential problems with mercury to test workers' urine samples for contamination. But they did not tell the workers they were exposed to hazardous materials, they did not significantly change production processes in order to limit workers' exposure, and they did not take serious steps to avoid environmental contamination. A Cold War mentality was at work: Atomic bomb production was going on at a feverish pitch, and nothing would be allowed to stand in its way.

That mentality continued among Oak Ridge scientists for many years. In 1977 a scientist from the Oak Ridge National Laboratories (ORNL) made a preliminary study of mercury releases into the environment and mercury contamination of Poplar Creek and the Clinch River. All of his fish samples for that year had mercury levels above the limit recommended by the Food and Drug Administration at that time. However, no action was taken to warn fishermen of the dangers of eating fish from Poplar Creek, and the report was quickly shelved. The head of the Department of Energy's (DOE) Environmental Protection Bureau, Jerry Wing, said, "Since the situation is quite sensitive from a public information standpoint, it is requested your report remain 'Business Confidential.' "

Nothing much happened between 1977 and 1982, except that the Oak Ridge officials lied to the state of Tennessee about the quantities of mercury that had been spilled over the years, admitting to a total of 100,000 pounds instead of 2.4 million pounds. In 1982 a junior scientist at the National Laboratories decided to try to get funding for a joint research project with his brother, who worked for the United States Geological Survey (USGS), by getting some preliminary data on heavy metal contamination on the Oak Ridge reservation. In their free time, the brothers Steven and Larry Gough walked along the banks of Poplar Creek gathering vegetation samples which Larry Gough took back to his USGS lab in Denver, Colorado, for analysis.

When Oak Ridge officials heard in April, 1982, of the extraordinary high levels of mercury beginning to be found in the plants, all hell broke loose for Steven Gough, the research biologist at ORNL. USGS was ordered to return the samples, without a cover letter so that there would be no record in the files of the incident. Steven Gough was reprimanded for insubordination, and a couple months later was removed from his job.

When the story hit the news a year or so later, amid massive publicity about Oak Ridge environmental damage, his superior stated that Steven

Gough had been reprimanded because he had taken on a study for which he was not qualified, and they did not want ORNL's scientific reputation damaged by substandard work. But those same ORNL scientists who were said to be "acclaimed nationally and internationally for their work on environmental aspects of mercury pollution" (*Science* 1983) had never carried out a study of Oak Ridge's own experimental pollution with mercury—or indeed with any of the rest of the toxic materials which have found their way into the Oak Ridge air, land, and water.

DOE's scientists seemed to be anxious only to downplay the significance of the high levels of mercury in fish from East Fork Poplar Creek. They suggested that Oak Ridge is a town of scientists and engineers, too affluent and too busy to fish for food. They ignored the fact that it was the poor black community of Scarbro that was "on the front line" of Poplar Creek's pollution, and that people from that community do indeed depend on fish and turtles from the creek as a source of food.

The Oak Ridge example has many aspects that are common to other cases of scientists ignoring problems that are a political nuisance. Scientists are often encouraged to become international experts on exotic subjects, but to leave strictly alone issues in their own backyards, and especially problems that may be vitally important for low-income and powerless people. For example, agricultural research on tomatoes has focused on production of fruits that can be transported across the country, or fruits suitable for mechanical harvesting. There has been no effort to find the perfect tomato for handpickers—the farm workers.

Increasing Specialization of Scientific Knowledge: The Holston River and Cherokee Lake

Back in 1978, trained as a researcher, anthropologist, and political scientist, but new to community struggles, I was asked to help a group of community residents document an environmental health problem. They lived in rural Scott County, Virginia, downwind from a large chemical manufacturing complex in Kingsport, Tennessee. Several of them worked with handicapped children, and had long felt that the number of babies born with birth defects in the community was exceptionally high. They suspected air pollution from the chemical plant, or occupational exposures of the plant's approximately 15,000 workers, many of whom live in rural areas around the plant. But they had little evidence for their suspicions. A group of us got together under the auspices of the "Kingsport Study Group" to try to gather what information we could about pollution in the area and its connections with human health.

At that time I, like most people, believed that someone, somewhere, had the answers to the questions we were asking. I had only to find the right scientists, whether in universities, research institutions, or government, and we would get the answers. But I was soon disillusioned. The state of Virginia's scientists were able to draw no conclusions from the birth defects records of Scott County. The numbers were too small for statistical manipulations. Almost no one was studying the complex of chemicals being emitted into the air from Kingsport's industries. I found that the scientists who were studying pollution of the Holston River downstream from the Tennessee Eastman chemical plant were interested primarily in temperature and bio-oxygen demand, aspects of pollution that affected fish and other aquatic life. They knew nothing about human health, and had little interest in chemicals in the river.

Scientists at the Tennessee Valley Authority were studying one chemical in the river, mercury, left in sediment along a 160-mile length of the Holston River from a disused chlor-alkali plant in Saltville, Virginia. But again, they looked at fish, not people. And it is significant that they studied only mercury from the closed-down plant, not the—politically sensitive—chemicals which are found in the waste streams from still-active Kingsport industry. Furthermore, even when mercury levels found in fish approached the "unsafe" levels determined by the Environmental Protection Agency, they did not feel it was their "place" to publicize the information they had or warn people who fished in the lake. They left that for the state of Tennessee to decide. And the state did nothing.

There were, of course, scientists whose primary concern was human health. Indeed, there was a Department of Public Health in the state government which had broad responsibility for safeguarding human health. But, at that time, its primary concern was with proper sanitation and drinking water, immunization programs, and the like. Pollution was largely out of their purview.

Then, and since, the organic chemicals and metals which are discharged into the Holston River by Kingsport's chemical companies were seldom monitored by federal or state government agencies, but mostly by the chemical companies themselves. It is very expensive to test water samples, especially for an unknown mix of chemicals. And the Reagan administration since 1980 had further slashed the Environmental Protection Agency's funds, making "self-monitoring" by the companies an even more attractive option for the agency.

In the case of the Holston River and Cherokee Lake, no one at that time was putting together a broad range of information from detailed specialist studies and assessing their overall impact on the health of people living near the river and lake, boating on it, and eating fish from it. This is a common deficiency we still live with. The fragmentation of scientific research has taken place in a world in which ever more complex combinations of chemicals surround our daily lives. Even detailed studies of single chemicals in laboratory tests are less and less useful in assessing the real problems people experience.

The fragmentation of scientific research has also done little to overcome the problems of "proof." Epidemiology, for example, lags far behind what people know in demonstrating harm from exposure to chemicals. Medical science, too, is outwitted by the classic symptoms of exposure to many chemicals like solvents—they may mimic other disorders, like flu, or may be interpreted as malingering, psychosomatic disorders, or hysteria. Science is a long way behind in the game of "catch-up" with the health effects caused by industrialization during the past forty years.

Difficulty to Non-Scientists of Obtaining Information

The arcane and highly specialized language used in communication of scientific research makes it hard for anyone not trained to get information they may need about particular problems. The availability of scientific journals is also restricted to university and other specialized or large libraries. For rural communities in Appalachia and the South, where the nearest public library may be in a small country town a thirty-mile drive away, such information is almost unobtainable. But there is more to the difficulty in getting scientific information than simply the restricted availability of journals and the jargon. Most scientists have little interest in or incentive for communicating with the general public. They may even have a real reluctance to do so.

Even fairly sympathetic scientists may have difficulty in giving information to citizens concerned about particular issues. They may believe that the citizens will not be able properly to understand and evaluate the information. They may be afraid that it will be used in a partisan cause and so threaten their own scientific reputation for objectivity. They may be instructed by their superiors to avoid public comment. Such instances are common among citizens struggling with environmental and occupational health matters.

One example concerned plans to build a synthetic fuels manufacturing unit in a rural area close to Oak Ridge, Tennessee. Members of a citizens' group, Save Our Cumberland Mountains, which had been active in the coalfield areas of east Tennessee for over a decade at the time, became concerned about the effects such a plant would have upon the community, and sought information. Oak Ridge at that time had a team of scientists who for some years had been researching the environmental impacts of various technologies for manufacturing liquid fuels from coal. It was an obvious source of information. But while sympathetic young members of the research team were prepared to meet with the citizens' group staff in private, and discuss the environmental problems likely to accompany the building of such a plant, they were not prepared to attend a public meeting called by the group and make public the results of their research.

Scientists' reluctance to become embroiled publicly in such issues stems in part from their internalized norms. According to their own self-image, scientists, like science itself, are supposed to remain politically neutral. The emphasis on objectivity in their research methods spills over into removing from them the right—or the responsibility—to hold opinions, to have values, and to exercise their rights as citizens.

Part of their reluctance stems from more external modes of social control in the profession. Scientists who become too closely associated with "causes" or with citizen groups tend to become regarded as "mavericks," eccentrics, and controversial figures. Such people may have difficulty in getting and holding positions, unless they already have tenure. They may have problems getting the research grants which are vital to their work. They may find the mainstream journals reluctant to publish their work, conferences reluctant to accept their papers. And at the most extreme, if they are young and vulnerable, they may find their jobs at risk.

"Fake Science" Is Used to Buttress Political Power

We talk about "fake science" when the high status accorded to experts and the notion of science as objective, disinterested, and pure are used to assure ordinary people of their own ignorance, in contrast to the power holders' ability to capture expertise for their own side.

In our study on the Holston River and Cherokee Lake, we talked to boat dock operators who made a living from people fishing the lake, and whose livelihoods suffered directly from the pollution which killed fish. We asked them about the series of public hearings the state of Tennessee had held on the condition of the lake. One man told us: "I didn't say a word during the meeting.... Eastman had fifteen lawyers, what's a man with a high school education going to say to a bunch of college professors?" (Kingsport Study Group).

Fake science has many uses for the powerful. It may be used to:

- Delay and defuse: "Doing a study on it" may have nothing to do with the merits of the problem; it may be simply a means of avoiding action while keeping people quiet. The studies usually take so long and have such inconclusive results that people have given up the struggle long before they are completed.
- Impress and bemuse: "Blinding them with science," that is, merely marshaling numbers of highly qualified experts, may impress people with their own inadequacy.
- Gloss and confuse: Political decisions are often claimed to be based on scientific procedures. Perhaps the best example of the last use of fake science is in the federal government's standard-setting procedures.

Workers who experience problems with exposure to particular chemicals in the workplace are usually assured by management that the levels of the chemical in the workplace are quite safe because they are at or below the

Threshold Limit Value (TLV) which has been set by the government. This limit value is expressed in terms of parts per million, or milligrams per cubic meter of air. It sounds good, sounds as if there must be some scientific reason to set it at that level, and that the level will protect workers.

But in fact standard setting is a bargaining procedure between representatives of corporations, unions, and government. Scientific studies may be used as chips in the bargaining, but the end result may not have much to do with protecting workers' health. At best, standards assume a young, otherwise healthy work force, which is not unduly sensitive. Workers who are no longer young, have other illnesses, are pregnant, or have been sensitized by prior exposures may not be "safe" when working under the TLV. But the standards are used to keep workers quiet and remove their grounds for complaint. Those who persist in reacting to chemicals at lower levels are blamed as victims, and may lose their jobs, or be moved to other positions with lower pay.

At worst, the standards may ignore long-term health hazards. Many scientists, for example, would argue that there can be no "threshold" for a cancer-causing chemical: no level below which exposure has no effect. But standards commonly allow limited exposure even to known cancer-causing agents like benzene and vinyl chloride. And then there are examples of standards which have been relaxed after vigorous lobbying from some affected industries. The standard for mercury in fish had been set at 0.5 ppm until 1977, when the tuna-fishing lobby stepped in: Suddenly the "safe" level for mercury in fish doubled, to 1 ppm (*Science* 1983). Let no one be comforted by the government's view of what is safe.

Accountability and Responsibility

Objectivity has a price tag, in more ways than one. While it may be acceptable for scientists to be the paid consultants of industry and government, it is seldom considered acceptable for scientists to become the unpaid consultants of communities or unions. They are considered to lose their objectivity if their labor is not paid for, and their evidence is tainted by the suspicion that their sympathy to the cause may have rendered them subjective and biased.

The problem is most commonly encountered in legal proceedings and government hearings. One case from our region involved Lewis Lowe, who sued the land company upstream from his small holding for damages caused by their strip-mining for coal, and subsequent siltation of the creek. The repeated flooding and deposition of toxic sediments affected his ability to grow food and be self-sufficient. It was a difficult technical case, to prove downstream damage from strip-mining; and a public interest group, the East Tennessee Research Corporation, played a lead role in marshaling expert research and testimony. Those experts who had donated their time to the case were accused by the land company lawyers of having lost their objectivity and credibility, and one expert witness refused to donate his time on the grounds that his professional reputation would be affected.

At the least, such arguments create economic problems for disenfranchised people. Despite the donated expert time, the public interest group estimated its costs to be around $50,000 (and they would have been far higher if they had had to pay all the experts). The case was won, but damages of only $3,000 were awarded. This was a poor person, who did not have much property to start with, and who was growing food. Property damages can never be high if you are poor to start with. But the case was a precedent-setting one: the first case to prove downstream damage from strip-mining.

These experiences, and the problems they reveal in the way scientific research is conducted and used, may seem a bleak picture indeed. But those who have been involved in such struggles know that there is another side. The barriers erected by the scientific establishment have led activists to seek alternative ways of meeting their goals. These alternatives, or the search for them, give us hope that there are ways to overcome the barriers, and even to begin a process of shaping a "new" science that is accountable and responsible to the needs of ordinary people. I will turn now to some examples of the alternative approaches that have been developed in our region in recent years.

CREATING ALTERNATIVES: PARTICIPATORY RESEARCH

Perhaps the strongest examples of alternatives to mainstream science have been in systematizing people's own knowledge and broadening their access to information produced by scientists. In many places, also, attempts have been made to develop cooperative relationships between scientists and citizens, with a view to research that meets people's needs. Both kinds of activities have often been difficult. Lessons from these experiences may help us develop further the beginnings of a "new science."

Systematizing and Giving Validity to People's Knowledge

People have knowledge of their own bodies, their own health. In a number of examples of projects to systematize and analyze this knowledge, both workers and communities have successfully carried out their own health surveys to document problems they suspect (and sometimes to uncover problems they had not suspected), and to give the validity of numbers to what they know. "Worker epidemiology" and the so-called "housewife epidemiology" have been important tools in organizing in many cases. They have their problems, of course, but they also have real strengths, as the case of Yellow Creek, Kentucky, shows.

The Yellow Creek flows from the pristine Fern Lake, past the town of

Middlesboro, and on downstream for some fourteen miles before joining the Cumberland River. From Middlesboro downstream, the creek is heavily polluted, the primary source of contamination being the Middlesboro Tanning Company. The tannery has been operating for many years, but until the mid-1960s used vegetable dyes which were biodegradable. They colored the stream, and sometimes used up so much oxygen in decomposing that the fish died. But they did not have as major an impact on the creek—and people's health—as the chrome tanning process which the tannery introduced in 1965. This process involved the use not only of chromium, which in its hexavalent form is very toxic, but also a couple of hundred other chemicals and minerals. Now the pollution of the stream began to be of a different order.

Along the stream people began to notice changes in animal, plant, and fish life. Domestic and farm animals died after drinking creek water, and people became concerned about their own health. Individually, residents along the creek tried to raise questions and express their concerns to local and state officials, but had little impact. In 1980, a small group of residents got together and decided to form a group to try to clean up the creek. From small beginnings the Yellow Creek Concerned Citizens (YCCC) grew rapidly.

One of the initial problems they faced was that the tannery was in the city of Middlesboro and sent its wastes to the city's sewage treatment plant, which was quite unable to deal with such industrial wastes. But the concerned citizens for the most part lived in the county, and their protests had little significance for the mayor or city council of Middlesboro. The Yellow Creek Concerned Citizens made repeated efforts to get the mayor and city council to listen to their concerns and answer their questions. Finally, out of frustration, the group held a sit-in at the council offices.

When they approached state and federal officials for answers and action, they found they needed ammunition. They needed to be able to show, with numbers, that there were health risks associated with the creek, and that it was not simply a question of color, of the water looking bad. It was out of this need for ammunition, some means of assessing the present and potential damage from the creek's pollution, that the group decided to conduct its own health survey.

A health survey committee of YCCC was formed and began to develop a questionnaire and plan the survey, with help from students at Vanderbilt University, through the Student Environmental Health Project of the Center for Health Services. They combined elements from earlier community and worker health survey questionnaires with their own particular concerns. The group's members themselves conducted the interviews, achieving a 99.5 percent success rate in almost three hundred households along the creek, involving almost 1,000 people.

The process of developing and carrying out the survey was exciting for the group and had some important effects. The Yellow Creek health survey did several things for the organization. First, it gave them a reason and an incentive to call at every household along the fourteen-mile length of the creek, and sit down and discuss with them the problems they were experiencing. Without the survey they might not have found the time and energy to do this. Second, it broadened and strengthened the leadership within the group. The prime activists in the health survey were women who became better informed and more vocal and confident through their work with the survey. And finally the process of doing the survey enabled the group to draw on and mobilize new outside resources.

The survey also gave them some information which they had not had before, and which they could use with state officials and the EPA, to persuade them of the seriousness of the situation at Yellow Creek. Now it was no longer a case of mere color, but of people's health. The survey found a statistically significant association between reported illnesses and exposure to creek water. Those who lived in areas prone to frequent flooding from the creek, and those who drank well water, reported higher levels of kidney problems and gastrointestinal problems than those who had alternative water supplies. The survey also found a statistically significant increase in the rate of miscarriages after 1970, five years after the chrome tanning process began.

The survey had its problems, both with the process and the end results. While the community was much involved in developing and administering the questionnaire, it had little involvement in the stage of data analysis because the questionnaires were taken away to Vanderbilt University for coding and computer analysis. That stage took a long time, because it depended on student time and labor, and access to university resources. And residents lost much of their sense of excitement and ownership of the project.

The survey, in common with others of its kind, also had problems with the end product. It was a hybrid between the rigorous proof requirements of epidemiology and the systematization of people's own knowledge. It went some way toward validating people's knowledge, but it did not really "prove" all that the community felt to be true. And although the survey was statistical, it was not a full-scale epidemiological study; and so the numbers, although statistically significant, did not really prove anything.

Dick Couto (1984), who directed the Center for Health Services at the time it cooperated with YCCC on the health survey, distinguishes between a "health risk assessment," which is what the YCCC health survey was, and an epidemiological study. Epidemiologists, he says, attempt to find statistically significant rates of illness, or relations with other factors. It is intrinsically a conservative approach, which prefers to err on the side of missing true correlations rather than to err by making false ones. It is limited to studying existing illnesses. And it is subject to mistakes and biases. Communities at risk, like the Yellow Creek residents, need to know what might happen, what is happening now, and what has happened. Epidemiology can meet only the last need of communities, and that often imperfectly.

Couto argues that health risk assessments, on the other hand, may meet community needs. They can assess if the degree of risk is such that a reasonable person would avoid it, and that is what is needed in political battles over risk. "Given the limited resources of a community at risk, members of that community are better off conducting assessments of the health risks— changes in the environment, indications of toxic pollution, and reported conditions of illness—and demanding that official agencies conduct the more rigorous epidemiological studies (Couto 1984, 21-22).

Broadening Access to Information

An important part of our work with the research program at Highlander has been to teach people how to gain access to information about problems that affect them. In the environmental health area this really began with the Bumpass Cove community. Prior to that, our staff had done research on chemicals and their health effects *for* people, and given them the results, but had not systematically taught them how to gain access themselves to the information they needed. Without that step, little empowerment took place. People might have the information they needed for a particular fight, but they were no better equipped to confront the next one. And they had not changed any of their perceptions about themselves vis-à-vis the scientific experts. It was only when the citizens themselves knew how to get information they needed that they felt able to challenge the experts on their own grounds, and felt that what they themselves knew could be validated. The importance of that became apparent to us with the Bumpass Cove experience.

Soon after the Bumpass Cove community organized and stopped the landfill from operating, a small group of residents came to a Highlander workshop. This brought together people from communities across Tennessee who were experiencing hazardous waste problems. The excitement with which they found that they were not alone, that other communities shared their problems and frustrations, and had knowledge from their experiences to share, is common to many Highlander workshops.

Later, a couple from Bumpass Cove traveled to Nashville, to the offices of the State Department of Public Health, to try to obtain all the documentation they could about the chemicals which had been buried in the landfill. They found the department's files in "a terrible mess," but after a couple of days' work obtained quite a stack of Xerox copies of correspondence between the landfill operators and officials, and a number of internal memos.

The problem they faced then was that much of the material was couched in technical and scientific terminology, and they had to assess its significance. They came to Highlander with another woman from the cove to use our library facilities. They wanted to begin to compile a list of chemicals which might have been placed in the landfill during its operation. Together we went through the mass of correspondence, memos, and test reports, making a three-by-five card each time we found a mention of a chemical having been dumped or found in tests, or where there was a request to dump the material from the operators with no indication that permission had been refused by the health department. Our supposition that it was quite likely that these materials had in fact been dumped at Bumpass Cove was later borne out by health department comments.

After compiling our list of chemicals, we needed to find out what the potential health effects were. And for this information we resorted to chemical directories, medical dictionaries, and Webster's. The chemical directories gave us information on potential health effects, results of animal testing done, and any standards for workplace exposure to the chemical. The medical dictionaries helped us figure out what the symptoms really meant, and the Webster's helped us translate the words of the medical dictionaries into language that we could understand.

Now, you have to remember that none of us were trained health scientists, and some of the people who were doing this research had not graduated from high school. They would have been—indeed were—regarded as scientifically illiterate by the "experts" employed by the state health department. But they had the incentive to struggle with the difficult material. It was *their* health at stake, and their children's. And with that incentive they were able to overcome the barriers placed in the way of their understanding by obscure language, remote sources, and lack of scientific training.

What came out of the exercise at Highlander was a list of chemicals suspected to have been dumped at the Bumpass Cove landfill, together with their potential health effects. But its impact was much more than a list. For the first time people began to feel that they had some control over the information, some beginnings of a feeling of power vis-à-vis the experts. That feeling was strengthened not long afterward by a confrontation with the health department inspector.

The health department had agreed to sample water in several drinking wells in the cove which were close to the landfill. An inspector then visited the citizens' organization to report on the findings at one well in particular, which was two hundred yards from the landfill. In a standard technique, he reeled off a list of chemicals with long names which had been found in the samples from the well, then hastened to assure the citizens that these chemicals were harmless. They pulled out their copy of a chemical directory which we had given them, looked up the names of the chemicals, and challenged the inspector. "This book says this chemical may cause liver damage, that one affects the central nervous system." The inspector left speedily, and the citizens, while disturbed by the nature of the information they had found, felt empowered to have been able to challenge an "expert" on his own ground. This small experience contributed to the citizens' growing feeling that they knew what the scientists did not, and that they had a right to speak out on what they knew.

Highlander has continued to do this kind of research training with citizens' groups, both in the field of environmental and occupational health and in other issue areas. We have found it an effective tool whenever there is a strong personal incentive to get the information. And people have devised their own creative ways of gaining access to information they need, in a process we call "guerrilla research." Tactics may range from raiding corporate garbage cans (useful sources for company records) to removing labels from chemical containers so that their chemical names may be looked up in libraries. Approaches to getting information from companies may be as subtle as leaving a chemical reference book casually on view to supervisors in one's lunch box to launching statewide campaigns for the "right to know" about chemicals being produced or used in one's state.

Education to Overcome "Fake Science"

From our experience with Bumpass Cove, and with similar experience from other areas in which the research program was working, we came to recognize the power in our society that goes with control over knowledge and information. It led us to begin to devise educational programs that could help people understand and challenge the uses of "fake science," science used to keep people ignorant and powerless, and to grow more confident about the validity of their own knowledge.

One example of an educational program which attempted to do just that was a curriculum for workers on occupational health which was developed for Highlander by David Clement, a British labor educator who had worked with a similar program in Britain compiled by the Trades Union Congress (TUC). The curriculum is designed primarily to train shop stewards and other activists on occupational health problems and how to confront them in their workplaces. It demystifies such issues as TLVs, and how to test for chemical exposures. It uses small-group problem-solving techniques to analyze problems ranging from what the Occupational Safety and Health Act itself says about protecting workers' health to how to deal with company officials. And it consistently looks at how organizing and education of the membership can help confront and resolve shop floor problems.

Highlander staff members were excited about the ideas behind the curriculum, feeling that it approached a merger between our goals of research and of education for social change. We published the curriculum and offered some workshops to train union staff and labor educators in using the curriculum. These had mixed results. Some were excited by what they saw, and felt there could be a real change in their approaches to labor education. Others felt that the workers could never deal with the level of technicality at which they were being asked to operate in the curriculum. These workshop participants were used to a top-down educational system as well as a science production system which denies valid knowledge and intellectual capacity to those who have not been officially trained.

Our own experiences with using the curriculum, as with other similar attempts to educate and teach research skills on technical issues, lead us to believe that ordinary people are more than capable of mastering technical skills when they really want to. And programs to teach such skills can be empowering, and have effects far beyond the utility of the information gained, when they change people's conceptions of themselves as actors, of science in society, and of what changes are possible. It is especially important to stress action—group action, not individual advancement—as a part of the learning process. "Scientific literacy," like literacy itself, may be a tool for social change when it is approached in an empowering way.

Cooperative Relationships Between Scientists and Laypersons

Science shops in the Netherlands were pioneers of cooperative relationships between scientists and laypersons (Groenewegen and Swuste 1984). These have been developed further in such European efforts as the Utopia Project, which brought together teams of workers and researchers in several Scandinavian countries to develop new technology in a way that did not de-skill workers (Utopia Project Team).

In the field of environmental and occupational health there have been a number of scientists who have joined with citizen or worker groups to address their concerns. The experience of the Love Canal residents and their health survey carried out with the help of Dr. Beverly Paigen has been well documented (see Levine 1982; Gibbs 1982). COSH groups (Committees on Occupational Safety and Health) have commonly allied health and legal professionals with union activists. In the more conservative political climate of the South, away from the major centers of scientific research, it has often been harder to find scientists willing to ally themselves with workers or citizens. But there have been some examples.

In 1985, the North Carolina Committee on Occupational Safety and Health (NCCOSH), with the Communications Workers of America (CWA), developed a study to document the effects of job stress on communications workers (Personal communication from Tobi Lippen, North Carolina Committee on Occupational Safety and Health). Many of the union and company officials did not believe that there were work-related health problems for telephone operators. This work had always been seen as clean and safe. But the mainly female work force knew there were problems, especially relating to stress from the use of new technology—video display terminals—and close monitoring of work by supervisors. The survey was designed with the help of an epidemiologist who was primarily interested in the incidence of cardiac problems related to stress.

The interviewing was carried out by CWA members over the telephone, and care was taken that the control of the research process should remain with the workers' research team. The survey did demonstrate many of the problems that they had expected to find, and some—notably relating to angina and VDT use—that had not been expected. In fact, the study documented the first known long-term chronic effect of VDTs. The real issue for most workers was not having control over their own work. The tyranny of the "average work times" which totally controlled their pace of work was what caused them the most stress.

The women's research team increased their leadership skills as a side benefit of the research project. There were some problems over ownership of the data and control of the publication process. The scientist involved was reluctant to pass control over to the union or COSH group. And the workers' team felt they had to make some compromises because of being involved in a "scientific" study. But on the whole it did represent a step toward the goal of defining new relationships between scientists and laypersons, and the beginnings of a new concept of science.

There are some crucial questions that must be asked about any relationship between scientists and laypersons:

- Who determines the need for the research?
- Who controls the process of research and makes decisions along the way which affect its outcome?
- Who controls the dissemination of results?
- Where does accountability lie?

We may not yet have any perfect example of participatory research on environmental and occupational health, but we do have examples where both citizens and scientists have worked for a new approach and which go as far toward citizen control and accountability as we can go, given the context in which we all work.

Participatory research has been done in the realm of popular knowledge, systematizing and analyzing people's knowledge of health or pollution. It has been harder to use participatory approaches to scientific knowledge, although various attempts at developing cooperative relationships between scientists and communities fall within this sphere. What we need to do now is break the link between scientific knowledge and elite forms of inquiry, and devise new approaches that combine essential elements of scientific research—the rigorous rules of proof, for example—with a process that is accountable to people. Only through such changes will we see a science that begins to meet the needs of ordinary people rather than the power holders, and only in such a way can we hope to see a constructive and humane science.

6

The Appalachian Land Ownership Study: Research and Citizen Action in Appalachia

BILLY D. HORTON

To understand the Appalachian Land Ownership Study and the subsequent action and research that it generated, one must first understand that it did not arise in a vacuum. Rather, the study, undertaken in 1979 and completed in 1981, was built on decades of popular knowledge about and struggle against the impacts of absentee land ownership. It also followed several other, less comprehensive land ownership studies that had been undertaken in the preceding decade.

In the decades between 1870 and 1930, residents of the Appalachian region lost control of their political, social, and economic destiny. This came about as absentee corporations, often assisted by local speculators, gained what in some counties was to become almost total control of the land, mineral, and timber wealth.[1] With the subsequent disruption of the land ownership and use patterns that had given meaning to both individual and communal life came a loss of power to influence the future course of social and economic development. In a real sense, that transfer of control left area landowners as "foreigners on their own land" (Appalachian Land Ownership Task Force 1983, ix).

During this century, the fact of absentee corporate control has manifested itself in numerous ways. Struggles to unionize the coalfields were made difficult because of the total control companies exercised over their work force, whom they had housed in company towns. Boom-and-bust cycles became a way of life in the central Appalachian coalfields. Political control by company-backed machines became a fact of life at the local level and often in state capitals as well. Forest lands were devastated, later to be bought up by the federal government, reforested, and turned into national forests and parks. In the middle part of the century, literally hundreds of thousands of Appalachians were "forced" to migrate to industrial areas of the North in order to survive economically.[2] This all became part of the popular history of the region, to be reflected in its music, literature, and folklore.

In the 1960s, public attention was focused on Appalachia to an extent never seen before. Persistent poverty in the region was used by federal officials to illustrate the urgent need for the War on Poverty and its associated programs. As expected, given the tradition of American liberalism out of which they arose, most of the programs were oriented toward changing individuals rather than the structures of ownership and control. Poverty warriors in the field (VISTA volunteers, Appalachian Volunteers, and others) were soon finding, however, that changing the individual was not enough.

They soon began to discover what had been part of the folk knowledge for decades—that a major cause of poverty in Appalachia was the absentee ownership and control of the land and mineral wealth, and the political power associated with it. By the late 1960s, the activists' focus had changed from individual uplift to political confrontation and community organizing. Battles against wanton strip-mining were undertaken; the rights of welfare recipients became an issue; taxation and the political control of educational systems were seen as critical; and the issue of absentee land ownership and control came increasingly to the forefront.[3]

One of the first attempts to document land ownership and taxation in the region was undertaken by Rich Kirby, then working for the Appalachian Volunteers in eastern Kentucky. Kirby, along with many others, had come to notice the irony in the fact that some of the country's poorest people lived on land possessing some of the nation's richest mineral reserves. The catch was that the surface owners seldom owned those mineral reserves. In order to document this, he undertook a study in the local courthouses of eleven eastern Kentucky counties. The findings—concentrated absentee ownership and low taxation—were to become familiar as others undertook similar studies in the coming decade. He found that thirty-one people or corporations owned about four-fifths of the coal in those counties. Also, about 86 percent of that coal land was owned by absentee interests who paid very little property tax on their land and minerals (Kirby 1969, 19-27). Over the next several years, other land ownership and taxation studies in Tennessee, Virginia, and West Virginia were to document similar patterns. Still other studies in North Carolina and Ohio demonstrated the negative impacts of absentee ownership in areas not so dominated by coal.[4]

So, the Appalachian Land Ownership Study builds on a long tradition of resistance struggles in the mountains and benefits from several earlier land ownership, use, and taxation studies. As with several of the other studies, it was also the confirmation and expansion of the already-existing reservoirs of popular knowledge. In a very real way we were documenting what was already well-known by Appalachian residents. The strength of the land ownership study was, then, its capacity and potential for documenting popular knowledge in such a way as to make it an effective tool for political struggle.

THE APPALACHIAN LAND OWNERSHIP STUDY

Since both the process of the land ownership study and its findings have been discussed extensively elsewhere, they will be treated only briefly here before turning to the action and research that occurred following its completion.[5]

As indicated earlier, throughout the late 1960s and the 1970s, there had been an increasing awareness among activists, scholars, and community people in Appalachia that the ownership and control of the region's natural resources was one of the key factors contributing to its persistent problems. A number of organizations and individuals confronted this realization as they fought to stop strip-mining, improve public education, attain better social services, and generally have their voices heard on community and regional issues. All too often, however, their struggles were frustrated by the lack of needed information to confront the expertise of those in power.

The immediate stimulus for the land ownership study came with the floods of 1977, when numerous communities in central Appalachia were devastated by rising flood waters. Many area citizens blamed the floods' severity on unregulated strip-mining in the watersheds. Such strip-mining, they argued, had led to erosion of the hillsides and subsequent siltation of the streams, thus decreasing their ability to handle heavy runoff during periods of extensive rain. One of the most devastated communities was Williamson, West Virginia, on the Tug Fork River just across the state line from eastern Kentucky. In response to their frustration at government and corporate inaction following the flood and the long history of such negligence, a group of citizens in that community called a meeting to bring together representatives from citizens' organizations around Appalachia to discuss some form of organized regional response.[6]

One of the results of that meeting was the formation of the Appalachian Alliance, a coalition of individuals and organizations, to develop a regional voice for the concerns expressed at the meeting. Members of that group most interested in the land ownership issue subsequently formed a task force to determine ways of documenting the extent and effects of absentee ownership and control. That task force—the Appalachian Land Ownership Task Force—composed of activists, regional academics, and community people, was eventually able to negotiate an agreement with the Appalachian Regional Commission, a federal agency, to provide partial funding for a land ownership study to be undertaken by the task force.[7]

After several months of discussion, the task force delineated the following goals for its land ownership study:

- to provide a model for citizens doing their own research, growing out of their local needs and concerns, rather than for professional consulting firms doing research based on needs and interests of government agencies.
- through the research process, to train local citizens and groups in obtaining information they need.
- through the research process, to develop a network of individuals and groups who are concerned with land-related issues and are committed to using the results of the study for constructive action.
- using the results of the research process to begin to educate and to mobilize a broader constituency of local groups for action on land-related questions in their own communities, as well as at state and regional levels.

With these goals in mind, the task force undertook a participatory research process which it hoped would enable the region's citizens to more effectively struggle against the abuses brought upon them through the existing ownership and taxation structure.

Almost two years later the results of the eighty-county, six-state study were released. The general findings of that research did not really surprise participants in the study, though the newly documented extent of absentee corporate ownership and lack of taxation may have. Area residents had known for decades that much of the land and minerals was owned by absentee owners. What they now had was irrefutable documentation of that popular knowledge. In brief summary, the research found:

- Ownership of land and minerals in rural Appalachia was highly concentrated among a few absentee and corporate owners. Only 1 percent of the local population, along with absentee holders, corporations, and government agencies, controlled at least 53 percent of the total land surface in the eighty counties.
- Appalachia's land and mineral resources were absentee-owned. That is, nearly three-fourths of the surface acres were held by out-of-country or out-of-state owners. Four-fifths of the mineral acres in the survey were absentee-owned. In one-fourth of the study counties, absentee-owned land in the sample represented over one-half of the total land surface of the county.
- Large corporations dominate the ownership picture in much of Appalachia.
- Mineral rights were greatly underassessed for tax purposes. Over 75 percent of the mineral owners in the survey paid less than 25 cents per acre in property taxes. Eighty-six percent paid less than $1.00 per acre. In the major coal counties surveyed, the average tax per ton of known coal reserves was at most only $.0002, or one-fiftieth of a cent (Appalachian Land Ownership Task Force 1983, 14-63).

As impressive as the findings of the land ownership study were, these are not the most important measure of its success as participatory research. Rather, the measure of the study's success hinges on the use of that information to further local and regional struggles and the extent to which the process created a model by which other citizens can research and act upon issues of importance to them. It is in the context of the general goals of the study outlined earlier—provision of a research model, training of local citizens and groups, networking of individuals and groups committed to use of the data as a basis for action with regard to land ownership issues, and education and mobilization of a broader constituency—that the project as participatory research must be evaluated.

Continuing in this vein, one can identify several aspects of the land ownership study follow-up that merit consideration. These are publicity of the land study findings, support for the work of already-established citizens' organizations, creation of new organizations to deal with land-related issues, increased networking, and provision of a model for use in studying land ownership and other issues. What follows is a description of some of those efforts.

INITIAL PUBLICITY AND CONTROL OF INFORMATION

From the beginning, the control of information was of concern to members of the task force, especially since it was working under a grant from a federal agency not known for its propensity to share information with grass-roots groups. In early negotiations with the Appalachian Regional Commission, members of the task force made it clear to the agency that the people of the region would control the information produced by the study. In fact, as suspected, the agency did make an effort to control the information released by refusing to release six volumes of state studies, choosing instead to release only the regional volume in limited numbers. The task force had prepared for this possibility, however, and released the state volumes through its own outlet and printed additional copies of the regional report as well.

As part of the research process, plans had also been laid for publicizing the study through regional media outlets once it was concluded. As a result, several of the major regional newspapers—the *Louisville Courier-Journal*, the *Nashville Tennessean*, and the *Charleston Gazette*—wrote strong editorials calling for change based on the study's findings and conclusions. Several local newspapers also picked up on the press releases and took note of the need for change. In fact, findings from the study had been included in articles in one county newspaper long before the study was officially released. That local newspaper eventually serialized much of the land study in its pages as a way of supporting local struggles over taxation of corporate land in the county. *Mountain Life and Work*, a regional magazine published by the Council of Southern Mountains, ran a series of articles on the regional findings and those in each state as well. After the articles had run, the council compiled them into a booklet for additional dissemination. In other areas land study participants took part in radio and TV interviews and debates, set up community forums, developed pamphlets, and engaged in other activities to insure that the study's findings were disseminated as widely as possible. These combined activities greatly increased the level of public awareness of and debate on land ownership and taxation issues in the region.

THE CREATION OF NEW ORGANIZATIONS: KENTUCKY FAIR TAX COALITION

The findings of the land ownership study were perhaps most dramatic in Kentucky. For all practical purposes, unmined coal was going untaxed there. In the twelve study counties in eastern Kentucky, which included some of the major coal-producing counties in the region, the total property tax on minerals was a meager $1,500. Researchers also found that a 1978 state law in Kentucky had established a uniform rate of one-tenth of one cent per $100 valuation on all unmined coal. The results could be demonstrated in most dramatic fashion in Martin County, one of the largest coal-producing counties in the state. In that county the Norfolk and Western Railroad (now Norfolk Southern) owned 81,333 acres, the equivalent of 55 percent of the county's surface, through its subsidiary Pocahontas Kentucky. That coal was valued at $7,604,963, but the annual tax generated was only $76.05.[8]

In June 1981, a couple of months after the land study had been released, a small group of people met in Berea, Kentucky, to discuss possible educational/organizing strategies on the issue of mineral taxation in Kentucky. Those present decided to focus on House Bill 44, a Kentucky property tax lid bill that would have to be changed to achieve new mineral tax revenues, and a property tax on unmined minerals. They planned to hold meetings in eastern Kentucky to discuss these issues and other land study findings. One meeting was held in July and a second one in August. At the August meeting the twenty-six persons present from twelve eastern Kentucky counties formally organized the Kentucky Fair Tax Coalition (KFTC).

The coalition developed a statement of purpose as follows:

Kentucky Fair Tax Coalition is a coalition of community-based organizations and interested individuals promoting more effective and efficient community services through a fair and equitable taxation system throughout the state of Kentucky with particular interest in the coal counties.

In the context of that statement of purpose, the coalition's members formulated three goals that would guide their activities:

• to maximize local control of the taxation process.

• to explore new avenues of mineral taxation.

• to monitor the policies of the Kentucky Department of Revenue with respect to the taxation of corporate mineral lands.

At this time KFTC had no staff or funds, though they did pass the hat and raise their first funds in the amount of $38. Later that fall, the Appalachian Alliance, the parent organization of the land ownership study, "lent" one of its two staff people to KFTC for organizational and other work.[9]

A crucial decision faced the coalition early in its history—whether to take the issue of an unmined minerals tax to the Kentucky legislature, which was to meet in January 1982. This consideration was particularly important since the legislature only meets biennially. Forgoing the conventional organizing wisdom that an organization focus on battles in which there is a high probability of victory, KFTC decided to push for an unmined minerals tax in the 1982 session.

An unmined minerals tax bill was drafted by KFTC and introduced in the legislature. KFTC used various tactics to generate support for the bill: mailing postcards and letters, making phone calls and personal visits to legislators; acquiring endorsements from other organizations, holding rallies, and using a little bit of sculpture titled "The Scales of Justice." The sculpture, created by one of the members of KFTC, showed the interests of the coal companies far outweighing those of the people. At one point a group of about fifty people met with the House Speaker and presented him with the "Scales of Justice." He accepted it with a certain degree of puzzlement and then proceeded to nervously give the group a lecture on civic democracy!

The bill was passed out of the House Appropriations and Revenue Committee by a vote of 11 to 1, but was subsequently bottled up and killed by various legislative maneuvers inspired by the House leadership. Later research showed that both the House Speaker and Speaker Pro Tem were lawyers in firms whose clients included some of the largest coal interests in Kentucky.

Rather than look upon this as a failure, KFTC moved ahead to develop the internal organization and public support necessary for the unmined minerals tax struggle in the 1984 legislature. At the same time the organization was consistently supporting local groups on whatever issues were of importance to them as well as assisting several groups in local property tax challenges. The KFTC approach to the development of local chapters and to other work in local communities has been an innovative one. Instead of foisting the unmined minerals tax issue upon local groups, it has urged those groups to define the issues of importance to them. As a result, KFTC has become a multi-issue organization, dealing not only with minerals taxation, but also with water quality issues and the broad form deed. The broad form deed has historically allowed mineral owners to strip-mine without first obtaining permission from the surface owner.

The platform that KFTC prepared in the fall of 1983 as its legislative program for the 1984 state legislative session reflected this multi-issue orientation. It included:

- taxation of unmined minerals at the same rate as surface property.
- abolition of the broad form deed.
- change in the severance tax distribution formula so that a greater percentage of revenue is returned to mineral-producing counties.
- adequate protection of our water resources through the development of strong laws and regulations.

KFTC approached the 1984 legislative session ready to do battle or offer support on several bills consistent with the above platform.

The outcome of legislative battles in which KFTC was directly involved or supported was a mixed one. A strong positive note was that legislation was passed that abolished the broad form deed. Beginning in July 1984, only methods "common to the day" the deeds were originally signed were to be allowed in mining. Surface mining can no longer be done without the consent and involvement of the surface owner. Expecting a series of challenges by coal interests, KFTC immediately set about establishing a fund for the defense of the new bill. A bill was also passed that would require the certification of all water-well drillers in the state.

In the case of the unmined minerals tax, the story was very different. A committee made up of representatives from coal associations, coal companies, and a few sympathetic eastern Kentucky county judges was formed to fight the unmined minerals tax. Whatever their impact, the bill failed to get out of the Appropriations and Revenue Committee on a vote of 13 to 6. The "rationale" given by several committee members for voting no was that they objected to "the heavy handed tactics" represented by a legal suit filed by KFTC against the Kentucky Revenue Cabinet, charging that it "systematically fails to fairly assess several forms of property belonging to coal, oil, and gas interests." So, the primary challenge to unfair minerals taxation now is in the court system.

Outside the legislative arena, KFTC has also had several noticeable successes in its short history. It has filed over a dozen actions in various courts to help remedy the inequities of the property tax system. In the area of water quality, it has had success in forcing the state to monitor coal operations for groundwater pollution. Several companies had to change their methods to prevent water contamination as a result. It has successfully assisted at least two communities in obtaining emergency declarations to make them eligible for grants to build new water systems. Its Citizens' Education and Water Monitoring Project has trained citizens in numerous communities to test and monitor water quality.

From that small group of twenty-six people who formed KFTC in 1981 it had, by April 1984, grown to a membership organization with nearly 700 members representing fifty-two Kentucky counties. Recently, the organization established an 85-95 fund to raise money for a special account that will not be touched until 1995. It has also developed an internal educational program focusing on leadership and development of organizing skills. This program will eventually use those already trained to train others. These activities and the successful record of KFTC suggest that it will be active on the issues identified in the land study for some time to come.

THE CREATION OF NEW ORGANIZATIONS: WESTERN NORTH CAROLINA ALLIANCE

The tie between the land ownership study and the Western North Carolina Alliance is not as direct as with KFTC. Follow-up to the study took a rather circuitous route in North Carolina. Members of the state task force did develop educational programs to be presented in local forums. However, other than a minerals leasing conference held in Asheville with participation of several persons previously involved in the land study, there was little follow-up in the counties that were part of the study. There may have been a couple of reasons for this. First, most of the researchers in western North Carolina were college students rather than community residents. Second, there had not been as much ongoing organizing around land issues there as in some other states. Whether these explanations account for it or not, little grass roots organizing immediately followed the study.

However, as must often be the case in participatory research, the issues and action come back around in the most unexpected ways. One of the concerns identified in the land study was the increasing leasing of minerals in the non-coal sections of the region. As it turned out, some people in western North Carolina were becoming concerned about oil and gas leasing in the national forests near their homes. One of those persons attended a conference in Tennessee at which one of the co-coordinators of the land study spoke. She went back home even more excited and concerned about what was happening, though still feeling very isolated in her opposition to minerals development in the public forests.

Not long afterward she wrote a letter to *Mountain Life and Work*, a regional publication of the Council of Southern Mountains. That letter was a plea for contact with others in the region who were dealing with minerals development issues. The Appalachian Alliance coordinator (and previous co-coordinator of the land study) responded and went to the community to meet with her and others; thus began a long process that would culminate in the formation of the Western North Carolina Alliance.

Several meetings were held (usually with no more than ten to fifteen people in attendance) to discuss how to deal with the issue of minerals leasing in the national forests, how to educate people in western North Carolina about the problem, and how to build an organization through which community people could bring pressure for change in current policies. After several meetings, the participants decided to form an organization with the following statement of purpose:

Western North Carolina Alliance believes that community people have a right to participate in decisions which have profound effects on the quality of life in our region. We believe our natural resources are our heritage and our future and need to be protected from uncontrolled commercial exploitation. To this end Western North Carolina Alliance has committed itself to a program of public education and community organization across the western counties.

Currently WNCA has representation on its steering committee from seven counties and a formal chapter in one of them. Current organizational building work includes plans for internal training and leadership development.

At the same time that WNCA was trying to build a broader organizational base, it plunged ahead with the task of educating Western Carolinians about the problems of mineral development. This has taken several forms. In September 1983 the organization sponsored a workshop titled "Water: Our Future," which brought in "experts" on uranium mining, brine pollution from oil and gas well drilling, olivine mining, and so on. Most of these "experts" were persons having personal experience in local struggles about these issues. The key strategy was to use the experiences in other areas of Appalachia, particularly those of citizens' groups having dealt with the numerous problems attendant to minerals leasing and development. The message was, "You can prevent this from happening here through education and community organizing."

Education has also been pursued in a number of other ways. WNCA has cosponsored workshops on water monitoring with other organizations in western North Carolina. They have done research and produced materials on minerals leasing and water quality as well as distributed documents prepared by other organizations that are relevant to the issue (Western North Carolina Alliance 1984; Linden 1983). They have also had considerable success in utilizing newspapers in the area to publicize the issue of minerals leasing on public lands.

In sum, WNCA, though having developed somewhat circuitously from the efforts of the land study, is no less a follow-up to the critical issues the study raised. It represents work on one of the priorities identified by the study—minerals leasing and new energy development. Though it does not yet have the track record of KFTC, it has provided a vehicle by which residents of western North Carolina counties can research and act upon issues of critical importance to them.

SUPPLEMENTING ONGOING WORK—SAVE OUR CUMBERLAND MOUNTAINS

Whereas KFTC and WNCA are relatively new organizations whose formation was stimulated by the land study, Save Our Cumberland Mountains (SOCM) had been involved in land and natural resources issues for nearly a decade before the land study was undertaken. The example of SOCM is perhaps the best one of both the research and findings of the land study meshing with the ongoing work of an organization. The beginnings of SOCM, a multicounty grass-roots organization primarily based in the coal counties of eastern Tennessee, date back to some land ownership and taxation research done in the early 1970s. For over a decade SOCM has remained active on these issues, whether through education, organizing, research, legislative action, or legal action. Tennessee was the only state involved in the land study in which an already-existent multicounty organization took sole responsibility for carrying out the land ownership research. That organization was SOCM.

One of the many recent activities of SOCM serves to illustrate follow-up to the land study. The activity is very specifically tied to taxation research as part of the study. It involves a challenge to the assessment of vast acreage of land and mineral rights owned by Koppers Company, a Pittsburgh-based energy conglomerate. The Campbell County, Tennessee chapter of SOCM first appealed the Koppers taxation in 1982, asking that the taxes on the large landholding company be raised to a level that would reflect the market value on the land it owns. Koppers owns about one-third of that coal county, which lies on the Kentucky-Tennessee line north of Knoxville. In 1980 Koppers bought 26,517 acres of Campbell County land for $26 million. SOCM argued that this purchase price should be used to set the market value of the property.

They first took the appeal to the local tax board, where the appeal was denied. The appeal was then taken to the State Board of Equalization, where it was heard by a hearing examiner. That examiner actually lowered Koppers's taxes to a yield of 96 cents per acre. He valued the land at only $150 per acre, although the company had in fact paid $980 per acre when it purchased the land. In early 1984, the State Tax Equalization Board lowered Koppers's appraisal in both Campbell and Anderson counties. Their ruling was essentially that the $26 million paid by Koppers in 1980 for the 26,517 acres did not establish market value for the property. The ruling was in favor of a company which according to SOCM's research did not pay any federal taxes on $268 million in domestic profits in 1983.

The battle and other tax battles go on. The Campbell County SOCM chapter has been researching new property appraisals in the county to see how they compare with previous years. The SOCM board has also established a tax committee to do research on taxation issues and appeals, and the organization continues to work on tax issues in several other counties. In addition to this, SOCM's members continue their ongoing work on strip-mining and other natural resources issues.

The Koppers example, only one of the many struggles SOCM has been involved in since participating in the land study, illustrates both the extent to which the land study was part of the organization's ongoing work and the extent to which the issues of ownership and taxation are interrelated. SOCM was active on land ownership and taxation issues before, during, and after the land ownership study. It remains so. Its participation in the land study was, thus, another link in a long chain of research and action on those issues.

VIRGINIA: AN ATTEMPT THAT FAILED

Much less success was seen in Virginia in the way of follow-up. While the results of the land study did serve to facilitate some local struggles (e.g., school finances in Buchanan County, tax assessment of coal lands in Wise County), it did not result in a multicounty organization as in Kentucky and North Carolina. Nor was there a single organization to carry on the struggle as in Tennessee. In Buchanan County, a small citizens/parents group was challenging the tax assessments that resulted in inadequate school financing. Findings from the land study were reprinted and distributed in the county with the help of the state coordinator of the land study. In Wise County, the woman who did the research and case study in that county used the information to challenge the county commissioners to reassess coal lands. However, that action did not result in any larger political organizing activities in the county.

There was an attempt in Virginia to form a multicounty organization, the Virginia Land Alliance, to deal with land ownership issues. Several members of the task force in Virginia expressed interest in the formation of such a group and appealed to the Appalachian Alliance for assistance in its formation. Several meetings and one all-day workshop were held to try to identify issues, participants, and the potential for such an organization.

The attempt was ultimately unsuccessful, though some work was done on leasing research in Washington County as an attempt to stimulate activity on an issue. There were probably several reasons that this attempt was unsuccessful. Among them were:

- inability to clearly define the land issue or issues on which the Land Alliance would focus.

- inability to define the scope of the Virginia Land Alliance (whether southwestern Virginia or the whole state).

- lack of financial resources and staff support (the Appalachian Alliance made a decision not to expend too much of its limited funds and staff time in Virginia, but rather to focus on Kentucky, where the issues were much clearer).

- lack of people resources (too few people ready to devote the time necessary to build an organization).

- lack of community support (inability to generate broad enough community interest in the effort).

- political considerations (already-existent inter-organizational relations having nothing to do with the land study).

After a several-month struggle to get the Virginia Land Alliance underway, the effort pretty much dissipated of its own inertia. To date those of us who participated in the land study have not fully analyzed whether or how the Virginia experience might have been different—whether the failure had something to do with how the Virginia Task Force was structured, the inadequacy of the Appalachian Alliance's assistance, or some other unknown phenomenon. The above list presents some of the more immediate and probable reasons.

THE LAND OWNERSHIP STUDY AS A RESEARCH MODEL

One of the goals for the land ownership study was to provide a model for citizen research. As a result of the example of the land study, land ownership research has been undertaken at several locations within Appalachia and elsewhere in the country. What follows is a brief discussion of those with which we are familiar.

Northern Appalachia

In the year following completion of the land ownership study, the Social, Economic, and Political Issues Task Force (SEPI) of the Commission on Religion in Appalachia (CORA) sponsored a conference in Pennsylvania bringing together church people from western Pennsylvania and southeastern Ohio. Several participants in the land study, including the two regional co-coordinators and a state coordinator, were invited to attend and present findings of the study as well as conduct a training workshop on how to do county-level ownership research. Conference participants were then to undertake studies in their home counties for possible later multicounty tabulation and analysis. Some local research followed, but to our knowledge the findings have not been tabulated on a multicounty basis.

Eastern North Carolina

Using the Appalachian Land Ownership Study as a model, the Institute for Southern Studies undertook a study of land ownership and control of wealth in several piedmont and coastal North Carolina counties in 1982-83. Preceding the study, the director of the institute consulted with both the co-coordinators of the Appalachian study. Also, the previous state coordinator of the land study in West Virginia became a staff person on this project and was involved in most of the county-level research. The results of this study have not been released as of this date.

Southeastern Ohio

The Appalachian Ohio Public Interest Campaign (AOPIC), an organization in Athens, Ohio, committed to building broad coalitions, researching and taking action on issues, and providing training assistance to local groups, has also undertaken land ownership research in that state. Activists and community people in this organization became interested in the land ownership issue in part due to the attendance of one of their members at the northern Appalachian conference in western Pennsylvania. They subsequently requested assistance from the Appalachian Alliance (1982) to do a workshop on how to research land and mineral ownership in local counties. The coordinator of the Alliance and the past coordinator of the land study in Kentucky conducted a workshop in Athens, Ohio. As a result, AOPIC members began gathering information on land ownership and taxation patterns in southeastern Ohio. They have now completed that research in six counties and in their words expect soon to be able to answer the question, "Who owns southeastern Ohio?" That information will be used to buttress ongoing campaigns for social change in that area.

Other Counties in the Region and Updating Information

Additional research has also been done in several counties in the region, both in new counties and in counties that were a part of the original study. The following are those of which we are currently aware.

- The Kentucky Fair Tax Coalition has assisted at least five additional counties in eastern Kentucky in land and mineral ownership research. They've also updated and expanded the data in several counties involved in the original land study.
- Research has been done in at least one other county in western North Carolina, as well as extensive additional research on mineral leasing in the national forests.
- Research was done on oil and gas leasing in Washington County, Virginia, showing that over half of the land was already under lease.
- Save Our Cumberland Mountains has offered assistance to other counties and has updated research in some of the original study counties in Tennessee.
- Students in Rabun County, Georgia, have researched land ownership and taxation in that northern Georgia county heavily influenced by second home and recreational development.

These examples illustrate continued interest in making land ownership research a part of social change efforts in Appalachia.

It should be stressed that the previous examples are the ones that we know about at the present time. Requests for information on how to do local land ownership research came to the Appalachian Alliance and Highlander Center regularly during the years following the study. Highlander still receives requests for information and assistance from communities and citizens' groups. So, there is continuing interest in how to use participatory land ownership research to empower people in their various struggles.

USING THE LAND OWNERSHIP MODEL TO RESEARCH OTHER ISSUES: SOUTHEASTERN WOMEN'S EMPLOYMENT COALITION (SWEC)

The Appalachian Land Ownership Study not only generated interest in the issues of land ownership and taxation. It also generated some excitement about the use of the participatory research model to look at other issues. Not long after completion of the study, there were discussions on undertaking a similar research effort in the area of education in Appalachia. The idea was to look at who owns and controls Appalachian schools. Preliminary discussions with Southern Appalachian Leadership Training (SALT) led to a grant proposal for such a project. However, for various reasons, including the lack of funding possibilities, the project never reached fruition. SALT did, however, continue to use a participatory model to do research on local education systems in several communities in which it worked.

In another case, though, the participatory research model was used by a regional organization to do research on a multistate level. The Southeastern Women's Employment Coalition (SWEC) had, since its inception, been concerned with the economic plight of women in Appalachia and the South. Continuing concern about the powerlessness of women in the face of a changing economy led them to obtain a private foundation grant to research the economic conditions affecting women in those areas. After reviewing the experience of the land ownership study, they decided to use a participatory research model for their study. This would enable them to both gather the research and empower local and regional women's groups.

Community research was undertaken by already-existing organizations such as the Women's Network in central West Virginia and the Institute for Community Living in coastal South Carolina. As part of the research, interviews were done with women in these communities so as to get beyond the standard evaluation of economic impacts. Though a standard questionnaire was prepared, the Women's Network chose to use in addition their own localized one, which also became a tool for building their organizational base. Additional research and analysis was done on the regional level by a SWEC staff person who also acted as regional coordinator for the project.

Both the local and more general research have been completed, though the results of the study have not yet been broadly disseminated. In the process of completing the study, SWEC confronted many of the same problems and challenges as the land study participants.

Now that two regional organizations in the same geographical area have completed participatory research projects, the level of discussion about it as a method of citizen empowerment has become more challenging. Some of the questions that have arisen were expressed at a recent Highlander workshop on participatory research attended by some twenty-five people from several Appalachian and southern states. Among that group were three people who had participated in the SWEC study and at least five who had been part of the land study.[10] Questions raised from the SWEC experience with participatory research helped to focus the discussions at that workshop. Some of those were

- In what cases does participatory research make sense as an empowerment strategy?
- Do we need first to identify the organizing goal so as to know what information we need or do not need?
- How do we tailor a participatory research process so that it meets both local and regional needs?
- What are the implications of funding sources and time constraints for the research process and product?
- How do we maintain inclusion in the analysis of research findings?

Many of these same issues had been confronted during the land study. Now, though, there is a reservoir of experience in participatory research developing in our region which will enable us to deal with them better in future research projects. In addition to the regional experiences of SWEC and the Appalachian Land Ownership Study, there are numerous other more local efforts now utilizing participatory research.

CONCLUSIONS

The preceding account of the land ownership study and its impacts has, of necessity, been a selective one. We have focused on the more obvious organizational activities, both the successful and the not so successful, and on the research projects that have looked to the study as a model. There are many other important activities as well. For example, several workshops were held at Highlander Center, bringing together people from the land study and elsewhere to deal with land-related issues. Two of the more important ones were a minerals leasing workshop and one on visions of the future. The latter workshop was an attempt by those involved in the land study to develop their ideas of how the region might look if they could design its future (e.g., what kind of ownership, educational system, politics, etc.).

There were also uncounted presentations at regional church meetings, some of which resulted in denominational bodies producing their own materials to educate their members about land ownership and taxation. In fact, church organizations played a very significant role in publicizing the findings of the study. In several instances they have also provided financial support for follow-up activities. There were also presentations by land study participants at numerous secular conferences in the region and elsewhere.

All of the above is important and contributed to the land study's success. However, it is still its use in political struggles and the model it provides for the empowerment of community people that make it unique. Most of the goals of the land ownership study have been met, though the battle over land ownership and taxation will be a long-term one in Appalachia. The Task Force was successful in amassing a significant body of information and making it available to the citizens of the region. It has provided a model that citizens' groups can use to research land ownership and other issues. Local citizens and groups were trained during and after the study in obtaining information on land ownership and taxation. That training still goes on in some of the organizations described in this chapter. There is now a broader network of individuals and groups in the region working on land-related issues. While some of the original members of the land study network have moved on to other things, many others have joined the network through the work of organizations like KFTC, WNCA, and SOCM.

In sum, land study participants can feel some pride that most of the goals were accomplished to some degree. One could always hope for more action, a greater network, more empowerment, more frequent political victories, and so on. At this writing, it has not yet been four years since the completion of the land study. This chapter has documented much, though certainly not all, of what has happened since then. Its impacts are still being felt; some of them may not have even yet become apparent. It has now become a part of the popular knowledge of the region and of the collective and personal histories of the groups and individuals who made it happen. It is now one more link in the ongoing struggle to attain justice in Appalachia and the country.

NOTES

The Appalachian Land Ownership Study was a project of the Appalachian Land Ownership Task Force of the Appalachian Alliance, a regional coalition of citizens' organizations and individuals. Administrative details for the project were handled by the Appalachian Center of Appalachian State University, Boone, North Carolina. The research was coordinated from the Highlander Research and Education Center in New Market, Tennessee. Billy Horton was a co-coordinator of the study, along with John Gaventa of the Highlander Center.

1. For excellent accounts of how this occurred and the effects it had on communities in particular and the region as a whole, see Donald D. Eller, *Miners, Millhands, and Mountaineers* (Knoxville, Tennessee: University of Tennessee Press, 1982); John Gaventa, *Power and Powerlessness: Quiescence and Rebellion in an Appalachian Valley* (Oxford: Clarendon Press, 1980, also Urbana: University of Illinois Press, 1980); and John Alexander Williams, *West Virginia and the Captains of Industry* (Morgantown, West Virginia: West Virginia University Library, 1976).

2. For a fictional account of this migration experience, see Harriett Arnow, *The Dollmaker* (New York: Avon Books, 1972). For a scholarly account, see Harry K. Schwarzweller, James S. Brown, and J. J. Mangalam, *Mountain Families in Transition* (University Park, Pennsylvania: Pennsylvania State University Press, 1971).

3. Accounts of social change efforts in Appalachia in the 1960s can be found in David S. Walls and John Stephenson, eds., *Appalachia in the Sixties* (Lexington, Kentucky: University Press of Kentucky, 1972); and David Whisnant, *Modernizing the Mountaineer* (Boone, North Carolina: Appalachian Consortium Press, 1980).

4. A brief summary of these and other studies can be found in Appalachian Land Ownership Task Force, *Who Owns Appalachia?* Lexington, Kentucky: University Press of Kentucky, 1983, pp. 10-13.

5. For instance, see Appalachian Land Ownership Task Force, *Who Owns Appalachia?*; John Gaventa and Bill Horton, "Land Ownership and Land Reform in Appalachia," in Charles C. Geisler and Frank J. Popper, eds., *Land Reform, American Style* (Totowa, New Jersey: Rowman and Allanheld), pp. 233-244; John Gaventa and Billy D. Horton, "A Citizens' Research Project in Appalachia, USA," *Convergence*, Vol. XIV, No. 3, 1981, p. 32; and "Who Owns Appalachia?" *Southern Exposure*, Vol. X, No. 1 (January/February, 1982), pp. 32-52.

6. One of the sources of immediate frustration came when there was no place to set up flood relief trailers provided by a federal agency. This was true because there was so little non-company owned land in the community.

7. A brief description of the intricacies involved in dealing with the Appalachian Regional Commission can be found in John Gaventa and Billy D. Horton, "A Citizens' Research Project in Appalachia, USA," *Convergence*, Vol. XIV, No. 3, 1981, p. 32.

8. A citizens' group in that county—the Concerned Citizens of Martin County, whose members were active in founding the Kentucky Fair Tax Coalition—had already been using the land study's preliminary findings to challenge the unfair taxation of Pocahontas Kentucky and had held a local tax workshop in 1980.

9. That "loan" was repaid by the Kentucky Fair Tax Coalition the following year, when their staff person assisted with some of the early organizational work that led to the Western North Carolina Alliance.

10. Also in attendance were persons from ten to fifteen other citizens' organizations who have engaged in participatory research either in the community or workplace.

7

Participatory Research as Critical Theory: The North Bonneville, USA, Experience

DONALD E. COMSTOCK *AND* RUSSELL FOX _____

Who has the right to create knowledge? Is this the sole prerogative of professional elites or should the people affected by new knowledge participate in formulating the problems to be studied, collecting and analyzing the data, and deciding how to use the results? This is the key question raised by participatory researchers, who argue that traditional social science creates knowledge that is used by elites to control, pacify, and manipulate people and that much modern science is, often unwittingly, a technical and ideological means for maintaining that control. To counter this, participatory researchers undertake studies designed to empower the oppressed. Local communities and workplace groups decide on the nature of the problem to be investigated and learn about their lives by collectively participating in the investigation of local and extra-local forces shaping their lives. Based on this knowledge, the community may take collective action aimed at social change. Investigation, education, and action are combined in participatory research as dialectical moments of a process of self-emancipation.

The initial characterization of participatory research was attempted by Hall (1977), who described it as research which (1) is of direct and immediate benefit to the community, (2) involves the community in the entire process from the formulation of the problem to the interpretation of the findings and the discussions of how to seek solutions, (3) is seen as part of a total educational experience which increases community awareness and commitment, (4) is viewed as a dialectical process, a dialogue over time and not static, (5) fosters mobilization of human resources for the solution of social problems, and (6) requires the researcher to be conscious of the ideological implications of research.

Since Hall's initial discussion of participatory research, numerous re-

searchers, adult educators, and community development workers throughout the world have contributed to this growing movement that is both a
critique of mainstream social science and an affirmation of the potential for
social research to be a progressive force.

We will provide an example and interpretation of participatory research
from the United States. First, we will focus on four major issues in participatory research and will argue that contemporary critical theory offers an
appropriate epistemology for participatory research. We will then report
on a project undertaken in the northwestern United States and attempt to
draw out of our experience with this project some tentative lessons which
we hope will be useful to others.

ISSUES IN PARTICIPATORY RESEARCH

A review of recent conceptual papers and case studies suggests four closely
related issues that should be dealt with in any discussion of participatory
research. The first is the question of whether participatory research is based
on a pragmatic epistemology or on historical materialism. Second is a concern for the proper position of popular knowledge, the common people's
conceptions of their world, in guiding participatory analyses. The third issue
focuses on the role of the outside researcher in maximizing community
participation in research. Finally, we will address how knowledge created
in the participatory process may be justified as valid and, in so doing, will
confront the relation between research and action. Throughout this section
we will try to extract the key perspectives that have been expressed in recent
analyses of participatory research and then compare these perspectives to
one derived from critical theory.

Is Participatory Research Pragmatism or Dialectical Materialism?

Is participatory research applied dialectical materialism or is it a method
of solving the immediate problems confronting poor and oppressed communities? This issue arose at the 1977 Cartagena Conference (Molano
1978), at the 1979 African Regional Workshop (Mbilinyi et al. 1979), and
at the 1980 International Forum on Participatory Research (International
Council for Adult Education and UNESCO 1980).

Those who advocate a pragmatic approach emphasize a dialogic method
of problem solving which requires a commitment by the researcher to the
people and a close involvement with the life and problems of a community.
They advocate a respect for the people's capacity to create progressive
knowledge by analyzing their own circumstances (Darcy de Oliveira and
Darcy de Oliveira 1982; Hall 1977). These pragmatic researchers seem
largely motivated by a general critical perspective drawn from the tradition

of Marxist studies but wish to remain open about the applicability of specific theoretical categories to any particular situation.

On the other hand, those viewing participatory research as a method of application of dialectical materialism seem to have in mind the Marxist-Leninist theory of the transformation of capitalist and dependent capitalist societies through class struggle based on a scientifically correct understanding of the necessary path of historical change. Yet, they also believe that it is necessary to move the participants toward a theoretical understanding of this process. Thus historical change has both an objective and a subjective moment. For example, Bryceson and Mustafa (1979) see participatory research as part of the development of class struggle, and Vio Grossi (1980) points out that historical materialism is a theory of the objective tendencies of capitalist social formations, while participatory research is the method of applying that theory to the actual transformation of capitalist society.

Part of the controversy lies in confronting epistemology and theory, that is, the logic of analysis with the content of an analysis, and part of it stems from problems with applying the theoretical content of historical materialism to contemporary social conditions. We believe that critical theory offers an epistemological foundation for participatory research and a theoretical focus that resolves some of these problems and controversies. Critical theory is both a development from the historical materialism of Marx and a critique of the dialectical materialism of many neo-Marxists. It preserves the logic Marx used in analyzing both religion and nineteenth-century political economy while applying that logic to the conscious transformation of the structures of domination that characterize the twentieth century.

Critical theory is an historically applied logic of analysis which provides a method for the immanent critique of domination (Schroyer 1973; Antonio 1981). An immanent critique compares a social reality characterized by domination with the ideology which legitimates and mystifies that domination. It gives priority to neither social reality nor ideology but focuses attention on the contradiction between them. It shows how that contradiction can be resolved only by consciously transforming the social relations of domination by applying existing progressive ideals. Immanent critique comprises the subjective moment of the historical dialectic by stressing the conscious struggle to create a more rational reality. As Antonio has put it,

immanent critique seeks, by revealing the contradictions of claim and context, to transform legitimations into emancipatory weapons. The goal is to replace inaction based on the false correspondence [between ideology and social reality] with emancipatory praxis aimed at making the ideal real. (1981, 338)

The method of an immanent critique of domination can be schematically presented as follows: (1) a comparison of an ideology with the social structures experienced by the people, (2) a critique of the contradictions between the ideology and the social structures it purports to describe, (3) the discovery of immanent possibilities for liberation by applying current ideals to the specific historical development of social structures, and (4) the negation and transcendence of both the ideological and material bases of domination. This transcendence involves both creating new understandings of social conditions and undertaking political struggle to alter these social conditions to more closely accord with progressive ideals.

Applying the logic of immanent critique to twentieth-century culture and social structure, critical theorists have been most concerned with a critique of the growth of instrumental reason, or means-rationality, which eliminates questions of value from the sphere of rational knowledge (Horkheimer 1974). Enlightenment thought overthrew the absolute reason of religion and replaced it with the instrumental reason of science and technology. The effect was to unleash enormous powers of human creativity to investigate, understand, and dominate nature. But the historical consequence of this instrumental orientation to nature has been the extension of rational domination to the social sphere. The increasing administrative power characteristic of our age is an extension of instrumental reason into spheres of social action and thought. As Horkheimer and Adorno expressed it,

In their [the masses'] eyes, their reduction to mere objects of the administered life, which preforms every sector of modern existence including language and perception, represents objective necessity, against which they believe there is nothing they can do. (1972, 38)

Through an immanent critique of instrumental reason, critical theorists have sought to reawaken a form of reason which focuses on moral values and ends. Called practical reason, such an interest in knowledge would restore to the public sphere a dialogue about the values served by instrumental thought and action. Instrumental reason would not be suppressed, but our scientific and technical knowledge would be recognized as means to the achievement of values consensually determined through public discussion. In such a dialectic of means and ends, or technical and practical reason, everyone can participate and contribute. In contrast to mainstream social science, participatory research incorporates both instrumental knowledge and moral values in the process of creating new knowledge. By involving the members of a community in creating social knowledge, participatory research subordinates technical knowledge to human values. In this way participatory research is the practice of critical theory and represents a method for practically transcending scientific and bureaucratic power based on an exclusive interest in instrumental reason.

Critical theory represents a transcendence of the controversy between pragmatic and dialectical materialist orientations to participatory research.

Those who pursue a materialist strategy are correct in their emphasis on dialectical analysis and political struggle. But dialectical materialism is ahistorical insofar as it fails to recognize the concrete conditions under which people *now* live. And it shares in the hypostatization of instrumental reason when it promises emancipation through the advance of science and technology under the guidance of a bureaucratically administered state. Finally, dialectical materialism gives too little weight to the processes of knowledge production and the importance of new understandings of social reality for action to transform that reality.

On the other hand, the more pragmatic participatory researchers are correct in their concern for dialogue with and among the oppressed as a method of creating new knowledge. They are also correct in their concern for the solving of practical problems of communities. But the pragmatic approach offers little to guide our evaluations of progressive solutions to immediate problems and seldom leads to fundamental changes in power and decision-making structures. It fails to specify a logic of analysis which moves the oppressed beyond ideologically distorted estimations of the actual and the possible.

Participatory research should be neither pragmatism nor dialectical materialism, although it needs to be informed by both. Participatory research based on critical theory can be an epistemologically grounded method of generating liberating knowledge and testing the validity of that knowledge in political struggle.

What Is the Position of Popular Knowledge in Participatory Research?

Here we find parallels with the division of opinion just reviewed. On the one hand we find researchers who look for a theoretical understanding of local issues in the people's own knowledge of their situation. On the other hand there are those who see this knowledge as ideologically distorted and in need of critique and transcendence.

The first position is exemplified in Hall's (1977) statement that theory should arise from the participants' own analysis of their situation, not from the researcher's analysis. Fals Borda (1979 and 1980) has struggled with this question in his attempt to facilitate the growth of a popular or common people's science, which he characterizes as "the empirical or common sense knowledge . . . belonging to the people in the social bases" (1980, 4). Yet, as Fals Borda also points out, the weight of ideology has systematically distorted the people's view of their world and their own capabilities. The result for most is passivity and a resignation to the status quo as an unchangeable and natural experience.

This is the point of departure for those who reject as "romanticism" the idea that the oppressed hold the truth for their emancipation (Bryceson and Mustafa 1979). For these researchers, it is crucial that participatory research offer a critique of popular knowledge. Reflecting this concern, Jackson, Conchelos, and Vigoda (1980) warn that "while professionals in participatory research may be directed by popular groups, they nevertheless must not permit false consciousness to dominate the process." But how not? The danger of assuming that the people are not dominated by false consciousness in need of correction is that "participatory" researchers may adopt an authoritarian form of interaction with the community which will reproduce domination and stifle the people's capacity for *self*-analysis and *self*-critique.

This problem has been addressed in several places. Conchelos and Jackson (1980, 7) assert that some sort of balance must be struck between the influence of the indigenous people's and the professional researcher's perspectives. Fals Borda (1980) points out that the intellectual who is committed to popular struggles must deal in two languages simultaneously, that of the people and that of the scientist of social change. According to this view participatory research is a process in which the people's "raw" knowledge—sometimes distorted and inadequate—is systematized by "reflected" knowledge, while control of this process remains with the local community (International Council for Adult Education and UNESCO 1980). Participatory research then is a nonantagonist dialectic, a dialogue between people with different perspectives, but the same interest in liberation (Himmelstrand 1977; Rader 1980).

If participatory research is conceived as immanent critique, popular knowledge plays a central role in generating new knowledge and motivating a community for political action. An immanent critique proceeds from an examination of the inconsistency of existing beliefs with historically changing social structures. Only by comparing existing beliefs, values, and understandings with the social reality they experience can people discover the contradictions of their existence and find the potentials for creating a more ideal existence.

This calls for a method of collective analysis and action which proceeds from, but criticizes and transcends, existing popular knowledge. Thus, through self-critique, members of a community improve popular knowledge and make their actions more rational. Critical knowledge must remain popular, that is, collective, knowledge in order to generate collective political action. Critical knowledge that is not popular knowledge invites alienation and renewed domination.

The participatory researcher plays a crucial and delicate role in guiding and encouraging the process whereby popular knowledge and values are brought to light, collectively studied, and compared to social reality, and whereby the potentials for emancipatory actions are discovered. We turn next to a discussion of the role of the outside researcher in participatory research.

Participation and Role of the Outside Researcher

Maximum participation by the members of a community in knowledge creation and use is a necessity because of the close connection between ideas and power. Power includes the ability to define what is factual and true, and the more powerful are able to impose a conception of the world that supports their power (Fals Borda 1980). Participatory research is a method of destroying the ideological bases of current structures of power by giving a voice to those who dwell in what Freire (1970c) calls the "culture of silence."

Participatory researchers have identified two additional reasons for maximizing community participation. The first is that participation in research encourages collective self-education. Jackson (1978), Mduma (1982) and Conchelos and Jackson (1980) have observed the horizontal transfer of skills and understandings among members of communities and between communities engaged in participatory research. Members with different skills and perspectives begin to share these with one another, and each participant becomes both a researcher and a teacher.

Another reason for maximizing participation in research and education is to re-create the conditions for collective social action. Collective knowledge creation is a political act that leads to collective action for social change (Barndt 1980). Tandon (1980) has argued that participatory social action must be based on participatory research rather than traditional top-down social research.

From the perspective of participatory research as the critique of domination, maximum participation is necessary to avoid re-creating the conditions for domination by the scientific or technical expert. Dialogic, participatory, and democratic methods are the only ones consistent both with the logic and the goals of critical theory.

Recognizing the desirability of widespread participation, several researchers have noted the constraints they faced in carrying this out in particular research projects. These constraints stem from the disparity between researchers and community members with regard to their resources (Moser 1980), expertise (Barndt 1980), and interests (Fals Borda 1980). Several researchers have also commented on the difficulties of overcoming internal power structures of communities and local cultures that restrict participation (Mduma 1982; Mbilinyi et al. 1979; Cain 1977). However, some have noted that the participatory research process tends to break down the local power hierarchies by developing a greater understanding and appreciation of the skills and commitments of various subclasses within the community (Hudson 1980; Conchelos and Jackson 1980). Finally, the participatory researcher must always be conscious of competing interests and activities that constrain the degree and types of participation that can be expected. As Barndt (1980) observes, people's priorities are often survival and entertainment above serious discussion. Thus some participatory researchers use theater, drawing, or music to stimulate participation.

In working to maximize participation, the relationship of the outside researcher to the community must be constantly evaluated. This topic has received considerable attention from participatory researchers. Questions have been raised about the values and attitudes of the researcher (Cain 1977), the class membership and interests of professionals (Bryceson and Mustafa 1979), the commitment of the researcher to the community and its problems (Darcy de Oliveira and Darcy de Oliveira 1982; International Council for Adult Education and UNESCO 1980), the activities appropriate to the role of the expert (Jackson 1978; Bryceson and Mustafa 1979; de Vries 1980), and the degree of equality between the professional and the participants (Jackson 1978; Bryceson and Mustafa 1979).

Many researchers feel that the primary contribution of the outside professional is to the research process, including bringing funds to the community, supplying technical research and writing skills as well as information not available in the community, and training community members in research and analysis (Jackson 1978; International Council for Adult Education and UNESCO 1980). The local community furnishes the content of the project, including locally available information and theoretical perspectives (Conchelos and Jackson 1980). De Vries (1980) has suggested that the researcher is primarily a supportive scientist who is a keen observer and describer of the local situation, responsible for mediating between the people and the systematic descriptions that emerge from the investigation. Bryceson and Mustafa (1979) advocate a more active role for the researcher. They suggest that the researcher should impart a theoretical awareness to the community and acknowledge a pedagogical role. They believe it is false and patronizing for the researcher to attempt to interact with the community on the basis of an assumed equality.

Jackson, Conchelos, and Vigoda (1980) and Cain (1977) suggest a more convergent relationship between the researcher and the community by pointing out that, while the researcher and the people in the community may not begin as equals, every attempt must be made to progress toward reciprocity and equality as the research proceeds. This can be accomplished by conveying information and skills to the people as rapidly as possible and by maintaining a dialogue with the people about their interpretation of the analysis. In this process both the people of the community and the researcher learn and grow.

We believe the focus of much of the work of participatory researchers should be on the process of immanent critique rather than the content of the analyses. This does not preclude the researcher from helping to gather data about the community and its environment, nor does it prohibit the researcher from helping the participants learn what they need to know to take political action. In all cases, however, these efforts by the researcher must be in response to the expressed needs of the community and they should always be subject to an evaluation of their relevance by members of the community in their own attempt to understand their situation.

How Do We Judge the Validity of Participatory Research Results?

The final issue we must address is how new knowledge collectively created by researchers and community members is validated as appropriate, correct, or true. A range of positions may be observed among participatory researchers, some of whom seem to hold different positions simultaneously. Three positions are worthy of noting here: the pragmatic, historical materialist, and critical.

The pragmatic criterion for knowledge is that it contributes to the solution of particular problems experienced by particular groups or individuals (Oquist 1978). This is exemplified in the statement by the Darcy de Oliveiras that "the degree of a theory's truth is in direct relationship to its capacity for providing answers to concrete problems of everyday life" (1975, 30). De Vries's (1980) advocacy of "process-validity," the contribution of knowledge to action, might also be interpreted as a pragmatic criterion.

A second position is that of historical materialism, which warrants knowledge as valid insofar as it contributes to class struggle by the oppressed (Bryceson and Mustafa 1979). Historical materialism adds political and economic dimensions to the pragmatic criterion of validity: It is not any solution to any problem but historically progressive solutions to the problems of powerless groups struggling against capitalist domination. This involves two standards according to Bryceson and Mustafa: On the one hand the results of participatory research must be correct from a theoretical point of view, that is, congruent with the theory of historical materialism. On the other hand, the information must be relevant to the situation of a particular group or class—it must be applicable to political action in their situation.

Finally, we can observe in several participatory research reports what we might call the critical criterion of validity. According to Moser (1977) truth becomes a task of revealing the underlying social forces and relations hidden behind a surface of harmony. Information gains importance by its ability to enlighten discourse or rational argumentation among participants about the relevance of different information and different perspectives. From the critical position, valid knowledge is not fixed but is a process of developing understandings in dialectical tension with a changing reality (Himmelstrand 1977; Fals Borda 1980). From this perspective, the goal of critical knowledge is praxis. It is not simply problem-solving activity, but new understandings which guide social groups in struggles to eliminate their domination. As Vio Grossi puts it, participatory research "is intended to change the fundamental conditions that engender poverty, dependence, and exploitation" (1980, 7). Praxis requires that theoretical insights generated by participatory research contribute to political action that reduces and eliminates oppression and gives power to the powerless and voices to the silent.

A further element of the critical criterion is the capacity for participatory research to generate a self-sustaining dialectic of reflection and action—a spiral-like process of self-criticism and theoretically guided political struggle. This makes the researcher increasingly redundant and unnecessary as members of the community gain knowledge and confidence in their ability to carry on the process themselves. Thus the object of participatory research is not only to generate liberating knowledge and practice but also to initiate a permanent process of action and reflection which leads communities to undertake further analyses and struggles on new issues. Surely it is necessary to address the immediate sources of powerlessness. But just as surely the solution of immediate problems must stimulate a process of self-emancipation and increasing autonomy for the oppressed. Participatory research must contribute to the transformation of the oppressed into historical subjects who are capable of critical reflection upon the conditions of their oppression and autonomous political action to overthrow those conditions.

Keeping these four major issues in mind—the epistemological basis for participatory research, the role of popular knowledge, the role of the outside researcher in the creation of new knowledge, and the criteria for evaluating participatory research projects—we turn now to a review of a participatory research project in the United States. We will try to see how our experience in this project may shed light on the issues we have just reviewed and the applicability of critical theory to participatory research.

THE RELOCATION OF NORTH BONNEVILLE

In 1971 the U.S. Army Corps of Engineers, after analyzing eleven potential sitings for a second powerhouse at the Bonneville Dam on the Columbia River, announced that the best location for the powerhouse (and a new channel in the river) would be the center of the town of North Bonneville in the state of Washington. Every family in the town, and many around it, faced eviction and relocation. With a population of 470, including one-third on fixed income and about 40 percent unemployed or only seasonally employed, a payroll of two (a sheriff and part-time clerk), and an annual budget of $39,000, the town seemed destined to be another insignificant footnote in the history of towns destroyed by Corps of Engineers projects. In this case, however, the grandeur of the geographic setting, the strength of the ethical values of the community, and the philosophy and tactics of a college resource it located combined to enable this community to take control of its destiny and, in fact, win every battle it fought with the Corps. In July 1978 the new city of North Bonneville, conceived, fought for, located, and designed by the residents of North Bonneville, was officially inaugurated.

Located in the majestic Columbia Gorge, where the Columbia River cuts through the Cascade Mountain Range of the states of Washington and Oregon, the site has a rich history as an important human settlement. It was the principal point of contact and trade among Indian nations of the Pacific Coast and the inland plains. As recently as the late 1800s, the community of Cascades, as North Bonneville was then known, was one of the largest settlements in the state of Washington, again because of its central role in the transfer of goods through the mountain range. The thundering rapids, the steep shorn bluffs, the legendary Bridge of the Gods, an imposing monolithic volcanic dike that reminds one of the Rock of Gibraltar, the colors, the winds, the salmon—all combine to make this the kind of natural environment that enables one to formulate deep, meaningful, and comforting answers to questions relating to the role and place of humans in the universe.

The residents of North Bonneville are fiercely independent and self-sufficient in their personal and family lives, yet were unified by the common threat to that relationship. Politically conservative and extremely patriotic, few residents expressed a desire to try to stop the powerhouse project. Many had settled in the area after working on the construction crews that built the first dam and powerhouse at Bonneville during the 1930s. Forty years of uncertainty and the sudden reality of a second powerhouse put tremendous stress on their personal and family lives. While most had accepted the inevitability of relocation, the limits of their ability to accept a disruption in their lives were reached when relocation meant leaving the Columbia Gorge and breaking the bonds they had with that particular environment.

When the Corps of Engineers told the town's residents in 1971 that they were going to have to move to Portland, Oregon, or Vancouver, Washington, or anywhere else they chose, the town found itself rallying around a common desire and goal—relocation as a community, where social bonds and a relationship with the majestic geographic features of the Columbia Gorge would be maintained. They formed North Bonneville Life Effort (NOBLE) and, with the assistance of the Bureau of Community Development of the University of Washington, completed a survey documenting that 64 percent of the residents preferred to relocate into a new North Bonneville as close as possible to their existing town.

There were two major obstacles: The Corps of Engineers interpreted the Federal Relocation Act of 1970 to state that it was not authorized to replace towns, only to compensate individual households by paying them fair market value for their property and up to $15,000 in relocation benefits. Owners of businesses were to be paid only the market value of their property. They could also receive up to $10,000 if they were terminating their business rather than relocating it. The Corps claimed that the only conditions whereby they would pay for construction of new town facilities were if the town purchased or provided a town site and paid for all of the planning for the new town. In addition, the Corps also claimed that they needed all of the available flat or accessible land in the narrow gorge for the twenty-three million cubic yards of earth they would remove from the construction site.

In its search for assistance in maintaining its identity, the town contacted the Evergreen State College in Olympia, Washington, in November 1972. Created by the Washington state legislature with the mandate to provide an "alternative curricular structure" within higher education, Evergreen was only in its second year of operation. The full-time, year-long, team-taught "coordinated studies" format enabled students and faculty to pursue problems or issues in an in-depth interdisciplinary context. Students in one such academic program during the 1972-73 school year had spent three months extensively studying the structure and function of communities, the philosophical bases and techniques of urban planning as vehicles of social change and community decision making, and the skills and strategies of community-based education and participatory research. The principal faculty member of the program, Russell Fox, had been strongly influenced by his participation in a Chilean government program designed to decentralize Ministry of Housing and Urbanization decision making, and by his role as organizer of a participatory research and land use planning project with a semirural community in Washington State. Fox and the Evergreen students were looking for projects that would demystify the planning process, decentralize community structures and decision making, and empower citizens through participatory research. The residents of North Bonneville discovered the faculty and students of Evergreen and a four-year participatory research project was underway by January 1973.

The students quickly discovered that, although the town's residents had extensive knowledge about their community and strong feelings and desires concerning their pending relocation, they did not understand the complex external political and social forces that were determining their future. They were not confident about accepting responsibility or initiating action outside of their experience. When Fox and fifteen students attended their first town council meeting in December 1972, the five councilmen avoided the crucial business of the evening—selecting a new mayor and talking to the Evergreen group about how they could help—for over two hours. Finally, among themselves—a motel owner, bartender, retired painter, truck driver, and tavern owner—they convinced Ernie Skala, the retired painter, to take over as mayor. Then they turned to the Evergreen group: "We know what we want. Can you help us?"

After discussing the general nature of the town's problem, goals, and commitment to active participation in the planning process, Fox and the students made the following proposal for a participatory research process.

(1) The objectives of Phase I of the project, to be completed at the end of the school year in June 1973, would be (a) to generate the information

needed to plan for the relocation of North Bonneville—a specific and detailed inventory of the town and the relocation options its residents faced; and (b) to develop the capability of the residents to use their understanding of this information in pursuing their goals. The report produced during Phase I would include information such as the town's historical and regional context, demographic and economic base data, sociological and cultural patterns, physical infrastructure and community facilities, geographic and natural features, use and ownership of land, and the laws and other external forces affecting the relocation.

(2) The general strategy would be for the students to live and work in the community, while creating and gathering the quantifiable planning data needed *and* engaging in ongoing discussions with residents so that the residents could create and discover their own understanding, expression, and use of the data. The data with which to make decisions, an awareness of the external forces affecting decisions in their lives, and the self-confidence and capacity to make their own decisions all needed to be developed simultaneously.

(3) The students, through informal discussions with residents, community workshops, and internships with principal agencies, would (a) share with the residents what they were learning about communities, the planning process, and the skills of participation; (b) compile, organize, and publish a report with pertinent information available about the relocation problem and the characteristics of the existing community; and (c) take leadership in coordination of information and involvement of governmental agencies interested in the relocation issue, while involving the town in discussions that would lead to political skills and strategies they could use in pursuing their goal.

(4) The town, initially through actions of its elected council, would (a) provide work space and assume some of the costs of travel and living expenses for the students, (b) actively promote the participation of residents, and (c) assure that the entire process be genuinely open to all groups and members of the community.

(5) The expected outcomes of the six-month project would be (a) the publication of a relocation planning study that the residents would understand and be ready to use; (b) an increased awareness on the part of all residents of the nature of their community, the nature of the relocation problem, and the options available to them, and (c) an increased readiness to politically participate in the pursuit of their goal to relocate into a new North Bonneville.

(6) While this group of students would only be involved until June 1973, the college would maintain its commitment to assist the town in whatever direction the project took after this initial phase.

After meeting and negotiating twice with the Evergreen team, the town council accepted the proposal and voted unanimously to allocate $1,000—

half of its first federal revenue-sharing check—to help pay student living expenses while the students worked in the town. The town also provided a storefront office for the students. The students welcomed residents dropping in to help add figures, to locate features of their community on maps, or to describe, in detail no outside researcher would ever identify, the social networks among community members or the special ponds or groves that different residents had claimed as their special places to fish or picnic. The students met with residents in their homes, in the post office, in the café, and on the river bank. The discussions were dialogues of sharing what they each knew of the community and its problem. The residents knew their community, how it worked, and what was special about it. The students shared what they were learning about the planning process; about the relocation laws; and about the technical data they were developing, or discovering through research (often involving a resident or two) into information available through different state or local agencies. In a few cases the students actually spent time working as interns in agencies such as the Underwood Soil Conservation District, the Skamania County Planning Department, and the Washington State Planning and Community Affairs Agency. More formalized contact between students and residents included scheduled coffee hours in homes where the particular relocation situation and options of each family could be discussed, weekly workshops and presentations of information being generated which were open to the whole community, and almost daily contact with the staff and elected officials of the town.

As residents reflected and talked about what they knew about their community, they began to realize the discrepancy between their knowledge of who they were and the very different perspective of the Corps of Engineers and the politicians who wrote relocation laws. They began to define their community as a complex network of social, natural, and spiritual relationships. They discovered that the government defined their community as abstract individuals and a quantifiable number of physical artifacts, such as a fire truck and so many lampposts. Similarly, as the residents learned about planning processes—both those imposed by external forces and those they were creating—they realized that planning was merely the creation of information to implement goals. They realized that the Corps planning was a meticulously designed and carefully controlled critical path for technical efficiency. To the contrary, the town's "process planning" was the creation of knowledge about themselves, including the potential for implementing their own, rather than the Corps's, goals. They discovered that their goal—survival of the social relationships that defined their community—was quite different from the government's goal—to build a powerhouse as quickly as possible.

These discoveries and the students' persistent encouragement and affirmation of the town's ability to control the situation gave the town's leaders the confidence and skill to act on their own perception of reality rather than be limited to fighting the Corps's perception of reality through the channels the Corps controlled. The members of the Corps of Engineers are masters— perhaps the best in the world—of construction logistics and pursuit of their goals. They have the skill and strength to out-professionalize anyone who challenges them at their own game. The Corps of Engineers were continually baffled and outmaneuvered, however, when faced with an entire town of residents who *weren't* represented by professionals but who knew the data, information, and processes themselves.

The first major example of the Corps's inability to understand or control this development of popular knowledge was the Corps's May 1973 reversal of their earlier claims about not being able to fund planning for a new town. Once the town's planning effort began gaining momentum, the Corps came to the town with a slick presentation of a planning process they would undertake for the town. The town's residents listened politely and responded with a firm "No, thank you." They recognized that they and the students were already doing everything that the Corps proposal included and that the town, rather than the Corps, was a client and owner of the study.

The students also helped the town council realize that one of the Corps's most effective strategies was to control and manipulate information and keep united fronts from forming by selectively telling different agencies and segments of the community different information. Over beer following a frustrating town-Corps meeting, students and town officials developed the idea of creating a relocation advisory board, where all of the principal agencies would meet regularly to share and coordinate information. The Corps resisted participation. However, once Governor Daniel Evans, Senators Warren Magnuson and Henry Jackson, Skamania County commissioners and port district officials, the Evergreen State College, and town of North Bonneville representatives all endorsed the idea and began meeting, the Corps had to attend—and give the same information to everyone.

Phase I concluded with the publication of the 230-page relocation planning study in June 1973. Its publication and wide distribution served as a major validation of the town's planning process, especially among skeptical professionals who had been watching and helping the town. The real power of the document, however, was that most of the residents of the town *already knew and understood* everything in it before it was published. As the authors of the study wrote in their introduction,

the planning program directed toward the development of a comprehensive plan for relocation must accept the responsibility for promoting direct community involvement as an integral part of the planning process. Disruption of human lives, community patterns, social functions and economic activity will be minimized only if the citizens directly affected experience an understanding of their relocation through their direct involvement. Planning information and analysis must therefore be set forth in a manner needed to make decisions with respect to relocating options. If there is to be any hope of maintaining an identity as a community, direct involvement of the citizens in relocation planning and decision making must be the primary goal.

Phase II began in the summer of 1973, when a small grant enabled five students, including Pollard Dickson, whom the town subsequently hired as planning director, to work in the town as interns. Another group of students and faculty then assisted the town during the 1973-74 school year. The focus of the students' work continued to be cooperating with the residents in ongoing education and research endeavors. They helped a newly formed planning commission design and train volunteers to complete a comprehensive relocation preference survey. They began to focus discussion and analysis of the planning information upon the issue of selecting a site for the new town. They worked with small groups of residents interested in studying specific relocation problems, such as the relocation of the school, the need for a medical clinic, and how the businesses would be able to relocate given the inadequate relocation benefits they would receive.

As one of their programs during Phase II of the project, the 1973-74 student group began working with different segments of the community on the initial conceptual characteristics and relationships that would lead to the design and layout of a new town that reflected their life-styles, values, and social and economic relationships. For example, school children drew maps and visual representations of their community. The real pathways and connections between important features of the community began to unfold. Grid street patterns became insignificant as thinking focused on relationships among activities in the town in a way that reflected actual living patterns. The children became more knowledgeable about their town than the Corps surveyors and bulldozer drivers ever could be. This groundwork in getting the community to think about the relationships of places and activities in their lives, and how they could be reinforced or inhibited by design of the new town, prepared the residents for the intense, fast-paced location and design decisions they were to face in Phase III of the relocation.

Members of the town council, meanwhile, had been turning their attention, knowledge, and emerging confidence to securing a site for the new town and to generating financial support for the increasingly complex and sophisticated relocation planning. During Phase II there were at least five significant actions that demonstrated both their emerging skill as political strategists and the success of the participatory process that was empowering them to act on the knowledge they were generating. First, the council and planning commission directed the staff to prepare an "optimum town statement"—a comprehensive statement of the town's position regarding the location, design, planning, and decision-making processes for the construction of a new town. Adopted as a formal resolution, this statement was a comprehensive and unifying presentation of the town's position. Second, the town drafted, and the Washington State congressional delegation introduced and helped pass into law, an amendment to the Rivers, Harbors, and Flood Control Act of 1974 that obligated the Corps to pay for a town site and detailed planning, while giving the town control over the selection and hiring of the planning consultants. The town then used its "optimum town statement" as the basis for a twenty-page scope of work which made the private consulting firms work in the town, involve all the residents in each step of the planning decisions, and, in essence, teach residents how to design their own community. Evergreen's original participatory criteria for providing technical assistance were now the town's.

Because the Rivers, Harbors, and Flood Control Act made federal funding contingent upon the town's demonstration of fiscal capability, the town annexed the eventual new town site but did not disincorporate the existing town that was soon to be a part of the river. Then they persuaded the Washington State legislature to amend the taxing laws so that towns their size could levy a sales tax on federal construction projects within their city limits. Although the sales tax was subsequently ruled unconstitutional, the Corps's $650 million project within the city limits was subject to a one-half percent business and occupation tax. This became the town's major source of revenue and fiscal survival once the old town was demolished and while the new one was being prepared for occupancy.

Phase III, which began in August 1974 with the signing of the relocation contract and the hiring of the private consulting firms, continued to be characterized by community-wide workshops that involved all residents in planning decisions. Although the Corps of Engineers subsequently tried to dissolve, ignore, and subvert the relocation contract, the town turned to the courts to force the Corps to fulfill its contractual obligations. In July 1976 the new city of North Bonneville was officially dedicated.

In 1982 North Bonneville is the home of 450 people. The design of the town reflects, far better than the original town did, the residents' relationships to each other and their physical environment. While all of the residual issues of relocation are not yet settled, the town has taken the increased consciousness of itself and its potential into new arenas of learning and action. For example, the town has secured grants for pilot drillings to explore the potential of geothermal energy as a source of the town's heat. The pilot wells were successful and the town is now pursuing public and private capital to install the country's first community-wide geothermal heating system. Although he recently faced a hotly contested reelection campaign that reflected the level and intensity of political involvement by residents in their community, Ernie Skala, the retired painter who was reluctant to assume leadership ten years ago, is still the mayor of North Bonneville. The 1982 city budget of $550,000 is fourteen times the 1971 budget. Planning Director Pollard Dickson continues to insist that the entire community be involved in decisions about its future as a community. With the city of North Bonneville firmly in control of its destiny as a community, the Evergreen State College has moved on to other participatory research projects.

DISCUSSION

What does the experience of North Bonneville tell us about the issues we raised at the outset of this chapter? We initially raised the controversy over the theoretical and epistemological bases of participatory research. Participatory research is neither pragmatism nor historical materialism but, instead, is an application of critical theory conceived as the method for an immanent critique of domination. Such a critique involves the community in a study that reveals the contradictions between ideology that maintains power and the social reality that offers possibilities for emancipation. Immanent critique leads to the discovery of possibilities for social change by applying progressive ideals to social conditions. These discoveries form the theoretical bases for the people's political struggle against their exploitation. We can find several aspects of such an immanent critique in the North Bonneville experience.

As early as 1971 the residents of North Bonneville confronted the disparity between ideology and social reality. Over the years they had learned that others defined their community as a temporary "shack town" destined to be destroyed by the expansion of Bonneville Dam. They could look about the town and see the physical evidence for this in the number of abandoned buildings and houses in poor repair. Yet, the NOBLE survey in 1971 demonstrated that residents felt a strong identification with the community and its locale. On the basis of this, they began searching for ways of preserving their community.

The residents also discovered a disparity between the Corps of Engineers' ideology of assistance to residents and businesses and the reality of relocation, which meant the destruction of the community and the dispersion, often with inadequate compensation, of its members. The Corps viewed the Columbia Gorge as a resource to be exploited—dammed, rechanneled, and harnessed for electrical power. But to the people who lived there the gorge was a source of personal and collective identity—a place in the world that gave meaning to their lives and relationships.

As they discussed the problems of relocation in 1972 and 1973, the residents of North Bonneville also began to understand that their goals differed from those of the Corps. For them, the maintenance of social relations and geographical and spiritual location were paramount. The Corps wanted to build a new powerhouse as quickly, cheaply, and efficiently as possible. Through their research into their community and the laws governing relocation assistance, the residents discovered that different information serves different relations of power. The technical criteria used by the Corps put the town at a disadvantage. As the residents learned this technical information, they could subordinate it to social and cultural information about their community. This enabled them to move the grounds for decision making away from those so thoroughly mastered by the Corps of Engineers.

Very early in the struggle, the residents discovered the contradiction between the Corps's meaning of community and their own. To the Corps the community was individuals and physical structures. This ignored the reality of community values, attachments to the land, and social networks. Through a careful description of their community, the residents gained a more articulate sense of their own identity and vitality as a community. This was physically embodied in the relocation planning study issued in July 1973. It systematized and documented the scattered knowledge of the residents of North Bonneville. Armed with this evidence of their own reality, the residents could challenge the instrumental rationality of the Corps and the ideology of domination based on treating people solely as individuals to be bought out or forcibly evicted.

The residents gradually discerned the progressive possibilities represented by the strength of their bonds to the gorge and to each other. Theirs was a moral rather than a technical interest in the land, and this struck a responsive chord among potential supporters in the state and federal governments. They were able to use their ideals to legitimate their political struggles.

Their values also were incorporated into their design for the new city of North Bonneville. Through research about their community, combined with their newly acquired skills in planning, the residents were able to discover the possibilities for creating a better community in a new location. The 1973 relocation planning study documented both the good and bad features of their old town and led to constant discussions of the desirable changes for the new town. When the time came, they demanded of the private planning firm the right to participate in planning the new town so that they could incorporate their knowledge and values into its design.

In this way the people of North Bonneville both discovered and created the possibilities for a shift in power: from the Army Corps of Engineers and from outside consultants, including the Evergreen students, to the town with its elected leaders and staff. They refused the Corps's belated offer to plan the new town for them, realizing they would have no control over such a process. They taxed the Corps's construction within the city limits and they gained federal legislation to require the Corps to pay for the design of the new town to be carried out under the community's control.

Throughout the residents' struggle to relocate as a community there is an implicit critique of instrumental reason exemplified by the Corps's treatment of the Columbia River, the gorge, and its people as means rather than ends. At one meeting a frustrated Corps official shouted at Pollard Dickson,

"Neither you nor this little town is going to tell the federal government what to do!" In the shocked stillness that followed, Dickson quietly asked, "Who is the federal government, sir?" This realization that others would treat the community and its people as means carried over into the residents' planning of the new town. Planning became more than a technical task; it became a project of incorporating, and subordinating, technical knowledge and criteria to the values and goals of the people themselves. For example, the school children's studies of pathways in the old town became the basis for planning the circulation system of the new town, where automobile roadways have been subordinated to paths and bikeways. In their own way the residents of North Bonneville discovered the dialectical relation between instrumental knowledge and practical-moral reason.

We also raised the question of the position of popular knowledge in participatory research and argued that if participatory research is seen as immanent critique, it must begin from the consciousness of the people and help the community sort out their reality from the ideologies that dominate them. The North Bonneville project began from the strength of local values and community attachments. The first phase of research organized their understanding of their community into a form available for everyone in the community to use as the basis for relocation planning. The people of North Bonneville separated their patriotic beliefs in economic growth and the necessity for increased electrical generation facilities from the reality of the Corps's attempts to destroy their community. And they created a new and more sophisticated popular knowledge that included an understanding of political power, community planning, and collective decision making. In the process, they preserved those values and understandings that make them a distinct community with the strength and sense of identity necessary for continued growth.

The experience of the residents of North Bonneville demonstrates that participatory methods of research and planning can create an effective basis for collective action. This town of fewer than 500 people challenged the U.S. Army and won. The data gathered and skills learned in 1972 and 1973 gave the community the self-confidence to challenge the Corps of Engineers. Their experience in working with the Evergreen students was used as a model for the participatory work plan required of the private planning firms. At each stage of their struggle, experience with participatory methods led to greater demands for a voice in, and eventually for control over, the process of re-creating their community.

The student researchers' roles consisted largely of guiding the research process, teaching some technical skills to the community members, and organizing the information provided by the residents. They also gathered technical information and shared this with the community. As de Vries (1980) suggests, the researchers played a mediating role between the knowledge scattered among the residents and the information systematically summarized in the relocation planning study. The community, however, remained responsible for analyses, decisions, and actions. The students from Evergreen initially coordinated relations between the community and outside planning and funding agencies. But as the project matured, more and more of these functions were assumed by the community itself. Eventually the student researchers found themselves redundant as the residents took over more and more of the research, planning, and fund-raising activities and carried them out with a sophistication unimagined in 1971 and 1972.

We have said that the validity of the results of participatory research can be gauged first, by the extent to which the new knowledge can be used to inform political action and second, by the degree to which a community moves toward the practice of a self-sustaining process of democratic learning and liberating action. At each phase of the project, the information created by the community and its student researchers was used as evidence to wrest economic and political assistance from government agencies and legislatures. Information about the community was also used to politicize residents and encourage their active participation in the town's struggle with the Corps.

Perhaps the most striking result of the North Bonneville experience has been the degree to which a self-sustaining political process was initiated. We see this in the early phases of the project, when the town led the way to the formation of an interagency relocation advisory board, annexed the new town site, and began taxing the construction project. The growth of self-direction continued as the residents, no longer content with their original demand that a new town be planned and built for them, demanded control over the design of their own community. The results of this process can be seen today in the political involvement evident in the recently contested mayoral election, and it is especially evident in the town's decision to study and develop the geothermal energy resources of their area. In this and other ways, the North Bonneville experience demonstrates the potential for participatory research to initiate a potentially revolutionary process in which members of a community gain control over the conditions of their lives and the creation of new understandings—understandings that represent an immanent critique of their oppression.

CONCLUSIONS

Several lessons might be drawn from the North Bonneville experience. First, it demonstrates the potential for participatory research to provide a basis for successful political struggle by a community. Other communities that may be faced with economic or social destruction at the hands of government agencies or private organizations can be encouraged by the example of North Bonneville. Collective research and education does create the conditions for collective action against exploitation.

Second, the North Bonneville experience shows that participatory research can initiate a sustained process of political organization by a community along with the personal growth of its residents. The people of North Bonneville have continued to learn about themselves and their environment. And they have put this knowledge to use in creating a new community that preserves such progressive values of the old as a respect for the land.

Furthermore, the North Bonneville project may also help us learn more about the method of participatory research. While epistemological presumptions cannot be tested against empirical evidence, we believe that the experience of the residents and the student researchers in North Bonneville demonstrates the usefulness and appropriateness of thinking about participatory research as the application of critical theory. Critical theory provides the epistemological foundations for an immanent critique of domination, and this may be the most appropriate way of characterizing participatory research. Critical theory also is a historically specific critique of our domination by instrumental reason. Thus it provides a historical justification for the progressive social science represented by participatory research—the negation of the one-dimensionality of mainstream social science. Participatory research as the praxis of critical theory may be able to demonstrate how a critical dialectic of instrumental and practical reason can be restored.

Critical theory developed as a critique of consciousness in the twentieth century—as a form of cultural Marxism. But it failed to develop a critical praxis. While critical theory has attacked domination, it has failed to describe the historical possibilities for new social formations. Participatory research may be the application of critical theory that can restore the positive movement to critical philosophy. The residents of North Bonneville learned that they could create knowledge, and by doing so, they transcended forty years of oppression by the Corps of Engineers. The North Bonneville experience demonstrates that an immanent critique by the oppressed can lead to emancipatory action.

NOTE

This article was originally prepared for ISA Research Committee 9, Innovative Processes in Social Change, Session 1: "Actors of Change and Action Research," at the Tenth World Congress of Sociology, Mexico City, August 1982.

8

Breaking Down Barriers: Accessibility Self-Advocacy in the Disabled Community

MARY BRYDON-MILLER

> That's what I resent more than anything else is the minute someone sees you're handicapped, they mentally pick you up, put you in a box, mark the box "Handicapped," and put you way up on that shelf up there. Well, I'm sorry, but I have kicked off the cover of my box and I'm sitting up on that shelf yelling. Screaming and yelling, "Get me down from here, I've got too much to do!"
>
> —Mary Jane Kerr

Negative and patronizing societal attitudes have long made people with disabilities the object of oppression and discrimination in every facet of life. While society may no longer condone the practice of abandoning disabled infants to die of exposure on barren mountainsides, we have created a modern Mount Taygetus by our practice of excluding persons with disabilities from our very social awareness. Educational and employment opportunities have been withheld, political and social involvement discouraged, and even personal relationships and intimacy denied on the basis of disability. Disabled people, like the members of other groups which have experienced such discrimination, have in recent years begun to recognize the inequities inherent in this experience and to demand recognition and equal rights. The Independent Living Movement, which has developed over the past decade into a powerful political force, has achieved important advances both in insuring the rights of disabled people and in developing services and programs to enable disabled individuals to live as independently and actively as possible. A central tenet of the Independent Living Movement has been its emphasis on individual autonomy and personal control. Disabled individuals themselves determine where and how they will live, work, and play, and take responsibility for coordinating the services they need to make this possible. Independent Living Centers provide training and peer counseling to individuals and act as advocates to see that the necessary services are available, and that the rights of disabled people are respected.

Architectural accessibility has been an important focus of these recent efforts on the part of people with disabilities to achieve independence and equal rights. Without access to town halls and governmental offices, people with disabilities have been excluded from participation in the political process. Stores, offices, and businesses which are inaccessible have forced disabled people to seek other, often more costly, alternatives or to rely on other people to transact their business for them. Architectural barriers in restaurants, theaters, concert halls, and other recreational facilities have made it impossible for people with disabilities to freely choose how they will spend their leisure time, and have encouraged continued segregation of disabled individuals from their communities.

Recent legislation, much of it the result of concentrated lobbying on the part of disability rights organizations, has acknowledged the importance of architectural accessibility and has established guidelines and requirements for insuring that new construction and large-scale renovation projects will be barrier-free. There is still much to be done, however. Enforcement has been lax due to ambiguity in the assignment of responsibility and insufficient funding of review agencies. Private homes and apartments, as well as many businesses which predate the regulations, do not fall within these guidelines, and there seems to be an overwhelming lack of concern on the part of many designers and planners to ameliorate the situation.

The Community Accessibility Project described here represents an effort to identify the accessibility needs of disabled persons in the western Massachusetts area and to determine what accessibility advocacy strategies might be developed to address these needs. The project then goes on to plan and carry out specific action on the basis of the results of this preliminary investigation.

Rather than approach this issue from a traditional research perspective, however, a participatory research perspective was employed, emphasizing the active and informed involvement of disabled participants. This alternative research approach was used in part because it seemed more consonant with the participatory-action orientation of the Independent Living Movement. At least as important, however, in making this choice is my conviction that traditional social science research has contributed to the continued powerlessness of oppressed groups. The participatory research approach, on the other hand, demands the active involvement of people in identifying and finding solutions to the problems they face, and requires a commitment from the researcher to make this involvement possible and effective.

SUMMARY OF PROJECT OBJECTIVES

In reporting a traditional research project, a neatly defined methods section describing what one did is followed by an equally well-defined results section. The very nature of participatory research makes such a distinction impossible because the research itself is an interactive process, the direction of later components of the work taking shape from the results of initial interactions. However, while the participatory research process is by design a dynamic one, this does not release the researcher from the responsibility of providing initial structure and direction. Unlike the statement of hypotheses developed in a traditional research method, the expectations with which the participatory researcher enters the research process must remain negotiable, must suggest rather than demand a possible context for the research process which can be amended in interaction with participants.

Stated briefly, the general objectives I held for this project can be considered in two categories. The first, having to do with specific outcomes, included such goals as (1) to provide participants with useful information and skills to conduct effective self-advocacy work, (2) to identify specific accessibility-related problems experienced by disabled people in the area, and (3) to plan and carry out advocacy efforts guided by a shared understanding of the needs of the local disabled community.

At a second level, overall project objectives must also address the process through which these concrete goals are to be achieved. It is these more process-oriented objectives which most clearly distinguish the participatory research approach from an applied traditional research method, which evaluates the process solely in terms of its efficacy in achieving certain outcomes. The initial process objectives of the project included (1) to encourage participants to see themselves and one another as legitimate experts in the field of disability, (2) to demonstrate the potential for advocacy efforts to achieve social change, and (3) to develop a sense of community among participants, and a sense of ownership on the part of participants in relation to the research process.

THE COMMUNITY ACCESSIBILITY COMMITTEE

The Independent Living Center which sponsored this research provides independent living services to disabled individuals in the western Massachusetts area. My initial, admittedly somewhat grandiose, plan was to organize an accessibility advocacy conference for participants in the center's programs. Local legislators and policymakers were to be invited and attendance would be open to all program participants. The conference would provide participants with an opportunity to meet with policymakers and advocate for their own interests and needs. In discussions with staff and with the board president of the center it became apparent that the chief obstacle to planning a successful conference would be generating enough interest to insure a reasonable level of attendance. In regard to this, the organization's executive director pointed out that I could always count on the people I had gotten to know on a personal basis. It seemed obvious, then, that in order to increase attendance I must get to know more people. On this purely pragmatic basis I determined to begin the research process by holding face-to-face interviews with individual participants. I discovered that this decision contributed more to the development and subsequent success of the project than perhaps any other.

In this first phase of the research, individual interviews were conducted with fourteen persons who had expressed an interest in participating in response to a mailed inquiry. Each interview lasted approximately one to one and a half hours and, apart from those conducted with staff of the center, all interviews were conducted in the homes of participants. The richness of these conversations and the references to specific examples are necessarily lost in attempting to condense these hours of interaction into a few pages. To summarize briefly, a variety of accessibility-related concerns, both specific and general, surfaced during the course of the interviewing, as well as a range of individual strategies for dealing with inaccessible environments.

The psychological and social importance of accessibility was a common theme. One participant observed that, while access was important "for my own growth and self-esteem," it was also important because "to be sort of highbrow about it, if I can't put my input into society by saying 'Yes, I'm here and have these views,' then they miss out, too." Another participant told me I should "emphasize how accessibility—what a difference it makes in people's lives. I know what a difference it made in my life. So maybe go into the psychological aspects of it. How accessibility makes me feel more independent and productive—contributes to society—whatever psychological terms you use."

In terms of accessibility planning priorities, there seemed to be general agreement on the importance of making public buildings and governmental offices accessible. At this level, accessibility is viewed as a basic right due to every citizen and a necessary link in achieving full participation in public and community affairs. Privately owned businesses were also mentioned frequently, as well as medical facilities, places of worship, and recreational facilities. Housing and transportation were other important concerns mentioned by many participants during the interviews.

However, the interviews were not designed solely for the generation of concrete information but were also meant to serve as a forum for participants to examine their own experience in relation to accessibility and to suggest possible avenues for future action as a way of beginning to define a participatory research process. Many of the participants I interviewed seemed already to have developed an awareness of the impact of inaccessibility and had been active in addressing these issues in various ways. In most cases these efforts had been limited to individual actions such as writing a letter to a bank requesting a ramp or, in a more extreme case, knocking over a large, aisle-blocking display to bring the problem of access to the attention of a store manager. For others it seemed that the interview provided their first opportunity to examine these issues and the first acknowledgment they had received that their experience and insight were valid and should be shared and acted upon.

For many, too, the interview provided an opportunity to reflect upon the ways in which architectural inaccessibility is linked to continued prejudice and discrimination against people with disabilities. This is often expressed in the failure of architects and designers, even those engaged in designing adapted environments, to work with disabled people in developing effective barrier-free design strategies. As one participant observed, "The thing that makes me the maddest about it is that they will never ask a handicapped person. Apparently if you're handicapped, you can't use your arms or legs, you can't use your brain or mouth either."

By this time it had become clear through my discussions with participants that my original scheme to plan an elaborate conference with political figures and policymakers was not of particular interest to potential participants, who felt that a more informal, information-sharing meeting with other disabled individuals would be more appropriate. In order to provide a common base of knowledge and an explicit recognition of the importance of the information provided in the interviews, I prepared a brief summary of the issues and ideas which had already been generated, and proposed to bring all of those involved together to discuss them. This summary emphasized the importance of involvement and suggested that solutions to some of the problems identified in the interviews might be found through joint action.

The workshop was held at the Independent Living Center office and was attended by twelve persons. The session was opened by the president of the center's board of directors, after which workshop participants were asked to identify important accessibility-related problems or issues. More than thirty specific problem areas were identified during the discussion, and the group decided to focus on a local shopping mall as a first accessibility advocacy target. This decision emphasized to me the obligation of the participatory researcher to accept the direction of project participants. On a personal level, shopping malls are a source of some horror, clearly places to be avoided. But to many disabled persons, especially those living in areas with fairly severe winters, shopping malls represent one of the few opportunities to get out, socialize, and move about independently for much of the year. Thus, insuring appropriate access at such locales is of great importance. A committee of five persons was appointed to conduct an evaluation of the site. The group also decided to meet on a monthly basis and, after some discussion, chose a name. The Community Accessibility Committee was officially established. After a short break, our invited speaker, one of the members of the Massachusetts Architectural Barriers Board, spoke about the role of the board in reviewing accessibility-related concerns on a statewide basis and stressed the importance of consumer involvement. He explained the procedure for filing a complaint, and concluded his presentation by telling participants that "the board will not take violations seriously until consumers do."

That first meeting was held in 1984. The Community Accessibility Committee continued to meet on a monthly basis, gained new membership, and was involved in a variety of accessibility-related projects throughout the area.

The shopping mall project which was proposed at the first meeting was finally resolved in 1989, and the development of this specific action provides a good example of the ongoing work of the committee. On the Saturday following our initial meeting, four members of the evaluation team met at the mall. I came with my tape measure, one of the members of the group offered to act as recorder, and we made a tour of the facility noting potential barriers to accessibility. The only real difficulty we encountered in making the evaluation resulted from the helpfulness of other mall patrons who insisted on opening doors for one team member in a wheelchair while glaring at me for standing by while the "poor woman" struggled with the door.

At the first Community Accessibility Committee meeting we had had a lengthy discussion of tactics. One faction supported the idea of staging an immediate demonstration protesting the lack of access. It was then mid-December, and a picket line of disabled and nondisabled people protesting accessibility problems would have made quite a stir among Christmas shoppers. One participant who had been on staff at the center for some time pointed out that two letters had already been sent to the mall management requesting accessibility improvements and that no response to these requests had ever been received. The time had come, they felt, to take a more active stance. I agreed with this group, in large part because I thought such action would serve to bring the group together and would give immediate visibility in the community. Besides, I thought we would all have a good time doing it, and I agree with Saul Alinsky when he notes that it's not worth doing if you don't have a good time doing it. The other faction noted that the letters, which had been sent a number of months earlier, might not have reached current management personnel, who might not be aware of the problems and, if they were, could easily deny any knowledge of earlier requests. To stage a demonstration, they held, would be premature and might make the group appear unreasonable. Cooler heads finally prevailed, and the results of the initial evaluations were drafted into a third letter to the mall management.

A letter from the mall management observing that there were, in fact, no access-related problems at the mall and a generous offer to make wheelchairs available to patrons if we would donate the wheelchairs did little to relieve our concerns. We wrote a follow-up letter to which we received no response. After discussing the situation at a committee meeting, we decided to file a complaint with the Architectural Barriers Board. After determining that the mall had been constructed after the regulations were put into effect, we drafted a complaint outlining all the violations noted during our initial evaluation. A series of letters and responses finally resulted in a few minor alterations and a request for variance of the code in regard to the more costly changes, including renovations to the restrooms, the provision of access to a lower-level eating area, and the installation of an elevator to provide access to the second floor of the facility.

This request for variance was considered at a hearing held in Boston in September 1984. Three members of the committee were present along with the manager of the mall, a corporate architect, and two corporate attorneys hired by the Pyramid Company, owners of the mall. This first hearing was fairly informal, consisting for the most part of a review of each of the items in our original complaint and discussion concerning those violations not yet addressed by the mall. At this time an agreement was reached concerning all of the violations with the exception of the installation of an elevator to the second floor of the mall. The state board determined that such action would not be technically impossible and that the benefits to disabled members of the community would outweigh the costs to the Pyramid Company, and hence directed the mall to develop plans for installing an elevator. The Pyramid Company disagreed and requested a formal adjudicatory hearing. Unable to hire an attorney of our own, we sought help from the Developmental Disabilities Law Center. While it could not officially represent us, it did provide technical assistance in preparing a response to the Pyramid Company's brief.

A second hearing was held in December 1984, and again we made the trip to Boston with four members of the committee. Two of the members had prepared testimony they would present in regard to the personal impact that lack of access to the second floor of the mall had created. However, when we arrived at the hearing the attorney for the mall launched into an objection to our participating in the hearing at all. We had failed to file motions to act as intervenors at what we thought was our own hearing. This initial dilemma was resolved by the board's attorney, who granted us the opportunity to participate contingent on our filing a motion following the hearing. The entire two hours of the hearing proceeded in like fashion, the mall's attorney objecting to everything any one of us said and going so far as to demand of both of our witnesses how, if they had never been to the second story of the mall (an impossible feat, since both travel in wheelchairs), they could be so sure that they would want to go if they could.

The board again decided in our favor, directing the Pyramid Company to submit plans for the installation of the elevator by March 1985 and to complete construction by July. We planned an Independence Day celebration to be held in the restaurant on the second story of the mall. The Pyramid Company appealed the board's decision to the General Court, a procedure which resulted in having personal summonses served on all those members of the committee who had acted as intervenors. The fact that these summonses were served during one of our regular monthly meetings was a source of great amusement and earned the sheriff a round of applause from the membership.

Again, the court remanded the issue back to the Architectural Barriers Board, which held yet another hearing, again denying the variance request. Another appeal by the Pyramid Company led to another decision in our favor and, finally, the decision was appealed to the Supreme Judicial Court of the Commonwealth of Massachusetts.

The final hearing in this case was held on April 6, 1988, in a large, wood-paneled, and very imposing chamber. Committee members who used wheelchairs had a particularly good view of the proceedings, since the only open space was near the front of the room. It all seemed a bit esoteric, but our general impression was that the hearing went well, though we realized it would be some time before a final decision was reached.

Finally, in August 1988 we received a letter from the general counsel of the Architectural Barriers Board. "After receiving the decision of the Supreme Judicial Court affirming the denial of variance . . . " The letter went on to direct the Pyramid Company to complete all work on the renovations by May 1989. We had successfully won the first accessibility-related case to be heard by the state supreme court.

Reactions of committee members throughout this long process were varied. Each victory was greeted with delight; each new setback seemed to generate greater frustration and less confidence that the final decision would be in our favor. Following our receipt of the decision of the formal adjudicatory hearing, one committee member who had been especially active and had testified at the hearing told me that she had never really expected it to work.

Altogether, this relatively minor change took a full five years to achieve. The Pyramid Company had all the time in the world to appeal decisions and, apparently, all the money in the world to spend on legal fees. We had a legal and moral right to equal access, but that does not pay bills. It took a herculean group effort to maintain pressure for a positive decision and, without the support of the Independent Living Center to finance our trips to Boston, we could never have continued to pursue this issue to its conclusion.

Certainly we were not idle in the meantime, and we gained a certain amount of visibility in the community through publicity regarding this and other projects. But the question remains, how to maintain group interest and support throughout protracted advocacy efforts such as this. On the other hand, we learned a great deal by participating in the full complaint-and-appeal process of the Architectural Barriers Board. Members of the group met with an attorney to discuss the preparation of a legal brief, submitted affidavits, testified in hearings, and became intimately familiar with the rules and regulations of the board. Despite the frustrations, these experiences will continue to be valuable to the committee and to individual members as they engage in actions in the future.

To evaluate the project more fully, it would be useful to consider our objectives and to examine the extent to which the project met these goals and the more general objectives of participatory research.

A SUMMARY OF ORIGINAL PROJECT OBJECTIVES

It should be clear from the preceding discussion that the outcome objectives outlined earlier were largely met during the course of the research, although further progress will be expected as the Community Accessibility Committee continues its work. The first of these objectives, which was to provide participants with useful information and skills to conduct effective self-advocacy work, was a major concern in preliminary workshop planning. The realization that many of those participating in the project, myself included, were uncertain as to the current enforcement regulations and complaint process of the State Architectural Barriers Board was a major impetus for inviting a representative of that board to appear at our first meeting. Thus, even had the project ended with this single meeting, participants would have gained important knowledge concerning their own accessibility advocacy rights. Participants who have been involved since the first meeting have had the opportunity to work with the regulations in performing evaluations, have been able to watch the advocacy process in action, and will continue to develop new advocacy skills through their involvement.

The second of these objectives was to identify specific accessibility-related problems experienced by disabled people in the area. Again, the Community Accessibility Project has been highly successful in achieving this goal. A number of accessibility priorities were identified during the course of the interviews, including public buildings and governmental offices, shops, restaurants, churches, private homes, and transportation facilities. These same priorities were also brought up in the course of the first workshop and helped to establish a common sense of the extent of the problem, as well as of shared concerns on which we might base joint action.

The third of these objectives was to plan and carry out advocacy efforts guided by a shared understanding of the needs of the local disabled community. This was the focus of both the accessibility project described here and of the ongoing work of the Community Accessibility Committee. The local shopping mall now has an accessible elevator to the second floor and, more important, the Commonwealth of Massachusetts has a legal precedent concerning accessibility in public spaces. More recent efforts, such as the development of an outdoor trail accessible to both physically disabled and visually impaired users, reflect the group's focus on concrete problem solving, while demonstrating a willingness to develop innovative strategies for addressing accessibility-related concerns in creative ways.

The second set of objectives reflects the more process-oriented goals of the project. These objectives provide a means of evaluating the impact the project has had on the participants on a more personal and experiential level. The first of these objectives, for example, was to encourage participants to see themselves and each other as legitimate experts in the field of disability. The importance of this expertise has been explicitly acknowledged at every phase of the project. The interviews, for example, provided an initial opportunity for participants to reflect on their experience with architectural barriers and to legitimate these experiences and their own reactions to them by communicating them to someone with an explicitly stated interest in just such experiences. For those participants who attended the workshop, this process of legitimation was extended in communicating concerns and experiences with one another and in seeing that what might have been considered a personal problem was shared by others and might be addressed on a group level. In addition, the vital role to be played by consumers in accessibility advocacy was a central theme in comments addressed to workshop participants.

Workshop participants were also aware that while they were expert in one sense, their present level of understanding of the legal status of accessibility issues and their general inability to deal with concrete design considerations might lessen their potential impact as effective advocates. With this concern in mind, participants showed little immediate interest in getting together with legislators and other policymakers, preferring instead to focus on becoming better informed. Plans were suggested for the group to get together with local building inspectors responsible for their enforcement. A request was also made for a workshop or training session to educate participants in how to read floor plans and other design drawings, and training in the Architectural Barriers Codes has been instituted in a program to establish community access monitors among members of the disabled population. I agree with the participants in their insistence on developing more concrete design and advocacy skills before addressing policymakers directly. In the meantime, the advocacy work which the committee has done has been seriously received and has been extremely successful.

In some ways, it is still too early to determine the extent to which the second of these objectives—to demonstrate the potential for advocacy efforts to achieve social change—will be successful. Certainly comments made by the representative of the Architectural Barriers Board instilled a sense that participation and self-advocacy can achieve positive change, but concrete achievements will be required to demonstrate that this is, in fact, true. The advocacy process is often very slow, as evidenced by the five years of effort required to have an elevator installed in the mall, and I am afraid that many people experience a feeling of frustration with the lack of immediate results. To a large extent, I believe the success of the committee in the future will depend on their ability to maintain momentum despite the laggardly nature of the advocacy process.

Finally, the third of this set of objectives was to develop a sense of community among participants, and a sense of ownership on the part of participants in relation to the research process. I have to admit to a degree of naive paternalism in having stated this objective. As I proceeded with the project, I discovered that a strong sense of community already existed among the participants, many of whom knew one another already or were at least familiar with one another's names. This is probably partly because all of the participants in the project are in some way associated with the local Independent Living Center, and also partly because those participants in the immediate area face a restricted range of available, accessible housing options. However, the "sense of community" extends beyond personal familiarity and is generated, I believe, by a sense of common experiences and shared concerns. A shared concern for accessibility brought participants into the project in the first place, and I think the first workshop was successful precisely because this sense of community was latent and needed only an opportunity to be explicitly acknowledged to coalesce into a more tangible sense of group cohesiveness. Thus, rather than establishing a sense of community, I have been allowed to share in a community which was in many ways already there.

In terms of meeting its internal objectives, then, the project has been relatively successful, and it is to be hoped that continued efforts will result in the further achievement of both concrete change and increased awareness on the part of participants of their own resources for implementing such change. Has the project necessarily, then, also been successful as a participatory research project? Hall (1981) notes seven fundamental characteristics of the participatory research process which can be used as criteria in evaluating this particular project.

1. The problem originates in the community or workplace itself. Accessibility is certainly an issue in the everyday lives of most disabled individuals. In one sense the research depended on the entrance of an outside researcher to focus attention on this concern. However, I do not believe that this outside influence contradicts the notion that the research actually originated in the community. The interest and concern regarding accessibility were already there; the response of participants to questions about this issue demonstrates that there was an existing concern and involvement. The research process simply provided a forum for individuals to consider the issue and to begin to identify common objectives and possible actions.

2. *The ultimate goal of the research is fundamental structural transformation and the improvement of the lives of those involved. The beneficiaries are the workers or people concerned.* Here again, I believe the Community Accessibility Project can be said to have been successful. It will, of course, take a more extended time to truly evaluate the project in terms of this objective. If the momentum which has been generated can be maintained and if further actions can be undertaken and brought to completion, the project will have achieved concrete benefits for participants and for other disabled individuals in the area.

Perhaps more important, however, as a source of community education and empowerment the project has already succeeded in providing participants with the information and support they need to pursue accessibility advocacy on an independent basis, and has demonstrated the potential power in group action.

3. *Participatory research involves the people in the workplace or the community in the control of the entire process of the research.* As I noted earlier, the original decision to conduct the research was based on my interactions with participants and on my experience with accessibility consulting over a period of several months at the agency. This original decision was mine and was not made with the active input of participants. Following this initial decision, however, the research process itself has been highly interactive and continues to build participant involvement as the project develops. But while a group of participants has been involved in the entire research process, I do not feel that the project has, to date, been successful in involving a wide range of participants. Hopefully, over time broader participation will be achieved.

4. *Focus in participatory research is on work with a wide range of exploited or oppressed groups: immigrants, labor, indigenous peoples, women.* It would be impossible to deny that people with disabilities have been and continue to be severely oppressed. Economically, figures show that "sixty percent of working age handicapped Americans exist near or below the official poverty level" (Nosek et al. 1982, 7), while estimated unemployment among qualified disabled adults is at approximately the same level (Nosek et al. 1982, 7). Architectural inaccessibility contributes to this oppression by making it impossible for disabled people to participate actively in community, educational, vocational, and recreational activities.

5. *Central to participatory research is its role of strengthening the awareness in people of their own abilities and resources and its support to mobilizing or organizing.* If the Community Accessibility Project has been successful in any way, I feel it has been most successful in making participants aware of their right to equal access and of their power to achieve that

goal. The initial interviews contributed to this process by providing an acknowledgment of the participants' reaction to architectural barriers and by recognizing accessibility strategies that the participants had developed to address this issue.

However, it was largely in terms of the interaction which took place at the workshop, especially in discussion with participants concerning their rights and power as a collective, that this awareness was developed. Subsequent organizing and action have served to cement this sense of ability and empowerment which, it is hoped, will continue to be put into action and be communicated to others.

6. *The term "researcher" can refer to both the community or workplace persons involved as well as those with specialized training*. This criterion relates closely to the third characteristic of participatory research, and as stated in the discussion there, participants have taken active roles as researchers throughout the entire project. Participants have identified issues, examined possible avenues for action, and have organized action to address these concerns. In many respects, in fact, disabled participants are "those with specialized training," since their experience with disability has made them experts in the field in a way I cannot be. I bring to the project an understanding of the research process and some organizational skills which help to guide the process; participants provide the content of the research and determine the product.

7. *Although those with specialized knowledge/training often come from outside the situation, they are committed participants and learners in a process that leads to militancy rather than detachment*. As I am sure is true of most of us involved in participatory research, I did not seek out this research situation in order to pursue an academic interest in participatory research, but rather I sought out participatory research as an expression of my existing commitment to participant involvement and empowerment, which I found were unacceptable in a traditional research perspective. Social science is an inherently political pursuit, and to deny this fact is, as Gaventa and Horton observe, "to obscure partisanship" (1981, 40).

I prefer to make my partisanship explicit and to make whatever knowledge and training I have received available to people to serve in the achievement of their own goals and interests rather than to pursue my own idiosyncratic research objectives or those currently in fashion in my field. However, the very fact that I do have specific research and academic objectives in addition to my concern for architectural accessibility has raised issues which have an impact on my role as a researcher and as a nondisabled person, which affect the way in which I am perceived by participants, and which are closely tied to issues of experimenter control and true participation. In concluding this summary of the project as participatory research I think it is important to consider these concerns at greater length.

This project is my first experience in participatory research, and while I am committed to this research method, I have to admit to some feelings of ambivalence in turning away from the more traditional research method in which I have been trained and in which I feel very competent.

The most dramatic, and most difficult, change from traditional research has for me been the relinquishing of control over the research process. Experimental control is the very bedrock of traditional research methodology; turning this control over to participants generated a great deal of anxiety on my part. This anxiety was created by my sense that, while I was giving up control I could not, at the same time, turn over responsibility for the project to participants. I felt that somehow I still had to see that "everything turned out all right" and that the project succeeded despite the fact that I could no longer determine what course the research process might take. Resolving this paradox by accepting the fact that for the project to be truly participatory both responsibility and control must rest largely in the hands of participants enabled me to develop a more relaxed, more accepting attitude toward the project which has, in turn, enabled me to enjoy my own participation in the process and to appreciate my relationships with the other participants more.

This is not to imply that I now feel absolutely no responsibility for the research at all, but rather that I have attempted to define this responsibility as a process- rather than product-oriented role. My tasks as researcher are to listen, to explore ideas and concerns with participants, to provide resources and references, to contribute to a shared educational process, and to assist in making opportunities for communication and action available to participants. My primary goal as a researcher is to enable participants to examine their situation and to take action to achieve change. I am responsible for these tasks; I am not responsible for the actions and decisions of the participants.

The relinquishing of control for the final outcome of the research process has been made especially problematic because of my decision to make this foray into the unknown the basis of my doctoral work. The specter of failure looms large in this particular situation and has been all the more potent to me because I have elected to pursue an alternative research approach which is largely unaccepted in my field.

And it was precisely because it was my perception that I had, in fact, taken a risk in deciding to pursue a participatory research approach in completing my doctoral work, that I was so dismayed when one participant, after reading a short section of my dissertation, told me that she had been "disappointed" and "hurt." No methodological or philosophical challenge could possibly have the impact on me that this observation had. She said she felt that she and the other participants had "been used." I was stricken. She said she had forgotten that I was only doing it as a research project and that when she read about herself and about the other participants as I described the workshop she realized that I was only using them as "guinea pigs" for my own academic achievement. If, despite all of my best efforts at creating an alternative research process, I was still perceived as a manipulative, self-serving social scientist, I felt I might just as well concede defeat.

The participant who shared these feelings with me is also a friend, and I felt her criticism, not as a personal attack, but rather as a direct, and angry, challenge to my involvement as a social scientist. We talked about her reactions and about my own intentions and response to this challenge for over an hour. I tried to explain that my interest in accessibility had preceded, and would continue beyond, my dissertation. I also asked her to review the edited draft of my dissertation to be certain that I communicated accurately and respectfully the events of the workshop and committee.

But I am also left with the realization that the distance between myself and the other participants in the project remains. I did have other reasons for my involvement, and though I feel I was straightforward about these other interests, I may not have achieved an appropriate balance between my roles as participant and researcher. This is a dilemma which I have not fully resolved even in my own mind, and one which has not resolved itself simply because I have completed my graduate work. As a researcher, I continue to have my own reasons for involvement in various projects, I continue to be interested in relating my work to a more general consideration of participatory research, and I continue to attempt to interpret the results of my work in the light of a critical theoretical perspective. I would not expect other participants to share these admittedly idiosyncratic interests; but, on the other hand, I would expect other participants to have their own reasons for involvement, and I do not believe that individual motivations for participation need denigrate the sincerity of one's commitment. I can thus justify my actions and my involvement as a researcher to my own satisfaction.

This does not, however, address the problem of possibly making participants feel used or manipulated if the results of the research are made the basis of a report or presentation. One possible solution would be to draft any report or presentation together with project participants. In some cases I think this approach would be quite appropriate and workable. Though again, I can hardly insist that the people with whom I work become conversant with the participatory research literature, as this would in no way address their needs or interests. Nor would it be in my own interests to abandon these issues in the interests of a forced notion of equality. Equality is not the question here; personal autonomy is, and I am unsure how best to project my own independence and freedom to act while maintaining my respect for that of others.

In this particular situation, there is a second factor which must be con-

sidered in regard to my role in the research process—I am not disabled.
How does this influence my interactions with disabled participants and how
does it affect the research process?

My first reaction to the issue of being a nondisabled researcher was
that it was an unavoidable liability to the project. I felt that it would
have been preferable had the researcher been disabled, but since I was
the only researcher interested and available, I would have to deal with
the situation as best I could. Besides, I reasoned, if I wished to pursue a
career as a participatory researcher, unless I satisfied myself with working with white, upper-middle-class American women, I would inevitably
be placed in situations of being an outsider, so I had better learn to accept this limitation.

I have discovered that, far from being a liability, the fact that I am not
disabled has in some ways contributed to my effectiveness as a researcher. This is not to say that a disabled researcher would not have
been able to do a similar research project, but rather that there are distinct advantages to being outside the sphere of expertise of the participants with whom you are working—it necessitates their involvement in
the research. I cannot know what it is to be disabled. I must base my
understanding of the experience of disability on the perceptions of others
whose experience is more direct and can better inform our research and
action. This demands the active involvement of disabled participants, in
identifying accessibility priorities, in suggesting appropriate action, and
in pursuing change. I have a set of technical skills I can make available. I
can represent the possibility of change by presenting alternatives, and I
can devote time and energy to bringing the research process to fruition,
but I can only do this in partnership with others.

These are certainly important issues to be examined further and, hopefully, resolved. However, I do not think that these concerns have undermined
the success of the project, nor do I believe that they argue against pursuing
participatory research as one alternative to traditional research. If anything,
I think that these problems stem, at least in part, from the expectations that
people have generated from their previous experience in research settings,
which would suggest that research is manipulative and does take advantage
of people. It is this experience and these expectations that we must consider
by developing an alternative.

GENERAL IMPLICATIONS OF THE RESEARCH

Indeed, it seems that the hold of traditional research on the thinking of
researchers and nonresearchers alike remains very strong, and it will require
an immense effort on the part of participatory researchers to effect change
in this system. What direction might that change take? I think our first task

must be simply to do more participatory research, to increase the number of participatory research projects which are conducted. For those of us working in more industrialized nations, I think it is imperative to demonstrate that participatory research is not a method applicable only in Third World contexts, to force a recognition that oppression and exploitation are very real phenomena in the Western world, and to successfully translate the participatory research method into these situations.

Second, we must improve our methods for communicating the results of our research not only to other participatory researchers but, equally important, to researchers working with more traditional methods. It will be difficult, perhaps, to gain any level of recognition, but if a number of researchers working in a participatory research perspective form subgroups within professional organizations such as the American Psychological Association or the American Sociological Association and demand a voice at national conferences and in professional journals, recognition will begin to develop.

Most important, perhaps, the effort will require an accessible and succinct epistemological critique of traditional method and a clear statement of alternatives to positivism. This effort must begin by demonstrating, as I hope I have at least begun to do here, that the assumptions underlying the positivistic model of research cannot be supported. However, the distinction must be clearly made between the untenable assumptions of positivism and the technical application of empirical-analytic inquiry which, as Habermas points out, is a necessary, though not sufficient, source of human knowledge (1972). To deny the importance of technical, instrumental knowledge in this way serves no purpose and, in fact, makes any alternative proposed seem naive. To acknowledge the role of empirical-analytic inquiry in solving technical problems, while recognizing that the problems facing humankind cannot all be reduced to this level, opens the way for a more balanced consideration of the alternatives. The social sciences, despite current myopia concerning the role of non-positivistic forms of knowing, do, in their focus on more interpretive methods, have a well-established tradition which competes with empirical research for recognition in the field. The presentation of a third approach to inquiry which incorporates the first two in the interests of achieving human emancipation seems to me to provide a long-needed synthesis of conflicting perspectives. Critical theory offers an epistemological basis for this synthesis; participatory research reflects the practice.

The methods used in conducting participatory research draw from each of these three knowledge-generation systems. When technical knowledge best serves the emancipatory interest upon which the research is based, empirical-analytic techniques will be utilized. This is the case with the work of Gaventa and Horton (1981). The work is non-positivistic in that it en-

courages those most affected by the problem to become involved in the
generation and use of knowledge, but the skills developed to perform data
collection and analysis are technically sophisticated.

On the other hand, methods which reflect the role of dialogue and human
interaction as forms of knowledge generation are also employed by participatory researchers. Much of Tandon's work with villagers in India (1981a,
1981b) reflects this type of inquiry.

Finally, there is participatory research which focuses on social action
as a form of knowledge generation. In most cases this research will incorporate empirical and interpretive techniques, but the knowledge
gained in joint social action is the ultimate objective here. As an example
of this type of effort, I think of the work on the women's health program (Chand and Soni 1981) in which women, through their common
effort in addressing health-related problems, begin to see themselves as
active participants in the research and to see their potential as active
members of society as well.

The Community Accessibility Project described here falls, I believe,
into this third category. We have used interpretive techniques such as
open-ended interviews and group discussion to identify issues and to
generate action, but at the same time these activities have been undertaken in the interests of the achievement of concrete social change and
the learning which accompanies participation in the social change process. It is quite possible that in the future we may also undertake a more
traditional, empirical inquiry into some specific problem; but again the
process will be participatory and the goal, the achievement of social
change.

An equally important translation process must be undertaken to increase the accessibility of critical theory to other researchers and students
as well as to community organizers and other members of the community. There seems to exist an irony in the statements of critical theorists
and many participatory researchers in that their message of liberation is
spoken in a language which is totally outside the experience of those it
seeks to liberate. As Billy Horton (1981) and others have suggested, a
variety of levels of communication must be simultaneously available to
make the results of participatory research and the ideas of critical theory
more generally available.

Finally, I believe we need to examine our attitudes and actions as researchers carefully. We must continue to follow examples set by Paulo
Freire, Myles Horton, and others who have explicitly made their professional and political lives one. Political activity must be recognized as an
integral part of our professional training and practice. We must insist on
becoming involved members of our communities, not in addition to our
practice as social scientists but as a critical component of that work. I
know that for me the temptation is still there to remake this new, still

intractable form of research into something more familiar, more manipulable, and more acceptable to peers and potential employers. I also know that it is only with the example set by others and with the support of the people with whom I work in these participatory research efforts that any of us can hope to succeed in creating a new, emancipatory approach to inquiry in the human and social sciences.

NOTE

I would like to express appreciation to the members of the Community Accessibility Committee and the staff and clients of Stavros, Inc., for their participation in this project. I would especially like to thank Ms. Seren Derin, the greatest advocate I know.

9

Aboriginal Organizations in Canada: Integrating Participatory Research

MARLENE BRANT CASTELLANO ⸻

Participatory research methodology has evolved from microlevel activities, often stimulated by intellectuals from outside the community, in environments where the population is disadvantaged or marginalized. Several writers (Jackson and McKay 1982; Tandon 1984; Rahman 1985) have observed that the vision of social change which inspires participatory research theorists is constrained in its realization by the macrostructure of the society in which the research takes place.

The language of participatory research often implies that macrostructural change through a liberation process will provide the optimum environment for people's empowerment. In the Third World context, where participatory research has been conceptualized and where social and political forms are more or less volatile, defining a prerevolutionary or postrevolutionary role for participatory research practice may be an appropriate way of gaining perspective on where the local activity sits in the larger sociopolitical scene. In practice among Native people in Canada the language of liberation has less intuitive appeal and practical value, for a number of reasons.

Canada is a liberal democracy in which the participation of all segments of society is ostensibly encouraged. The constitutional underpinnings of the Canadian federation, drawn from two founding nations, explicitly support bilingualism. As the ethnic mosaic in the nation has become more pronounced in recent years, the official attitude to cultural diversity has become more than permissive. The positive value of multiculturalism is actively communicated by a number of state agencies, both federal and provincial.

Encouraged by official tolerance of diversity and recent success in gaining recognition of their unique status as Aboriginal peoples, Native people tend to deny intent to change fundamental structures of Canadian society. They emphasize, rather, the compatibility of their goal of self-determination with the pluralistic ideals of the state and the affirmation of Aboriginal rights in the Canadian constitution. Still, in the experience of most Native people, disparities persist between the ideal of participation and the reality of exclusion. The reduction of these disparities is the focus of much of the political activity and development effort undertaken by Native communities and organizations.

Communal interests in mainstream Canadian society are entrusted to institutions which are conservative in nature and which, like all systems, tend to dampen and exclude external initiatives. Because these public institutions are relatively stable, the possibility of displacing them with alternative forms is severely limited. A further limitation on the prospect of macrostructural change to accommodate Native priorities is the minority status of Native people, representing two to three percent of the population, and their geographical dispersion in small rural settlements and urban neighborhoods. Native people in the far North are an exception to this demographic norm, since in some regions they constitute a majority.

Participatory research methods have proven to be effective in various projects mobilizing Native people to analyze their experience, articulate indigenous knowledge, and devise strategies to meet their needs (Castellano 1983; Jackson and McKay 1982). The problem of how to integrate the products of participatory research into the ongoing life of the minority community has been more resistant to solution, at least in the short term.

This chapter highlights some conceptual issues related to the expression of people's self-reliant consciousness and knowledge in the implementation of practical plans. To elaborate the issues I examine the efforts of specific Native groups in Canada to create institutional forms through which the products of their participatory research can be applied with continuity beyond the span of brief experimental projects.

INUIT BROADCASTING CORPORATION

The Inuit of the eastern region of the Canadian Arctic number 20,000. They are located in widely scattered settlements, most of which are accessible from the south by air transport only. Until the middle of the twentieth century they were exposed only minimally to acculturating influences of southern Canadian institutions of government, education, law, and social services. It is estimated that 90 percent of Canadian Inuit still speak their maternal language and many, particularly older generations, speak only Inuktitut. With the advent of satellite communications in the 1970s the Inuit were subjected to an abrupt and massive onslaught of southern cultural influence through the medium of television originating in southern Canada and the United States. The response of the Inuit was to undertake a campaign which has been sustained for the past twelve years, to gain a degree of control over the structure and content of television broadcasting in their homelands.

Until the late 1940s the Canadian government displayed little interest in the isolated northern reaches of the nation. Canada's alliance with the United States to establish defense outposts to defend against possible encroachment by the Soviet Union and the later discovery of substantial fields of oil and gas reserves brought an end to the period of benign neglect and introduced administrative and industrial activity to the northern regions. Demand for entertainment by transient workers in the North and interventions of corporate employers prompted the Canadian Broadcasting Corporation in 1967 to extend television broadcasting of videotape packages to industrial and administrative centers. Unlike earlier development of radio communications, which had allowed the Inuit to some extent to adapt usage to their own needs, no consultation with Native northerners was conducted and one-way transmission of programming from south to north made no provision for Inuit language or cultural content. The launching of the first Anik satellite in 1972 extended the coverage of broadcasting to isolated communities and increased the number of broadcasting hours.

At a public hearing in 1982, Rosemarie Kuptana, president of the Inuit Broadcasting Corporation, declared:

We might liken the onslaught of southern television to the neutron bomb. This is a bomb which kills the people but leaves buildings standing. Neutron-bomb television is the kind of television that destroys the soul of a people, but leaves the shell of a people walking around. This is television in which the traditions, the skill, the culture, the language, count for nothing. (Inuit Broadcasting Corporation 1985, 3)

Without control over local distribution of southern television and without Inuktitut programming, the Inuit feared for the survival of their language and their culture. In a 1985 position paper they cited research which indicated that "extensive television viewing decreases communication between the generations, causing stress in some communities and reducing the time children spend engaged in traditional activities with their parents." The paper deemed it most significant that "studies suggest that prolonged television viewing leads to a decline in the use of aboriginal languages" (Inuit Broadcasting Corporation 1985, 5).

Until 1971 the Inuit were without a regional political organization to advocate their views in transactions with the institutions of mainstream Canadian society. With the formation of Inuit Tapirisat of Canada (ITC) in 1971, an organization established to represent Inuit interests in negotiating with the federal government for settlement of Aboriginal claims to extensive homelands, the Inuit of the central and eastern Arctic acquired a lobbying voice.

From its inception, ITC perceived the crucial role that electronic communications would play in fulfilling its mandate to authentically represent Inuit community views. As early as 1973 ITC was recommending that licenses to broadcast in Inuit settlements be withheld until such time as the CBC was prepared to broadcast 80 percent of its programming in Inuktitut.

Throughout the 1970s ITC and other Native organizations mounted criticism of the policies and impact of public television broadcasting in the North. In 1980 the national broadcast licensing body, the Canadian Radio and Television Commission (CRTC) established a committee to investigate the extension of satellite television services in northern and remote regions of Canada. At the committee hearings ITC presented a proposal calling for the establishment of an Inuit broadcasting system. The CRTC supported the proposal and in 1981 the Inuit Broadcasting Corporation (IBC), serving central and eastern Arctic communities, became a reality. A federal government grant of $3.9 million provided the initial funding base for television production by several northern Native communications societies including IBC. Satellite facilities were shared with the CBC. The first IBC program was aired on January 11, 1982, reaching twenty-six northern communities.

Acquisition of the technical capability to assume responsibility for Inuit-controlled broadcasting had been proceeding in parallel with political action. Beginning in 1971 the CBC had sponsored experimental projects in community television production in northern Native communities. These typically involved training of Native personnel in the use of hand-held cameras and videotaping equipment, and providing access to community transmitters for broadcast of community events and exchange of videotapes between communities. Another federal agency, the National Film Board, had also conducted training workshops in media techniques and equipment usage in two Inuit communities, and several other communities had been involved throughout the 1970s in projects sponsored by the federal Department of Communications testing the use of technology to link communities interactively via satellite radio signals, rebroadcasting signals for community viewing, and producing Inuktitut language programming for broadcast by the CBC.

By 1978 one community, Pond Inlet, strongly supported by the communications arm of ITC, had successfully negotiated with the CBC to gain access to training and a transmitter to establish a community television station which would produce local programming to selectively replace CBC broadcasts and promote Inuit culture and intra-community communication.

In 1980 a major project in satellite broadcasting coordinated by ITC was initiated. The Inukshuk project, named for the humanlike stone cairns used traditionally to guide Inuit hunters, established video production units at five northern sites, video transmission facilities at one site, and video reception facilities at five other sites. Inukshuk became operational in 1980, broadcasting 16.5 hours of television programming per week, much of it produced by local video and film crews.

The licensing of the Inuit Broadcasting Corporation in 1981 built, therefore, on considerable technical expertise and extended the range of a broadcast capability which had been thoroughly tested. In the years between 1982 and 1987 the Inuit Broadcasting Corporation continued to document its accomplishments in producing quality programming in Native language, culture, education, and public affairs, gaining high audience acceptance, and doing so at a fraction of the costs of CBC programming. IBC also established collaborative links with six other northern Native communications societies and two territorial governments. In June 1987 a new body, Television Northern Canada, representing all of these agencies, submitted a new proposal to the government of Canada for the creation of a broadcast network having access to satellite facilities dedicated to northern service and managed by a board of directors drawn from the sponsoring northern agencies.

At the time of writing the federal government has not made a response to the Television Northern Canada request. The government has, however, responded to a parallel initiative requesting that the precarious status of IBC, supported by limited-term funding, be altered. IBC has now been granted ongoing-program status, insuring that for the foreseeable future it will have the resources to carry out its community mandate to strengthen the cultural and social fabric of Inuit society.

DISCUSSION

Internal Community Conditions

In the example cited, a major basis for mobilization of community effort was a collective sense of cultural distinctiveness deriving from historical roots, Aboriginal language traditions, and varying degrees of social and physical separation from mainstream Canadian society. The activities of mainstream institutions were perceived as incompatible to some extent with local priorities and, to counter intrusive effects, action was initiated to create self-determined forms of broadcast communications.

The norms which prevail in the realm of public broadcasting in Canada required that the Inuit create a new structure for carrying forward their initiative, one which explicitly distanced itself from the political mandate of their preexisting regional organization.

Development of appropriate organizational forms was essential to sustaining momentum over the months or years that elapsed between the conception of various goals and their implementation. Participation in organization activities over time allowed participants to gain expertise in planning and problem solving as well as specialized knowledge pertinent to the development project. The accumulation of expertise by key participants based in their home communities tended to counterbalance the influence of external technicians and consultants drawn into the projects. Decisions and directions were regularly evaluated in a forum of peers in the community; and delays and disappointments, as well as successes, in negotiations with external agencies could be put into perspective through community discussion.

The economic base of most Native communities in Canada has been severely eroded by the loss of their traditional lands and resources and the encroachment of external economic agencies. Native people have been only marginally successful in gaining access to economic benefits of the larger society. Lacking revenue to support local services and institutional development, Native communities are, for the most part, dependent on government grants which typically are targeted to specific programs sanctioned by government administrators. In the past decade, the adoption by the government of policy overtly supporting more self-determination for Native communities has created some flexibility in application of funds for development purposes, although such funds still represent a small proportion of administration budgets for Native affairs and are usually granted on a short-term, experimental basis.

The lack of independent income sources to support alternative programs and institutions limits autonomous research and planning in several ways. A great deal of ingenuity is required to package innovative initiatives in such a way that they will be approved for funding. Accountability for applying funds to the achievement of predetermined goals enforced by granting agencies deflects attempts at heuristic planning. The short-term nature of project funding precludes sustained commitments to project staff and inhibits the phased development of stable programs or the creation of institutional structures. Within these constraints, however, Native agencies engaged in development are free to innovate and challenge conventional ways of doing things.

The success of organizations in the eastern Arctic in securing resources for research and planning is not exceptional in the Canadian Native context. The Inuit Broadcasting Corporation, after seven years of experimental projects and fixed-term commitments, was accorded the status of a recognized agency eligible for ongoing public funding. The focusing of community effort over an extended period and the mobilization of political support within the communities and their regional organizations were instrumental in accessing the external resources required.

Socio-Political Context

The products of participatory research—self-reliant consciousness, indigenous knowledge, and practical plans—will be most viable where the state authority has a commitment to devolving responsibility to community institutions. However, even where local initiative is overtly encouraged, covert values inimical to participation often prove problematic. State action may limit and direct spontaneous initiative so that only participation which reinforces the social and political status quo is legitimized. If development goals are loosely formulated, the resultant laissez-faire attitude may fail to provide adequate support for local action. Technocrats with authority to enforce rigid ideals of administrative efficiency can also undermine spontaneous participation (Midgeley et al. 1986, 40-43).

In the early 1980s Canadian policy affirming the goal of devolving more authority to Native institutions was in a formative stage, characterized by vague hypotheses of what Indian self-government might imply and skepticism in many quarters of government that it was practicable. By 1987, public attitudes toward the principle of Native self-determination were more positive. However, the practical means of achieving it are still open to debate. The approaches to specific sectors of government by Inuit broadcasters received a generally positive response. These proposals were couched in terms of complementing and rendering more effective government-supported efforts to meet recognized needs. Therefore, they did not require any fundamental change in policy. There is the danger that such efforts to emphasize the congruence between local initiatives and societal values will result in compromises which subvert the goal of self-determination. The critical factor in avoiding cooperation would seem to be maintenance of means for participatory communities to continue to assess impacts and modify implementation of programs originating from their designs.

The values which prevail in societal institutions are only partially determined by public policy. They are also the product of persons with individual perspectives interacting in an environment which may be more or less constraining. In the Canadian context we consistently find within mainstream institutions individuals with reformist consciousness who support community initiatives. Those advocates who have been skillful in reconciling their innovative goals with the constraints of bureaucratic service and who have achieved influential positions are often crucial in creating space within institutions for minority initiatives to gain a foothold. Maximum utilization of the goodwill of these institutional advocates requires trust on the part of minority organizations, usually achieved through personal networks. The degree of disclosure of their activities which Native organizations are willing to provide is, in each case, a matter of judgment, since the advantages of thorough understanding of community goals and strategies by institutional allies must be balanced against the threats of co-optation or blocking of participatory goals which are judged incompatible with institutional priorities.

Inuit lobbying for a community-controlled television broadcast service was carried on in public view in consultative conferences, committee inquiries, hearings of the Canadian Radio and Television Commission, and through the publication of briefs. The principal argument set forth by the Inuit was that Native northerners should be accorded the means to shape the structure and content of broadcasting so as to mitigate the disruptive social impacts of culturally intrusive programming. Private lobbying efforts, carried on over a decade, secured support in principle from federal politicians responsible for broadcast policy, the broadcast regulatory body (CRTC), and officials in the CBC. Briefs putting forward the Inuit position skillfully used public statements by influential personnel recognizing the justice of their cause to break through the administrative roadblocks on the way gaining access to financial and technical resources.

In a highly institutionalized environment the task of instituting alternative organizational forms which provide a congruent vehicle for implementing community-based planning is rendered difficult if command of resources in the field is already held by agencies of the larger society. In any competition for resources and power, young minority organizations are at a distinct disadvantage, and their narrow resource base often does not allow for the diversion of personnel and funds to the struggle. It is important, therefore, to make a careful analysis of whether the institutional ground is occupied, whether the mandate to meet particular needs is uniformly acted upon, and whether space can be created for inserting alternative institutional forms.

In the successful case of Native institutional development cited, concerted effort by political organizations was instrumental in creating space for new initiatives. Inuit political organizations took the lead in highlighting the past inability of the CBC to provide a northern television service which met Inuit communication needs. The CBC acknowledged its difficulties in extending basic Canadian services to northern settlements and welcomed the possibility of a partnership in which federal government departments, northern regional governments, communications agencies, and peoples of the North would share responsibility for developing a more comprehensive program service. The Native planners proposed to establish services complementary to those of existing institutions, by creating a new institution, the Inuit Broadcasting Corporation, in parallel with the CBC.

Issues of Relationships

Even if the community proposing to implement change is vital and elements in the external environment are amenable, there remains the challenge of establishing effective relationships between the community and external institutions. The power relationships which prevail represent possibly the most critical factor.

Native people in Canada have been relatively successful over the past decade in securing recognition in principle of their right to pursue a self-determined path of social and political development. However, the distribution of administrative decision making through layers of bureaucracy and widely separated regional agencies often impedes the application of principles in practice. Because legislation and regulations affecting Native affairs are designed by federal institutions for national application, community groups typically encounter resistance in local and regional agencies to community-sponsored proposals to vary the application of inappropriate rules. Political organizations linking small, dispersed Native communities have emerged as effective instruments of policy and program change. Where consultative strategies lead to the articulation of regional priorities, Native communities are becoming increasingly effective in advocating their priorities. Still, the cost of maintaining communication over the vast expanse of the Canadian landscape and the difficulties of synthesizing the diverse cultural perspectives of village societies with a tradition of autonomous decision making often makes united action problematic. The Inuit's use of communications technology to develop intercommunity consensus and the critical mass to credibly challenge the broadcast monopoly of southern institutions is therefore particularly impressive.

A second issue is management of communications between communities and institutions when the actors operate from differing styles of communication. In general, the greater the distance between the cultural forms prevalent in the community and the cultural forms recognized or legitimated in the institutions, the more difficult it will be for both sides to recognize the commonalities that permit accommodation of community proposals by the institutions. If congruence between community proposals and institutional priorities is not easily identified, advocates within the institution will be subjected to personal risk in attempting to sell the ideas to their colleagues. The packaging of community proposals to emphasize points of congruence between new approaches and accepted practices, and the identification of persons or units in the institutions with a mandate to act in the field are strategic imperatives. The Inuit were aided substantially in pursuing their goals by the presence of the Canadian Radio and Television Commission, which from the early 1970s acknowledged the justice of the Inuits' bid for influence in northern broadcasting and was in a position to pressure particular agencies to accommodate to new relationships with the Inuit.

The final issue to be discussed is the role of brokers between local communities and institutions. The preferred mode of communication in Native communities is oral, whereas institutions of mainstream Canadian society rely heavily on written communications. Community priorities typically have to be transcribed, organized, and presented in the language of program planners. Regional Native organizations have taken a leading role in providing staff to carry out communication functions, though local communities are acquiring their own technical staff as more community members pursue formal education. Over the years, the Inuit have utilized the services of consultants, including southern academics, to facilitate the packaging of their views and plans for presentation in mainstream forums.

Brokers are more than passive channels of communication between cultures. They can exercise considerable power in identifying and selecting the points of contact between community agencies and external institutions. They are often in a critical position to assess when readiness for action within the community coincides with receptiveness to change in the external environment. To counter the danger that technocrats in their employ might preempt the communities' right to direct development, Canadian Native people try to avoid the hierarchical organizational structures favored by mainstream institutions. Regional organizations operate as loose federations, with multiple lines of accountability flowing back to constituent communities. As in the case of Inuit broadcast training, communities set a priority on preparing local personnel to assume technical roles as early as possible in new development projects.

CONCLUSION

Native people in Canada generally subscribe to the view that realization of their social and cultural goals can be achieved within the democratic structure of the larger society. Case material has been used here to illustrate strategies adopted by the members of one specific Native group to assert their development priorities.

The internal conditions discussed are cultural vitality, organizational infrastructure, and availability of economic resources to support participatory development. The external conditions include prevailing social values, the contribution of reformist advocates within mainstream institutions, and the extent of the monopoly exercised by mainstream institutions in relevant sectors of minority life. Interface issues include strategies to modify the effects of power imbalance between minority communities and institutions, facilitation of intercultural communication, and the strategic use of intercultural brokers.

Various Native communities and organizations in Canada have used participatory research methods to stimulate self-reliant consciousness and affirm the value of indigenous knowledge in charting a course for the future. In attempting to implement plans emerging from their knowledge and consciousness they have adopted a pragmatic approach to institutional innovation. Rather than seeking to displace mainstream institutions they have emphasized the complementary nature of their intent and the legitimacy of their proposals for institutional variation.

Participatory research methods have been particularly effective in stimulating self-directed change in small-scale societies. For purposes of Native development in Canada the challenge now is to adapt these methods of analysis and decision making to the larger context of regional community networks, intersocietal relations, and institutional development so that local participatory action may be complemented and enhanced.

NOTE

The author wishes to thank the colleagues and students who, in the spirit of participatory research, contributed materially to the preparation of this chapter: Lynne Davis, Ann Hobday, Sandy Lockhart, René Maillet, and Gail Valaskakis.

10

Challenges, Contradictions, and Celebrations: Attempting Participatory Research as a Doctoral Student

PATRICIA MAGUIRE _____

Participatory research asserts itself as an emancipatory approach to knowledge creation available to even the most oppressed people of the world. Yet, in the early 1980s, I found myself, an Anglo, middle-class, college-educated, North American feminist obsessively questioning: Was this approach available to me as a doctoral student? Could I do it?

Participatory research is a process of collective, community-based investigation, education, and action for structural and personal transformation. Because of the explicitly communal nature of participatory research, the question became not whether I could do participatory research, but rather, could I get involved in a collective participatory research effort as part of my doctoral research.

The purpose of this chapter is to reflect on the challenges, contradictions, and celebrations of attempting participatory research within the framework of doctoral work in a North American university while living in the small, multicultural southwestern community of Gallup, New Mexico, a border town to the Navajo Nation and Pueblo of Zuni. Reflection on the struggles I encountered in practice will inevitably illuminate some of the theoretical and methodological contradictions still to be worked out within participatory research. This is the essence of praxis. Likewise, reflection on the concrete details of the Former Battered Women's Support Group Project will vividly illustrate the phases or components of the ideal participatory research process as tempered by the less than ideal conditions we encounter in reality.

I purposefully titled this article "attempting" participatory research because some say that the Former Battered Women's Support Group Project was not *real* participatory research. By many standards, in the end, it may not have been. Nonetheless, reflection on the flaws and inadequacies, and even the modest successes of *attempting* this alternative research approach may help others find the courage to learn by doing rather than being immobilized and intimidated by ideal standards. Equally important, perhaps, it will help us, deep in the seriousness of our critiques and criticisms, to come up for air to examine and find ways to encourage small-scale efforts.

THE BEGINNING

In April 1984 I left Interstate 40 and entered Gallup. Certainly I entered the community with a notion of stimulating interest in participatory research. But I entered as more than a novice participatory researcher. I came to Gallup to live and work, love and play. It was to be my home, not merely a site for field research. Because of the move, not only because of the eventual research, I had to come to know the community.

Gallup, with a population approaching 20,000, is the largest town in McKinley County. The county, larger in area than Connecticut, is primarily rural. It is one of the poorest New Mexico counties, with 33.2 percent of its families below the poverty level. Unemployment, often higher than the national average, hovered near 11 percent in mid–1984. The last of the region's uranium mines closed that summer; the ripples of the subsequent unemployment were felt throughout the region's economy. The formal education level of McKinley residents is low; fewer than 30 percent of the people over twenty-five years of age have high school diplomas. Not quite 11 percent are college graduates.

The county is racially and culturally diverse. Native Americans, primarily Navajo and Zuni, compose 66 percent of the county's 56,000 people. Another 26 percent are Anglo, 6 percent are Hispanic, .7 percent are African-American, .3 percent are Asian-American, and the other 1 percent include those of East Indian and Middle Eastern origin. While the county is racially and culturally diverse, racism, subtle and overt, individual and institutional, is pervasive.

Gallup is the service center for a 15,000-square-mile market area. On pay weekends, Gallup's population may swell to 70,000, with people in town to shop, receive medical care, use water-related services such as laundromats and car wash facilities, and to seek entertainment.

Gallup suffers from a poor self-image as well as a poor image within the state and nationally. Alcohol abuse, extensive and particularly visible, contributes to this. However, it is a problem of substance, not merely "image." High alcohol abuse among both the Native American and non-Native population takes a great toll, personally and collectively. While the relationship between alcohol abuse and related problems is complex, it is safe to say that emotional, mental, and physical health problems, unemployment, motor vehicle and pedestrian fatalities and accidents, assault and battery, child neglect, and violence against women and children are exacerbated by alcohol abuse.

No visible social justice-oriented, community activist, or popular people's organizations existed in Gallup in that spring of 1984. There were no mainstream or radical feminist organizations. The American Association of University Women was the major concentration of feminist-identified women. Individuals with progressive, even radical politics and analyses existed, but they were not organized nor did they form any visible, vocal critical mass. The 1,400 students of the two-year University of New Mexico branch and area vocational school are primarily "worker-students," juggling the demands of family, full- or part-time work, and college studies. Within this context I began establishing relationships and commitments within Gallup.

My real immersion in the community and one of its problems came from my work, first volunteer and later in a part-time, grant-funded position, with Battered Families' Services (BFS). In fact, I first came across information about BFS, a plea for volunteers, on a laundromat bulletin board. My relationship with BFS was not motivated by my participatory research or dissertation intentions. Instead I was motivated by personal needs for camaraderie and meaningful interaction in the community. During this time I was still doing some training and consulting work which required travel outside the community. The consulting work allowed me to do the participatory research groundwork with no "sponsor."

Battered Families' Services is a nonprofit organization which provides twenty-four-hour services to battered women and their children, and public education about domestic violence in McKinley County and the surrounding reservations. In 1984 there were no shelters within the entire Navajo Nation, the size of West Virginia, or in Zuni Pueblo. BFS provided shelter and services to those areas, primarily the southern and eastern areas of the Navajo Nation. The 1983-84 United States Attorney General's Task Force on Family Violence noted that BFS might be serving the largest rural area of any shelter in the country. The warm family atmosphere of BFS impressed me. The small staff managed to avoid the distant, bureaucratic attitude characteristic of many social service agencies. They were committed to helping women help themselves.

The domestic violence in Gallup is typical of the problem in the country as a whole. It is estimated that over 2 million women were battered in the United States in 1984. Battered women account for nearly 50 percent of women seeking hospital emergency room treatment. Yet medical personnel recognize only one in four of these women's injuries for what they are: injuries sustained at the hands of their partner. Of the women committing suicide in 1984, at least 25 percent were battering victims. Likewise, 50 percent of female homicides are women killed by their husbands or boyfriends, from whom the women may have already separated. Gloria Steinem observed that women are safer on the streets than in their own homes (Roy 1977).

Throughout the spring and summer of 1984, the Office of Navajo Women, part of the tribal government structure located in Window Rock, Arizona, about 30 miles from Gallup, and the Council of Navajo Women, an advocacy group also operating out of Window Rock, unsuccessfully lobbied the Navajo Tribal Council for funds for shelters on the reservation. Battered women on the vast rural reservation often travel great distances under extreme circumstances to shelters in the off-reservation border towns of Flagstaff, Arizona, or Farmington and Gallup, New Mexico. Reflective of the county population makeup and the lack of shelters within the Navajo Nation, in 1983 73 percent of BFS clients were Navajo and 47 percent lived within the Navajo Nation.

My involvement with BFS grew and changed during my first year in Gallup. My initial work was as an on-call volunteer. Volunteers handle after-hours phone calls and go out to escort battered women and their children to a safe house. We often did this in the middle of the night, usually meeting women at area hospital emergency rooms or the police department lobby. These locations were picked for security reasons, as it is not unusual for a violent, angry man to pursue the victim as she flees the attack and her attacker. At that time, the shelter was located in an old, run-down house near the old house I rented. I spent time there talking with women and transporting them to various social service and medical appointments. Only 10 percent of BFS clients had private transportation, and, except taxis, there was no public transportation in Gallup. Social service agencies were located on the outskirts of town. A battered woman, perhaps traveling in inclement weather with small children, fears the public exposure of walking when she knows her violent partner, who may have threatened to kill her, the children, or himself if she leaves him, may come looking for her and the children.

Shortly after I began volunteering with BFS, they received a small grant from the Chicago Resource Center to hire a part-time coordinator of volunteers. The position entailed recruiting, training, and managing the small volunteer pool; writing a volunteer training manual and handbook; and doing community education. BFS staff asked me to apply. Initially I was reluctant. I was getting great satisfaction from the volunteer work, which of course could still continue if I accepted the paid position. But I was reluctant to tie myself down to a time-consuming, low-wage job, with a lot of potential headaches, when I thought I would eventually get deeply involved in an equally time-consuming, unpaid participatory research project with some as yet unidentified community group or organization. At that time I did not see BFS as an organization with which to do participatory research. Eventually I accepted the grant-funded, one-year volunteer coordinator position, which I held from August 1984 until August 1985. I continued working as an on-call volunteer for nineteen months. I accepted the position for two reasons: the satisfaction and nourishment of being part of the small agency staff whose work I philosophically agreed with, and the identity and "place" it gave me in the community.

TRYING TO INITIATE A PARTICIPATORY RESEARCH PROJECT

I talked informally with BFS staff about doing some type of participatory research with former clients as part of my graduate work. However, I was reluctant to try to work directly with BFS. BFS was a nonprofit social service agency serving the needs of battered women and their children; it was not an organization of battered or formerly battered women. Its clients and former clients had no power base or organized voice in the agency. Certainly at that time staff respected clients' opinions, but no structured channel or mechanism existed for clients to have a say in agency decisions on a regular basis. (The lack of power or a collective voice for battered women within BFS wasn't unique to that agency. Within the battered women's movement, a loose coalition of people and organizations, battered women themselves have little power and participation in comparison to the increasing role of social service professionals and advocates (Schechter 1982).) Then, after two years with a stable staff, BFS began undergoing many personnel changes. The agency had five executive directors from the time of my initial involvement as a volunteer in May 1984 to the project presentation to its board of directors in late 1986.

I thought that the ideal participatory research project, which would hold empowerment, liberation, and social transformation as long-term goals, should work as directly as possible with battered or formerly battered women. A very small, informal network of ex-clients living in town had stayed in touch with BFS. Staff told me that several women had expressed interest in forming a client support group. Since no organized or identified group of such women existed, the project began by determining interest in starting a group, which I hoped might evolve into an independent battered women's organization. While a "community" of women did emerge, no enduring organization did. In retrospect, trying to mobilize formerly battered women to form an independent organization through the strategy of beginning with a support group format was probably misguided.

Although Park's description of participatory research now so clearly articulates the necessary organizer or mobilizer role of the participatory researcher, the extent of that role was less clear to me then (see Park this volume). I realize now that the degree of organizing and mobilizing that will be required of the participatory researcher will vary greatly according to the type of organization which is involved in the project initiation. For example, if the initiating organization *is* a popular people's organization, the researcher won't have to do the grass-roots mobilizing that will be necessary if no such collaboratory organization exists or if the possible collaborating organizations do not directly represent people's interests. At the time, I didn't understand these distinctions.

I had difficulty juggling the participatory researcher's triple roles of organizer, educator, and researcher. I was not sure how involved to get in the organizer role. When we eventually got a support group rolling, I did play the major motivating role. Yet I felt uneasy with it, which may have been complicated by the fact that I was doing this in part as my doctoral research. For example, by working hard to motivate women to become active and regular group participants, was I trying to make the project, also incidentally part of my dissertation, a success? Was this "contamination" of a true participatory research project? Was that fear itself a holdover from the old research paradigm? Since ultimately project control was a key issue, I knew I should increasingly step back and see what happened as I relinquished the organizer/motivator role and some of the women took it up. I did try, by fits and starts, to step out of the organizer role over the year the group worked together. Yet none of the women followed through or apparently wanted this role.

I saw another difficulty: How could I write a dissertation proposal with its problem statement unless I did it unilaterally—the antithesis of participatory research? I was tinkering around with a proposal focused on trying to identify the characteristics of participatory research projects that actually lead to participants' empowerment.

At this point, a year into the community and into my relationship with BFS, I felt stuck. The "beginning" phase of a potential participatory research was becoming very elongated. Further immersing myself in the participatory research literature with its emancipatory and extensive agenda for social transformation, and its sometimes pretentious rhetoric, only heightened my confidence crisis.

ACKNOWLEDGING THE ANDROCENTRIC FILTER

Continued immersion in the literature had another effect, at first just a "feeling" that produced low-level irritation and annoyance on my part. Where were the women and our issues in participatory research? A feminist perspective helped me to see the many androcentric or male-centered aspects of participatory research. In the most widely circulated participatory research literature of that time, the voices and observations of women participants were largely unheard. Women were often invisible, submerged, or hidden in case study reports or theoretical discussion. Gender was usually rendered indistinguishable by terms such as the *people*, the *campesinos*, the *villagers*, or simply, the *oppressed* (Park 1978b; Horton, B. 1981; Marshall 1981; Masisi 1982; Mustafa 1982a; Swantz 1982; Vio Grossi 1982b). Only by reading several accounts of the same project (for example, the Jipemoyo

Project [Mbilinyi 1982a; Mustafa 1982a and 1982b]) or by reading between the lines did it become apparent that many projects worked only with male community members, yet the benefits were generalized to women's exclusion or marginalization within the participatory research project (Mduma 1982; Mustafa 1982b; Vio Grossi 1982a). Where women were excluded from or silenced in community problem-posing forums, their perceptions and definitions of local problems were ignored, and they were often excluded from subsequent benefits. This left few reports of successful inclusion of women, usually all-women projects.

Feminist theory and issues were largely absent from participatory research theoretical debates, focused on historical materialism and critical theory. Full discussion of the androcentric bias of early participatory research is beyond the scope of this chapter. However, I found indications of male-centered language, unequal access for women to project participation, inadequate attention to or discussion of obstacles to women's participation, subsequent unequal access of women to project benefits, an absence of feminism from participatory research theoretical debates, and finally, exclusion of gender from the participatory research agenda of issues (see Maguire 1987, chapters 4 and 5).

The absence of feminist theory and women in the bulk of early participatory research work and publications was dangerous. Participatory researchers were trying to develop a research approach with the potential and intention to empower people and transform social systems; but exactly which people and which social structures? I also began to wonder if some of the things which made participatory research unique, for example, involved participation, organization creating, and action aimed at structural change, might not make different demands of women than men. Even in the North American context, men less often struggle with a "double day" of work which includes child care, housework, and care of the sick and elderly, and enjoy a more privileged position in the public arena. I wondered if women might view emancipation and transformation differently from men. For example, with these battered women, men's brutalization of women and the systems which support it were things to be transformed. Although participatory research wanted to break the monopoly on knowledge creation, it seemed to be duplicating or colluding with the monopoly of male-centered traditional social science research. You will have to judge for yourselves how the situation differs from what I found in 1984.

Exploring participatory research's male biases led me to feminist research. Among other similarities, participatory and feminist research agree that knowledge, which is socially constructed, is power, and both are committed to empowering oppressed peoples. Participatory research has highlighted the centrality of power in the social construction of knowledge, yet it has largely ignored the centrality of male power in that construction. In fact, reading the alternative paradigm research literature, including participatory research, I would never have known that women played any role in challenging dominant, positivist knowledge creation. The hidden message was that only men create research alternatives.

GETTING STARTED

After a year in Gallup, I wrote a dissertation proposal to conduct a somewhat nonparticipatory examination of a participatory process. I unilaterally identified the overall dissertation problem, but project women would identify the actual research problem of the project. I envisioned a three-phase participatory research project. Phase I would include dialogue and the initial group organizing and problem formulation. Phase II would include formation of the women's group and the actual research process. Phase III would be a collective assessment of the participatory research project. The solitary final phase would be writing and defending the dissertation.

PHASE I: DIALOGUE, INITIAL ORGANIZING, AND PROBLEM FORMULATION

As there was no organized group of battered women to begin a participatory research project with, the first phase involved determining local interest in such a group, trying to mobilize it, and doing initial problem formulation. Once formed, the group would then define the actual problems they wanted to investigate and take action on.

To begin this process I went through Battered Families' Services' board of directors to get their permission and help to contact former clients. I went through BFS because at the time it seemed the most expedient way to gain access to the unorganized, scattered, hidden, isolated, and often ashamed battered and formerly battered women "out there." Once the group got established BFS would tell women in the shelter about the group. This would be one way of incorporating new women on a regular basis. Otherwise BFS was not expected to contribute any resources to the project.

After the meeting with the board of directors, the staff subsequently sent out a letter to former clients in the Gallup area describing the project. There were dilemmas in going through BFS to get to the women. For example, BFS would not send the initial letter concerning the project to former clients who had "burned" BFS by returning to the shelter drunk, revealing its location, or threatening staff or other clients. If you have never been intimately involved in battering, it is hard to fathom the life-threatening nature of some of these behaviors. On a near weekly basis, the news media present stories about abusers who, having tracked down the victim who has left them, murdered these women in private homes or public places, even when the abuser is under a court order or temporary restraining order not to make any contact with the victim. Hence, things like revealing the shelter's secret location are not mere breaches of courtesy, they can be life-threatening to the battered women, children, and staff, who depend on the safety of the shelter. The security issue aside, there were difficulties and contradictions trying to start a "people's" organization by going through a social service agency.

The project's relationship to and with BFS underwent numerous changes and was sometimes confused. I think that initially this was in part due to my own limited understanding of the realistic range of possible organizational bases for initiating a participatory research project. This led me to believe that ideal participatory research should try to work as directly as possible with the powerless, even if unorganized, rather than indirectly through a nonprofit social service agency which was already in place. Over time the relationship was primarily a function of the frequently changing leadership. In particular, one woman, executive director during most of the period of the group's existence, often felt threatened by the group members, most of whom had been clients during a previous administration, and their input.

Although BFS was not the collaborating organization in the usual sense, the group project had two sets of goals, one of which involved BFS. One set of goals was eventually established by the women themselves. The other set was negotiated by the BFS board and myself before the group was established. This was to have the group provide experience-based information to BFS about the problems women faced after leaving the shelter and for the group to assess and make recommendations about a support group format as one mechanism for dealing with these problems. I hoped that if former clients were able to organize themselves, they might gain some power and place in agency decision- and policy-making by virtue of the confidence and skills gained from organizing as well as the useful collective information they could contribute.

Through BFS letters, my own personal contacts, and referrals from other women, I met individually over a two-month period with fourteen formerly battered women, past BFS clients, to determine and build interest in the group. I used the Freirian problem-posing format for initial dialogue with them about problems they faced in their daily lives, about problems they thought other such women faced, why the problems existed, what could be done about them, and their interest in forming a women's group.

Why did I begin by meeting individually with these women? Replies to the BFS letter came in spurts. I went out to talk with women as soon as I got a reply to try to build some interest and momentum. Additionally, a number of people, including Navajo social workers, cautioned that "you'll never get Navajo women to talk in a group." Sometimes people feel ashamed to admit their problems, especially when they have been made to feel responsible for them. This is especially true with battered women, who, on the whole, are made to feel that somehow they have provoked, caused, and hence deserve their partners' physical, emotional, and sexual abuse. Along these lines, women who left the shelter and its supportive services and counseling were sometimes ashamed to admit that it was difficult to "make it on their own." When the violence stops or the violent relationship is ended, women have a whole new set of problems to contend with. When I went to talk with one woman, a Navajo mother of five and high school dropout, she told me, "This is really the first time I'm communicating with somebody since I left the shelter nine months ago."

If women were fearful, embarrassed, or shy about talking in groups, starting with individual dialogue might be less threatening. The problem-posing format would give women a chance to begin reflecting on their daily realities. I knew that many of the women who had left the shelter felt isolated by lack of transportation, lack of telephones, relentless child care, and the general isolation of being separated from extended family in an alienating, often racist community and society. Besides the difficulties of being afoot in a "car and truck culture," many women still feared being seen in public by the violent partner they had left. I hoped that talking with another caring and concerned adult might demonstrate the power of breaking silence and isolation to work with others. It did.

The dialogue process was powerful and poignant in other ways. Although I began by asking women to talk about the problems they experienced in their daily lives, they began somewhere else. Almost without fail women began by talking about the violence they had experienced and survived. Besides the usual beratings, beatings, punchings, and kickings, the violence they and their children had survived included everything from having a loaded gun put to their heads to having their clothes burned. One woman had stabbed and killed her partner in self-defense after he put her head through the kitchen wall then ripped the phone out of the wall as she tried to call for help. The women did something else with the problem-posing format. Again, without my asking, they talked about what was going right in their lives. It seemed important to identify not only their problems but also their successes and strengths.

At the end of each individual discussion, I asked women if they would be interested in forming and joining a women's group and, if so, what would they want and need from the group. What did they think such a group's purposes should be? They named such purposes as getting together to talk, support each other, and share ideas for handling their problems. No one said, "Let's do research." Several women suggested using the group to help other battered women, particularly those still in abusive relationships. They also suggested social activities which included their children.

Most of these individual meetings took one to two hours. I had asked each woman's permission to tape our dialogue; transcribing each meeting took about seven hours. I hand-delivered the transcript, which each woman kept. Out of the fourteen women with whom I had individual meetings, I had a follow-up meeting with eight, using the transcript of our dialogue as a stepping-off place.

PHASE II: FORMATION OF GROUP AND THE RESEARCH PROCESS

The initial dialogue led to the starting of a formerly battered women's support group. Eleven of the fourteen women wanted to form a group, and eventually thirteen different women participated to some degree, with another five women participating during their stay at the shelter. In addition to me, six Navajo and two Anglo women formed the consistent core of women who met for nine months on a biweekly schedule with various breaks. I had developed a personal relationship with seven of the eight core women from my year's work with BFS. None of the women had ever belonged to any kind of organization as an adult (with the exception of one woman active in her church group), nor had any of the women ever been involved in any kind of women's group or organization. In its three years of existence, BFS had never tried to organize any kind of support groups or former client groups. Our effort was a personal first for all the women and the area's first formerly battered women's support group.

The formal education of the group ranged from a master's degree (not including me) to completion of the fifth grade, with the majority of women having a high school diploma or less. Three women were employed full-time, eight received some combination of public assistance (AFDC, food stamps, WIC, housing or fuel subsidies), and two women went back and forth between employment and public assistance during the course of the group. Only one woman received sporadic child support payments. All of the women, except me, had children. All but one woman were separated or divorced from their abusive partners when the group began.

Lacking conceptual clarity about ideal participatory research, I ended up organizing a formerly battered women's group which became primarily a consciousness-raising support group, not a "research" group. Our group did not evolve into a more formal independent organization with a politicized action and research agenda. Due to my notions about "ideal" participatory research, I avoided a formal collaborating relationship with the one in-place agency interested in battered women. In retrospect, my concerns about a "reformist" approach were misguided. It's possible that if I had gone ahead and developed a formal project with BFS, I could have outlined conditions for real participation of staff and clients in a research project. That approach might actually have resulted in an organizational commitment to and mechanisms for democratization and meaningful, institutionalized participation of battered women in agency policy and decision making. Sometimes the seemingly "reformist" approach might eventually lead to the most significant change, for clearly participatory research takes an organizational base of some kind to implement and sustain change.

Having been blinded to that possibility, perhaps I should have headed directly for trying to organize an independent advocacy, research, and action organization. At the least, I should have been direct in asking the group if they would be interested in identifying a research problem and then designing and conducting a formalized participatory research process. This tack seemed contradictory to me after I started by asking women what purposes they would want a formerly battered women's group to serve. Now I understand the ideal nature of the organizing and researching aspects of participatory research to mean that the purpose is to organize people specifically to do participatory research, not merely to organize people and hope that somewhere along the line a research need will emerge. It might also mean to try to use a participatory research project as a means by which to organize the unorganized and voiceless. However, I believe this is a more challenging and more doubtful task. Most ideally, it would mean to work with already-organized people to do participatory research to meet their organizational information needs. The linkage between the organizing and research goals of participatory research is troublesome, particularly given the range of relationships that oppressed people will have to various possible organizational bases.

Seven women attended our first meeting. The first half of the meeting was spent introducing ourselves, sharing reasons for being in the group, discovering commonalities, and sharing problems and resources for solutions. The second half was devoted to organizational decision making. Everyone participated in deciding to meet every two weeks, rotating homes, and in setting the next four meeting dates. The issue of child care was raised when I noted that one woman, known by many in the group, hadn't come because her child care arrangements fell through at the last minute. When organizing the group I knew that child care would affect many women's ability to participate. After volunteering transportation for many women, I didn't want to unilaterally solve or even raise the child care issue. Everyone was concerned that no one be excluded by lack of child care or money to pay for it. The group started a child care fund. Each woman paid fifty cents per child per hour or what she could afford, if anything. One woman agreed to be treasurer and arrange the next meeting's child care. The group subsequently took total responsibility for child care and later rotated the treasurer role.

Everyone agreed to one woman's suggestion that the biweekly format include half the time on a pre-chosen topic and half of the time for open-ended discussion of current problems. I asked how to decide on those topics. Several people said, "You do it." I had brought to the meeting some large flip chart pages with lists of all the problems women had identified in our individual discussions. My intention had been for the group to identify generative themes. But time ran out as several women needed to get home to relieve baby-sitters. Someone said, "Well, you interviewed us all," and another person joked, "Besides, it's your dissertation." I agreed to choose topics for the next four meetings based on interview themes with the understanding that then we'd use a group process to decide. The group ended on a festive note and those who could stayed for refreshments.

Our meeting pattern fell into place during the next two months. The first half of the meeting was spent on our topic and the second half was spent talking about our current lives. The topics included recovering from the effects of abuse (psychological more than physical), difficulties raising children as single mothers, and difficulties becoming and feeling independent. The problems discussed varied greatly, including difficulties in school (college and GED programs), sexual harassment at work, loneliness, and current love relationships.

Members demonstrated increasing investment in the group. Several women tried to recruit new members who had expressed interest in joining, but lack of transportation remained an obstacle. The group continued to organize and pay for child care, which was on-site. We had refreshments with the children when meetings ended. While members took increasing control of logistical arrangements, except transportation, they were slow to take leadership in discussions. I was still the prime organizer of the group.

An externally initiated chance for group action came along. The new director of the Office of Navajo Women agreed to speak at the Introduction to Women's Studies course I was teaching at UNM-Gallup. In the course of making the arrangements, I mentioned the group. She invited the group to make a presentation at the upcoming Conference on Navajo Women. Very excitedly, I took her request to the group.

Few women were enthusiastic. Many of them came from the reservation area where the conference would be held. They expressed fear of talking in front of a large group where they might be recognized, see in-laws, or be the object of gossip. One member observed, "It's like being invited to speak at the White House your very first time in public." They declined the offer— a small reminder that a participatory researcher cannot make people do anything they aren't ready for.

After several months we had a meeting to plan for the new year. The group brainstormed topics for the new year and essentially moved from discussing their pasts to considering the present and future. One member suggested that members take more responsibility for facilitating the discussion when the meeting was held in their homes. Yet when we scheduled the next four meetings and places, only two women volunteered to facilitate. As we scheduled the next two months, I tried to get the group to schedule a meeting during a week I would be gone in January. No one wanted to. I also suspect that the only two women besides myself with vehicles didn't want to coordinate transportation. But a group member did facilitate the next meeting.

The next month was a turning point in the group, representing a major low out of which came new direction and momentum. Few women attended the February meetings and the volunteer facilitators weren't prepared or willing to facilitate the discussion. Those who came were dissatisfied with all the talk and little action. They seemed to want me to solve the problem. I kept turning the question back to them: What do you want the group to do and what are you willing to do to make it happen? The discussion turned into how to "get the work off Pat." In many areas they did.

One of our members was also on the BFS Board of Directors. At the winter meeting, the new BFS executive director proposed that men be allowed to be on-call volunteers. Our member suggested that the board get our group's opinion on the matter because all the women had been battered and had experienced being escorted to the shelter by a volunteer, a stranger to the women. The board agreed and the request was brought to our group. It was our first opportunity to have input into agency policy.

The group discussed their ideas and put together an impressive list of reasons why men should not be allowed to be on-call volunteers. They did not rule out roles for men in the agency. Their data came from direct experience. "Imagine yourself being met at the police station by a man you never saw, never met . . . and he says, 'I'm here to take you to the shelter.' Would *you* go with a total stranger?" "If he hears your story, he may think, 'I would beat her up too in that situation.' "

Our member on the board agreed to take the information to the next board meeting, but no one else would agree to go with her. I too declined. The day after the meeting she called to tell me about the board's mixed reactions. Out of curiosity, I subsequently talked with most board members about their reactions. The strongest discounting of the group's input came from the new BFS director, whose idea it had been to have male on-call volunteers. She discounted their ideas with reasons right out of traditional research criteria: "The information wasn't objective. . . . They had discussed it in a group so they biased each other. . . . It wasn't scientifically collected." One of the two male board members had commented at the meeting that their information represented paranoid and neurotic thinking. But most of the board listened and gave the input weight. Another board member, conscious of the attempts to discredit the group's data, observed:

That's just part of the human services mentality, you know, clients don't know enough to make their own decisions. The trouble with asking clients their opinion is they might have one, and it might not agree with yours!

The immediate outcome was that the issue was never brought to a vote after the data were presented by our member. The director suggested that more information be sought by polling other regional shelters about their policies on male volunteers, thereby essentially saying, Let's talk to other experts, not actual battered women. The issue was never brought back to the board. Our group's input essentially killed the move when the vote was postponed.

When our member finally reported back to the group, members viewed the board's reactions as a defeat, a discrediting of their experience. Three women observed, "It's because they don't know how it is. They've never been beaten up." I observed that they had at least temporarily halted the decision. They discussed the importance of having more battered women and group members on the board. One of two members who expressed interest joined for a short period.

After the interaction with the BFS Board, the members continued the earlier discussion of how to take on more of the group's work. They agreed to share the transportation, rotated the baby-sitting treasury to another woman, and talked of holding meetings in late May and early June, when I would be gone. There was even a little discussion of electing officers, but no one agreed to serve in that role. One of the most active members commented that she was reluctant to take on much more of the group's organizational work. "I like having something I can just come to and get something for myself without having to worry too much about it." Others agreed and talked about their responsibilities of child raising and work, inside or outside the home. They implied that because I had no children or a full-time job I had more time for organizational tasks. They were also saying that because control and participation take time, the benefits have to be weighed against the time costs.

Despite these concerns, the group started taking more action. They brainstormed ideas for a meeting they were requesting with BFS staff. They wanted to exchange information with BFS on two topics: how the group could be more of a resource to BFS and how BFS could best help women once they left the shelter. The subsequent meeting with two BFS staff, the director and child counselor, was facilitated by a group member and all the women participated. It was exciting. Fourteen women attended, including two women who were living in the shelter at that time. The group presented their ideas on the two topics and essentially told BFS that the initiative to help women once they left the shelter and to better prepare women for that transition would have to come from BFS. They noted that once women left the shelter, many felt ashamed to go back for counseling or advocacy assistance. Members were excited by BFS's openness to their ideas. It seemed like some sort of partnership might develop. Members took pride in being role models to the shelter residents who attended.

Several members started going to the shelter to talk with shelter residents, an informal "peer counseling" effort. The group then organized an early Easter celebration for women and children in the BFS shelter because they

knew how depressing and lonely holidays in the shelter can become. We
fed forty-four people at the in-shelter celebration: fifteen women and twenty-
nine children. Group members brought the food for a turkey dinner and
BFS provided Easter candy for the children. Small groups of women sat
around talking and sharing their stories.

The group had also decided that it could be helpful in educating local
social service, medical, and criminal justice personnel and teenagers about
problems of battered women. After the upbeat meeting with BFS staff, some
momentum seemed to gather on the possibility of several members working
with staff on a domestic violence workshop for the Navajo police. The
group had me invite a local mental health therapist to a meeting for the
purpose of exchanging information. The therapist was asked to talk about
dealing with depression, and the women would share information that might
help the therapist better understand what battering survivors deal with.
That particular meeting was disastrous because regardless of the number
of times I had told the therapist that these women were no longer in violent
relationships, she never got the point and ended up preaching about fleeing
violent partners. We had a good laugh when she left.

It seemed that the group's momentum was building. Yet most of the
attempted joint BFS-group endeavors fell through, due to lack of follow-
through or miscommunication from one side or the other. For most of this
I stayed out of the communication, planning, and follow-up loop. I felt that
if the group's independence and relationship with BFS were to grow, I had
to get out of the way. In the end, building an agency commitment to, and
mechanisms for, meaningful, ongoing battered women's inclusion or building an independent battered women's organization took more of a sustained
effort or commitment than existed.

The group meanwhile planned to meet twice during a period when I would
be gone. Members volunteered for transportation, hosting, and facilitating
the meetings. A meeting was planned the week I returned. When I got back I
learned that none of the meetings, for various reasons, had taken place. I realized that at the upcoming meeting we needed to evaluate how and if we
should continue. I also knew that I would not push for continuation.

At the meeting several of the most active members suggested that it would
be a good time to stop, even if only for the summer. A few quieter members
offered no opinion. Two members, who had no transportation nor had
offered any active leadership throughout were adamant that we continue.
But the majority won out. After an evaluation discussion, we ended with a
fried chicken dinner.

PHASE III: ASSESSMENT—BUT WAS IT PARTICIPATORY
RESEARCH?

After deciding to end the group, we evaluated the project, including what
the group had meant to each woman and what recommendations we should

make to BFS about the value and format of a support group for women leaving the shelter. I also talked individually with each member after the final June 1986 meeting. Members had an active role in the assessment phase but they did not design it nor, apart from the final group discussion, did they conduct it. Due to another change in BFS leadership, it was five months before the group's final recommendations could be presented to the BFS Board of Directors. Because of the delay, some member relocation, and work schedules, no group member attended. The board composition at the November 1986 meeting was totally different from the board I initially approached in May 1985.

The group recommended that Battered Families' Services take on the ongoing sponsorship of a support group for women leaving the shelter. By offering support and problem-solving opportunities and resources, the group experience could help decrease the number of women returning to unchanged violent relationships and help minimize the difficulties of struggling in isolation. Members said a group could be a valuable resource to BFS, both by talking with in-shelter women and by participating in community education events. They made other recommendations about the purpose, format, value, and logistics of a BFS-sponsored support group. Many of these recommendations came out of the group evaluation of the strengths and limitations of our group. They generated information about the kinds of problems women face immediately upon leaving the shelter and after being out of the shelter for a while. Members also made specific recommendations about how BFS could do more to help clients, both in and out of the shelter, deal with alcohol abuse.

In the traditional sense you can conclude that the group did not do "research." Even in the participatory research sense, the group did not formulate an explicit research problem or collectively design, conduct, and control a participatory research investigation. So what did we do?

Initially the women produced knowledge about themselves. They moved from discussing and informally investigating the problems in their own lives and helping each other, to beginning to reach out collectively to other battered women and to provide a diversity of battered women's perspectives to BFS. In addition to nine months of support group meetings, a variety of things were accomplished. Through individual dialogue and then group discussion, the group provided a data base on the problems women face upon leaving the shelter. They then made very specific recommendations to BFS out of their own group experience about an agency-sponsored group as one mechanism for dealing with those problems. They generated and provided information to BFS on the possible use of male on-call volunteers. Their input essentially blocked that decision. They also provided information to BFS on how the agency could better meet clients' needs and how a support group could be a valuable resource to BFS. They began taking some small actions to reach out to currently battered women and tried to begin

some orientation of local social service personnel about the problems battered women deal with.

Our actions or insights were not revolutionary, nor did they contribute
to major social transformation. But we did begin to challenge the oppression
of silence and isolation. Although we could not sustain it, we did create the
area's first support group for formerly battered women. On a very small
scale the group began to affect BFS policy and generate information for
various recommendations to BFS.

In their comments and evaluation, women indicated that the project did
meet the rehumanizing goals of collective knowledge generation. Group
members made such comments as "I no longer felt alone," "I realized I had
courage," "I learned I could go on," and "I felt supported by others and
supported them." We began shifting the traditional power relationship between an agency for battered women and its clients.

While the women didn't develop a structural analysis of patriarchy, capitalism, or racism, they gained a more critical understanding of the problems
they face "as women" and a better understanding of battering as an expression of male control. They examined how isolation contributed to their
problems and gained a firsthand appreciation of the value of collective
problem posing and solving. The group experience built their confidence
that they could be active problem solvers and decision makers, both individually and collectively.

The women did not have to wait for the application of project information
and benefits to eventually, if ever, filter down to them. They observed that
they benefited directly from project participation. One member noted:

I think our experiment was a success. I really appreciate just being with a group of
women. One benefit of the project is that I appreciate women far more. I never had
this much contact with different women. I have far more respect for women now
than ever before.

Other member-identified benefits from participation included learning
they were not alone in their struggles, problem and solution identification,
increased self-confidence and self-awareness, increased understanding of the
problems other women face, more appreciation of women's strength, courage, and mutual support, and help in current love relationships.

It became clear that resources, human and material, and organizational
structures are necessary to sustain collective reflection and action over time.
Likewise, to initiate *real* participatory research, whatever mobilizing is required for beginning the project must ultimately and clearly lead to an
explicit "research" effort with greater group control and decision making
at each step in the process.

SO WHAT DOES IT MEAN FOR A DOCTORAL STUDENT?

Developing caring relationships with people, oppressed or otherwise, takes time for meaningful involvement in each other's lives and nurturance of the relationship. There is no way to short-circuit the process. Nor, besides your own time schedule, is there any reason to. It is those involvements which sustain and nurture you, the researcher. Likewise it takes that same time and meaningful involvement for those participating in the project to develop relationships with each other, not simply with the researcher.

I was never a detached social scientist. I became involved in the women's lives, and they in mine, on a day-to-day basis, not simply during "project time." I cared about them, laughed with them, cried with them, and worried with them. I was proud of them yet certainly at times annoyed and irritated with them, as they may have been with me. They spent time in my home and I in theirs. I went to court with a woman, sat up nights with a suicidal woman, and helped numerous others connect to appropriate community resources. The participatory research process is engaging, invigorating, and likewise, exhausting. But then, that is the beauty of it. You will not be detached. You too, not merely the participants, will be rehumanized.

Participatory research is not only about trying to transform social structures "out there" and "the people," it is about being open to transforming ourselves and our relationships with others. Just as I examined the dilemmas and contradictions in participatory research, I was challenged daily to consider the dilemmas and contradictions of my own life choices. I was forced to question my part in the social construction and maintenance of the larger social structures, systems, and relationships. And relentlessly, I found myself asking, How am I choosing to be in the world? I was often disappointed in myself.

By way of advice to others I'd say try to head off some of the academic disappointments by being careful and deliberate about the dissertation committee you put together if, like I did, you have control of it. Seek out faculty promoting, or at least open to, alternative paradigm research approaches. The ideal is to find faculty as open to learning with you as they are to teaching you. You might also be very prudent about the setting in which you work. It may be easiest and most instructive to try becoming involved in an ongoing or established participatory research project, in which you can contribute your work without having to mobilize the entire project from scratch. You might consider trying to put together a team, even of other graduate students, to work in a context in which you're already established. Don't overlook the organizations, groups, or agencies in which you are already involved, regardless of how "reformist" you may initially assess them. You will inevitably make choices based on time constraints. The dissertation should be an integral part of your life work, but don't let it expand to become a lifetime project. However, make no mistake, the entire participatory research process takes time.

Although the dissertation shouldn't become a lifetime project, it cannot be disconnected from your values and philosophy. Like many others, I started out looking for ways to make my dissertation research more congruent with my beliefs about empowerment and social justice. The decision, then, to attempt participatory research grows out of a deep belief in the ability of people, ourselves included, to grow, change, challenge injustice and oppression, and take increasing control of our lives and communities through collective action, however small. Yet we live within the very structures and relationships we seek to transform. It is not a neat intellectual exercise. Collective work is messy and time-consuming. People may decide not to take action. They will surely not become empowered, liberated, or transformed on our schedules. When possible, get involved in a "problem" that you feel passionate about. For even if the participatory research work you engage in is not ideal, you will have the satisfaction of working on life issues close to your heart, not merely dissertation issues. Your life passions and interests will enrich the process, not detract from it. For example, my own concerns about women's oppression helped me to see the androcentrism of much participatory research.

The primary lesson for me is that the redistribution of power, among and between the world's women and men, is a long-haul, collective struggle in which there is work for each of us. Participatory research is but one tool in that struggle. However, transformation, social and personal, is not an event. It is a process that we are living through, creating as we go. It's dangerous to compare our modest beginnings and exhausting middles to the successful, documented endings of others' work. For we never know when we begin where the work will take us and those involved. Perhaps that is what allows us to even begin. Learn from others' work, but don't be intimidated by it. It is too easy to be seduced into comparing, then trivializing or discounting your efforts. The point is to learn and grow from doing, and to celebrate the doing, no matter how flawed, small-scale, or less than ideal.

Appendix: Contact Organizations

If you are interested in getting more information about participatory research, feel free to contact any of the editors or you might want to write or call one of the following organizations:

Center for Community Education and Action
17 New South Street, 1st Floor
Northampton, MA 01060
United States

E. T. Jackson and Associates, Ltd.
858 Bank Street, Suite 100
Ottawa, Ontario K1S 3W3
Canada

Department of Adult Education
Ontario Institute for Adult Education
252 Bloor Street West
Toronto, Ontario M5S 1V6
Canada

Highlander Center
1959 Highlander Way
New Market, TN 37820
United States

International Council for Adult Education
720 Bathurst Street, Suite 500
Toronto, Ontario M5S 2R4
Canada

Lindeman Center
188 W. Randolph, Suite 2817
Chicago, IL 60601
United States

North American Popular Educators
School of Education
University of California at Berkeley
Berkeley, CA 94720
United States

Participatory Community Development Project
Institute for Economic Development and Policy
East-West Center
1777 East-West Center Road
Honolulu, HI 96484
United States

Bibliography

Alinsky, S. D. *Rules for Radicals: A Pragmatic Primer for Realistic Radicals*. New York: Vintage Books, 1971.

Angus, M. *And the Last Shall Be First: Native Policy in an Era of Cutbacks*. Toronto: NC Press, 1991.

Antonio, Robert J. "Immanent Critique as the Core of Critical Theory: Its Origins and Development in Hegel, Marx and Contemporary Thought." *British Journal of Sociology* 32(3):330 (1981).

Appalachian Land Ownership Task Force. *Land Ownership Patterns and Their Impacts on Appalachian Communities*. Washington, D.C.: Appalachian Regional Commission, 1981.

———. *Who Owns Appalachia?* Lexington, Kentucky: University Press of Kentucky, 1983.

Apple, Michael W. *Education and Power*. Boston: Routledge and Kegan Paul, 1982.

Barndt, Deborah. "Connecting Immigrant Workers: Community Self-Portraits." Presented at the International Forum on Participatory Research, Ljubljana, Yugoslavia, 1980.

Bell, Daniel. *The Coming of Post-Industrial Society*. London: Heinemann, 1974.

Berger, T. R. *Report of the Commission on Indian and Inuit Health Consultation*. Ottawa: Health and Welfare Canada, 1980.

———. *Village Journey: The Report of the Alaska Native Review Commission*. New York: Hill and Wang, 1985.

Bobiwash, L., and L. Malloch. *A Family Needs Survey of the Native Community in Toronto*. Toronto: Native Canadian Centre, 1980.

Bottomore, Tom. *The Frankfurt School*. London: Tavistock Publications, 1984.

Brice-Bennet, C., ed. *Our Footprints Are Everywhere: Inuit Land Use and Occupancy in Labrador*. Ottawa: Queen's Printer, 1977.

Bronfenbrenner, Urie. "Lewinian Space and Ecological Space." *Journal of Social Issues* 33(4) (1972).

Brown, David L., and Rajesh Tandon. "Ideology and Political Economy of Inquiry: Action Research and Participatory Research." *Journal of Applied Behavioral Science* 19: 227-294 (1983).

Brubacher, John S., and Willis Rudy. *Higher Education in Transition: A History of American Colleges and Universities, 1636-1968.* New York: Harper and Row, 1968.

Bryceson, Deborah, and Kemal Mustafa. "Participatory Research: Redefining the Relationship between Theory and Practice." Presented at the African Regional Workshop on Participatory Research, Mzumbe, Tanzania, 1979.

Cain, Bonnie J. "Participatory Research: Research with Historical Consciousness." Toronto: Participatory Research Project of the International Council for Adult Education, 1977.

Callaway, Helen, ed. *Case Studies of Participatory Research. Proceedings of the International Forum on Participatory Research. Ljubljana, Yugoslavia, 1980.* Amersfoort, The Netherlands: Netherlands Center for Research and Development in Adult Education (Studiecentrum Ncvo), 1981.

Castellano, Marlene Brant. "Canadian Case Study: The Role of Adult Education Promoting Community Involvement in Primary Health Care." Unpublished manuscript, Trent University, 1983.

———. "Collective Wisdom: Participatory Research and Canada's Native People." *Convergence* 19(3):50–53 (1986).

CENTRAD (Centre for Training, Research and Development). *Small Business Management: Instructors' Manual.* Prince Albert, Saskatchewan, 1973.

Chambers, Robert. *Rural Development: Putting the Last First.* London: Longman Press, 1983.

Chand, A. D., and M. L. Soni. "The Pachod Health Programme." In W. Fernandes and R. Tandon, eds., *Participatory Research and Evaluation: Experiments in Research as a Process of Liberation.* New Delhi: Indian Social Institute, 1981, 127-150.

Cheong, Ji Woong. "A Women's Cooperative Store." In Helen Callaway, ed., *Case Studies of Participatory Research. Proceedings of the International Forum on Participatory Research. Ljubljana, Yugoslavia, 1980.* Amersfoort, The Netherlands: Netherlands Center for Research and Development in Adult Education (Studiecentrum Ncvo), 1981.

Chervin, M., and D. Norman. "Getting Out to the Trapline: A Resource for Discussion and Action." Trent University and Kayahna Area Tribal Council, 1982.

Colorado, P. "Bridging Native and Western Science." *Convergence* 21(2–3):49–68 (1988).

Community Careers Resource Center. "Nonprofits Enter the Computer Age." Washington, D.C.: Community Careers Resource Center, 1985.

Conchelos, G. *Participatory Oral History Research in Native Communities: Some Problems and Emerging Guidelines for Doing It.* Prepared for the Conference on Participatory Research for Community Action, University of Massachussets at Amherst, 1985.

———. "Knowledge Systems, Environmental Impact Assessment and Participatory Research." Draft manuscript, Carleton University, Peterborough, 1988.

Conchelos, Greg, and Ted Jackson. "Participatory Research for Community Education: Comparing Urban and Rural Experiences." Presented to the Canadian Community Education Conference, Brandon, Manitoba, 1980.

Cornish, M., and L. Ritchie. *Getting Organized: Building a Union*. Toronto: The Women's Press, 1980.

Council for Yukon Indians. *Comprehensive Training Plan for the Yukon Indian People*. Whitehorse, 1981a.

————. *Land before Money, Co-operation before Competition: Report of the Alaska Study Tour*. Whitehorse, 1981b.

Couto, Richard A. "Failing Health and New Prescriptions: Community-based Approaches to Environmental Risks." In Carole E. Hill, ed., *Contemporary Health Policy Issues and Alternatives: An Applied Social Perspective*. Athens: University of Georgia Press, 1984.

Cove, J., and S. Clark, "Rethinking Ethics: Anthropological Research and Native Politics in Canada." Draft manuscript, Carleton University, Ottawa, 1984.

Daniels, D. *Indian Government: Middle Class Dream or Working Reality?* Presented to the Annual Meeting of the Western Association of Sociology and Anthropology, Saskatoon, 1982.

Darcy de Oliveira, Rosisca, and Miguel Darcy de Oliveira. "The Militant Observer: A Sociological Alternative." In Budd Hall, Arthur Gillette, and Rajesh Tandon, *Creating Knowledge: A Monopoly. Participatory Research in Development*. New Delhi: Society for Participatory Research in Asia, and Toronto: International Council for Adult Education, 1982.

de Vries, Jan. "Science as Human Behavior: On the Epistemology of the Participatory Research Approach." Presented at the International Forum on Participatory Research, Ljubljana, Yugoslavia, 1980.

Dewey, John. *Experience and Education*. New York: Collier Books, 1963.

Dobbs, Carolyn E. "Community Development: A Proposal for Involving Citizens in the Planning Process." Unpublished Ph.D. dissertation, University of Washington, 1971.

Dubell, F., T. Erasmie, and J. de Vries, eds. *Research for the People—Research by the People. Selected Papers from the International Forum on Participatory Research in Ljubljana, Yugoslavia, 1980*. Linkoping, Sweden: Linkoping University, Department of Education; and Amersfoort, The Netherlands: S. V. E. The Netherlands Study and Development Center for Adult Education, 1981.

Ellis, Patricia. *Participatory Research: An Integral Part of the Developmental Process*. Barbados: WAND Unit, The Pines, St. Michael, 1983.

Equipe das Comunidades de Base e de Agentes da Diocese de Goias. "O Meio Grito. Um Estudo sobre as Condicoes, os Direitos, o Valor e o Trabalho Popular Associados ao Problema da Saude en Goias." In Carlos Rodrigues Brandao, org., *Pesquisa Participante*. Sao Paulo: Editora Brasilense, n.d.

Fals Borda, Orlando. "Investigating Reality in Order to Transform It: The Colombian Experience." *Dialectical Anthropology* 4:33 (1979).

————. "Science and the Common People." Presented at the International Forum on Participatory Research, Ljubljana, Yugoslavia, 1980.

————. "Participatory Research and Rural Social Change." *Journal of Rural Co-operation* 10(1) (1982).

————. "The Application of Participatory Action-Research in Latin America." *International Sociology* 1:329–347 (1987).

————. *Conocimiento y Poder Popular. Lecciones con Campesinos de Nicaragua, Mexico, Colombia*. Bogotá: Siglo Veintiuno Editores, n.d.

Fals Borda, Orlando, and Muhammad Anisur Rahman. *Action and Knowledge: Breaking the Monopoly with Participatory Action-Research*. New York: Apex Press, 1991.

Fay, Brian. *Social Theory and Political Practice*. London: Unwin Hyman, 1975.

Fernandes, Walter, and Rajesh Tandon, eds. *Participatory Research and Evaluation. Experiments in Research as a Process of Liberation*. New Delhi: Indian Social Institute, 1981.

Feyerabend, Paul. *Against Method. Outline of an Anarchistic Theory of Knowledge*. London: Verso, 1975.

Food and Beverage Trades Department, AFL-CIO. *Manual of Corporate Investigation*. Washington, D.C.: AFL-CIO, 1984.

Foucault, Michel. *The Order of Things: An Archaeology of the Human Sciences*. New York: Random House, 1970.

Freire, Paulo. "Conscientization and Cultural Freedom." In *Cultural Action for Freedom. Harvard Educational Review*. Monograph Series No. 1, 1970a.

————. "Cultural Action and Conscientization." *Harvard Educational Review* 40:452–477 (1970b).

————. *Pedagogy of the Oppressed*. New York: Seabury Press, 1970c.

————. "Creating Alternative Research Methods. Learning to Do It by Doing It." In B. Hall, A. Gillette, and R. Tandon, *Creating Knowledge: A Monopoly. Participatory Research in Development*. New Delhi : Society for Participatory Research in Asia, and Toronto: International Council for Adult Education, 1982.

Gaventa, John. "Land Ownership in Appalachia, USA: A Citizen's Research Project." In F. Dubell, T. Erasmie, and J. de Vries, eds., *Research for the People– Research by the People. Selected Papers from the International Forum on Participatory Research in Ljubljana, Yugoslavia, 1980*. Linkoping, Sweden: Linkoping University, Department of Education; and Amersfoort, the Netherlands: S.V.E. The Netherlands Study and Development Center for Adult Education, 1981.

————. "Participatory Research in North America." *Convergence* 24(2–3):19–28 (1988).

Gaventa, John, and Billy D. Horton. "A Citizens' Research Project in Appalachia, USA." *Convergence* 14(3) (1981).

Gayfer, Margaret, and Anne Armstrong. *Women Hold Up More Than Half the Sky*. Toronto: International Council for Adult Education, 1981.

Geertz, Clifford. *Local Knowledge. Further Essays in Interpretive Anthropology*. New York: Basic Books, 1983.

Geisler, Charles C., and Frank J. Popper, eds. *Land Reform, American Style*. Totowa, New Jersey: Rowman and Allanheld, 1984.

Gergen, Kenneth J. "Feminist Critique of Science and the Challenge of Social Epistemology." In Mary M. Gergen, ed., *Feminist Thought and the Structure of Knowledge*. New York: New York University Press, 1988.

Gibbs, Lois. *Love Canal: My Story*. Albany: State University of New York Press, 1982.

Gramsci, Antonio. *Selections from the Prison Notebooks*. New York: International Publishers, 1971.

Greever, Barry. "Tactical Investigation for People's Struggles." Washington, D.C.: Youth Project, n.d.

Griffith, R. "Northern Park Development: The Case of Snowdraft." *Alternatives* 14(1):26-30 (1987).

Griffith, William S., and Mary S. Cristarella. "Participatory Research: Should It Be a New Methodology for Adult Education?" In John Niemi, ed., *Viewpoints on Adult Education Research*. Columbus, Ohio: ERIC Clearinghouse, 1979.

Groenewegen, Peter, and Paul Swuste. "Worker-Scientist Cooperation: A Case Study from the Netherlands." *Science for the People* 16(6) (November–December 1984).

Habermas, Jürgen. "Toward a Theory of Communicative Competence." In Peter Dreitzel, ed., *Recent Sociology*, vol. 2, *Patterns of Communicative Behavior*. London: Macmillan, 1970a.

———. "Scientization of Politics and Public Opinion." In *Toward a Rational Society: Student Protest, Science and Politics*. Boston: Beacon Press, 1970b.

———. *Knowledge and Human Interest*. Boston: Beacon Press, 1972.

———. "Dogmatism, Reason, and Decision: On Theory and Praxis in Our Scientific Civilization." In *Theory and Practice*. Boston: Beacon Press, 1973.

———. "Legitimation Crisis in the Modern Society." In *Communication and the Evolution of Society*. Boston: Beacon Press, 1979a.

———. "What Is Universal Pragmatics?" In *Communication and the Evolution of Society*. Boston: Beacon Press, 1979b.

Hall, Budd L. "Participatory Research: An Approach for Change." *Convergence* 8(2):24–32 (1975).

———. "Creating Knowledge: Breaking the Monopoly." Toronto: Participatory Research Project of the International Council for Adult Education, 1977.

———. "Knowledge as Commodity and Participatory Research." *Prospects* 9(4) (1979a).

———. "Participatory Research: Breaking the Academic Monopoly." In John Niemi, ed., *Viewpoints on Adult Education*. De Kalb, Illinois: Northern Illinois University, 1979b, 43–69.

———. "Participatory Research, Popular Knowledge and Power: A Personal Reflection." *Convergence* 14(3):6–19 (1981).

Hall, Budd L., A. Gillette, and R. Tandon. *Creating Knowledge: A Monopoly. Participatory Research in Development*. New Delhi: Society for Participatory Research in Asia, and Toronto: International Council for Adult Education, 1982.

Hall, Budd L., and Yusuf Kassam. "Participatory Research." In T. Husen, ed., *International Encyclopedia of Education*. Oxford: Pergamon Press, 1985, 85.

Harris, Kevin. *Education and Knowledge: The Structured Misrepresentation of Reality*. London: Routledge and Kegan Paul, 1979.

Heaney, Thomas W. "Power, Learning and 'Compunication.'" In David G. Gueulette, ed., *Microcomputers for Adult Learning: Potentials and Perils*. Chicago: Follett Publishing Co., 1982.

Held, David. "The Reformulation of the Foundation of Critical Theory." In *Intro-*

duction to Critical Theory: Horkheimer to Habermas. Berkeley: University of California Press, 1980.

Heron, John. "Philosophical Basis for a New Paradigm Research." In Peter Reason and John Rowan, eds., *Human Inquiry: A Sourcebook of New Paradigm Research*. New York: John Wiley and Sons, 1985.

Himmelstrand, Ulf. "Action Research as Applied Social Science: Scientific Value, Practical Benefits and Abuses." Presented to the Symposium on Action Research and Scientific Analysis, Cartagena, Colombia, 1977.

hooks, bell. *Feminist Theory: From Margin to Center*. Boston: South End Press, 1984.

——. *Talking Back: Thinking Feminist Thinking Black*. Toronto: Between the Lines, 1988.

Horkheimer, Max. *Critique of Instrumental Reason*. New York: Seabury Press, 1974.

Horkheimer, Max, and Theodor W. Adorno. *Dialectic of Enlightenment*. New York: Herder and Herder, 1972.

Horton, Billy. "On the Potential of Participatory Research: An Evaluation of a Regional Experiment." Paper presented at Annual Meeting of the Society for the Study of Social Problems, Toronto, 1981.

Horton, Billy, David Liden, and Tracey Weis. *Who Owns It? Researching Land and Mineral Ownership in Your Community*. Prestonburg, Kentucky: Appalachian Alliance (c/o Kentucky Fair Tax Coalition), 1985.

Horton, Robin. "African Traditional Thought and Western Science." *Africa* 37 (1969).

Howlett, Dennis. "Social Movement Coalitions: New Possibilities for Social Change." *Canadian Dimension* 23(8):41–47 (November–December 1989).

Hudson, Grace. "Women's Participatory Research in the Kayahna Area." Presented at the International Forum on Participatory Research, Ljubljana, Yugoslavia, 1980.

International Council for Adult Education and UNESCO. "Report on the International Forum on Participatory Research." Toronto, 1980.

International Council on Adult Education. *Convergence, Special Issue on Participatory Research* 8(2) (1975).

——. *Convergence. Special Issue: Developments and Issues* 14(3) (1981).

——. *Convergence. Focus on Participatory Research* 21(2–3) (1988).

Inuit Broadcasting Corporation. "Population Paper on Northern Broadcasting." Ottawa, 1985.

Jackson, T. "Clearcutting Canada's Forests." *Alternatives* 6(2) (1977).

——. "Resisting Pipeline Imperialism: The Struggle for Self-Determination in the Canadian North." *Alternatives* 7(4): 40–51 (1978).

——. "Environmental Assessment for Water and Sanitation in Big Trout Lake, Canada." In H. Callaway, ed., *Case Studies of Participatory Research in Adult Education*. Amersfoort, The Netherlands: Centre for Research and Development in Adult Education, 1980, 43-52.

Jackson, Ted, Greg Conchelos, and Al Vigoda. "The Dynamics of Participation in Participatory Research." Presented at the International Forum on Participatory Research, Ljubljana, Yugoslavia, 1980.

Jackson, T., D. McCaskill, and B. Hall. "Introduction." *Canadian Journal of Native Studies* 2(1):1–9 (1982).

Jackson, T., and G. McKay. "Sanitation and Water Supply in Big Trout Lake: Participatory Research for Democratic Technical Solutions." *Canadian Journal of Native Studies* 2(1):129–145 (1982).

Kassam, Yusuf, and Kemal Mustapha. *Participatory Research: An Emerging Alternative Methodology in Social Science Research.* New Delhi: Participatory Research Network, 1982.

Kassi, N. "This Land Has Sustained Us." *Alternatives* 14(1): 20–21 (1987).

Kayahna Area Tribal Council. *"We Know What We Want": Report of a Workshop on Land Use and Economic Development.* Big Trout Lake, 1980.

Kemp, Ray. "Planning, Public Hearings, and the Politics of Discourse." In John Forester, ed., *Critical Theory and Public Life.* Cambridge: MIT Press, 1985.

Kentucky Fair Tax Coalition. *Struggling for Tax Justice in the Mountains: The Story of the Kentucky Fair Tax Coalition.* Lovely, Kentucky: Kentucky Fair Tax Coalition, June 1982.

———. *Taxing Unmined Minerals in Kentucky: Questions and Answers.* Lovely, Kentucky: Kentucky Fair Tax Coalition, October 1983.

Kerr, Clark. *The Uses of the University.* Cambridge: Harvard University Press, 1963.

Kingsport Study Group. "Smells Like Money." *Southern Exposure* 6(2) (n.d.).

Kirby, Richard M. "Kentucky Coal; Owners, Taxes, Profits: A Study in Representation without Taxation" (prepared for the Appalachian Volunteers, 1969). See also excerpt in *Appalachian Lookout* 1:19–27 (October 1969).

Knight, R. *Indians at Work.* Vancouver: New Star, 1978.

Krotz, L. *Indian Country: Inside Another Canada.* Toronto: McClelland and Stewart, 1990.

Kuhn, Thomas. *The Structure of Scientific Revolutions.* Chicago: University of Chicago Press, 1962.

Kumar, Krishan. *Prophecy and Progress: The Sociology of Industrial and Post-Industrial Society.* Harmondsworth, England: Penguin Press, 1978.

Lather, Patti. "Research as Praxis." *Harvard Educational Review* 56(3): 257–277 (August 1986).

Levin, Morten. "A Trade Union and a Case of Automation." In F. Dubell, T. Erasmie, and J. de Vries, eds. *Research for the People—Research by the People* Selected papers from the International Forum on Participatory Research in Ljubljana, Yugoslavia, 1980. Linkoping, Sweden: Linkoping University, Department of Education and Amersfoort, The Netherlands/S. V. E. The Netherlands Study and Development Center for Adult Education, 1981.

Levine, Adeline Gordon. *Love Canal: Science, Politics and People.* Lexington, Massachusetts: Lexington Books, 1982.

Linden, David. "This Has Gone Far Enough." *Southern Exposure* 10(1):52 (January–February 1982).

———. *Rights: Yours and Theirs (A Citizen's Guide to Oil and Gas in Appalachia).* New Market, Tennessee: Appalachian Alliance, 1983.

———. "Pulling the Pillars: Energy Development and Land Reform in Appalachia." In Charles G. Geisler and Frank J. Popper, eds., *Land Reform, American Style.* Totowa, New Jersey: Rowan and Allanheld, 1984, 111.

Lindquist, Sven. "Dig Where You Stand." In Paul Thompson and Natasha Bur-
    chardt, eds., *Our Common History.* Atlantic Highlands, New Jersey: Hu-
    manities Press, 1982.
Lockhart, Alexander. "The Insider-Outsider Dialectic in Native Socio-Economic
    Development: A Case Study in Process Understanding." *The Canadian Jour-
    nal of Native Studies* 2(1):159-168 (1982).
Loney, M. "A Political Economy of Citizen Participation." In L. Panitch, ed., *The
    Canadian State: Political Economy and Political Power.* Toronto: University
    of Toronto Press, 1977, 446-472.
Lowery, David. *Fair Taxation in the Commonwealth: A Progressive Tax Agenda
    for Kentucky.* Lexington, Kentucky: Commonwealth Tax Policy Education
    Group, 1984.
Loxley, J. "The 'Great Northern' Plan." *Studies in Political Economy* 6:151–182
    (1981).
McDermott, P. "The New Demeaning of Work." *Canadian Dimension* 15(8):34-
    37 (1981).
Machlup, Fritz. *The Production and Distribution of Knowledge in the United States.*
    Princeton: Princeton University Press, 1962.
———. *Knowledge and Knowledge Production.* Vol. 1 of *Knowledge: Its Creation,
    Distribution and Economic Significance.* Princeton: Princeton University
    Press, 1980.
McRae, Duncan. *The Social Functions of Social Sciences.* New Haven: Yale Uni-
    versity Press, 1971.
Maguire, Patricia. *Doing Participatory Research: A Feminist Approach.* Amherst,
    Massachusetts: Center for International Education, 1987.
Marcuse, Herbert. *One-Dimensional Man.* Boston: Beacon Press, 1966.
Marshall, J. P. "Participatory Research: A Model for Initiating Problem-solving
    Education in the Community." Paper presented at Annual Meeting of the
    American Sociological Association for the Study of Social Problems, Toronto,
    1981.
Masisi, Y. K. C. "Demystifying Research: A Case Study of the Chiwand Nutrition
    Education Project." In Y. Kassam and K. Mustafa, eds., *Participatory Re-
    search: An Emerging Alternative Methodology in Social Science Research.*
    New Delhi: Society for Participatory Research in Asia, 1982, 179–197.
Mbilinyi, Marjorie. "My experience as Woman, Activist, and Researcher in a Project
    with Peasant Women." In Marie Mies, ed. *Fighting on Two Fronts: Women's
    Struggles and Research.* The Hague: Institute of Social Sciences, 1982a, 30–
    48.
———. "The Unity of Struggles and Research: The Case of Peasant Women in West
    Bagamoyo, Tanzania." In Marie Mies, ed. *Fighting on Two Fronts: Women's
    Struggles and Research.* The Hague: Institute of Social Sciences, 1982b, 102–
    142.
Mbilinyi, Marjorie, Ulla Vuorela, Yusuf Kassam, and Yohana Masisi. "The Politics
    of Research Methodology in the Social Sciences." Presented at the African
    Regional Workshop on Participatory Research, Mzumbe, Tanzania, 1979.
Mduma, E. K. "Appropriate Technology for Grain Storage at Bwakira Chini Vil-
    lage." In Y. Kassam and K. Mustafa, eds., *Participatory Research: An Emerg-*

ing Alternative Methodology in Social Science Research. New Delhi: Society for Participatory Research in Asia, 1982, 198–213.

Midgley, James, with Anthony Hall, Margaret Hardiman, and Dhanpaul Narine. *Community Participation, Social Development and the State.* New York: Methuen and Co., 1986.

Molano, Alfredo. "Introduction." *Critica y Politica en Ciencias Sociales: El Debate Teoria y Practica.* Bogotá, Colombia: Punta de Lanza, 1978.

The Moment. "The Native Right to Self-Government." Winter 1987 (published by the Jesuit Centre for Social Faith and Justice, Toronto).

Moser, Heinz. "Action Research as a New Research Paradigm in the Social Sciences." Presented at the Symposium on Action Research and Scientific Analysis, Cartagena, Colombia, 1977.

———. "Action Research—Experiences from a Swiss Project." Presented at the International Forum on Participatory Research, Ljubljana, Yugoslavia, 1980.

Moyers, B. "The Adventures of a Radical Hillbilly: Parts I and II." Transcript of radio broadcast of "Bill Moyers' Journal," New York: WNET, 1981.

Mustafa, Kemal. "The Jipemoyo Projects." In Y. Kassam and K. Mustafa, eds., *Participatory Research: An Emerging Alternative Methodology in Social Science Research.* New Delhi: Society for Participatory Research in Asia, 1982a, 214–229.

———. "Tanzania: Jipemoyo Project—Role of Culture in Development." In Participatory Research Network, ed., *Participatory Research: An Introduction.* New Delhi: Society for Participatory Research in Asia, 1982b, 30–33.

Nahanni, P. "The Mapping Project." In M. Watkins, ed., *Dene Nation: The Colony Within.* Toronto: University of Toronto Press, 1977, 21–27.

National Science Foundation. *Federal Funds for Research and Development.* Surveys of Science Resource Series, vol. 32, 1984, 170.

Nazko-Kluskus Study Team. *Report to Nazko and Kluskus Bands of Carrier Indians from the Nazko-Kluskus Study Team.* Nazko Village, British Columbia, 1974.

Nelkin, Dorothy. *Science as Intellectual Property: Who Controls Research?* New York: MacMillan Publishing Co., 1983.

Nelkin, Dorothy, and Michael Brown. "Knowing about Workplace Risks: Workers Speak Out about the Safety of Their Jobs." *Science for the People* 16(1) (1984).

Norman, Colin. *Knowledge and Power: The Global Research and Development Budget.* Worldwatch Paper 31. Washington, D.C.: World Watch Institute, 1979.

Nosek, P., Narita, Y., Dart, Y., and Dart, J. *A Philosophical Foundation for the Independent Living and Disability Rights Movements.* Houston, Texas: The Independent Living Research Utilization Project, 1982.

O'Brien, Rita Cruise, and G. K. Helleiner. "Political Economy of Information in a Changing International Economic Order." In R. C. O'Brien, ed., *Information, Economics, and Power: The North-South Dimension.* London: Hodder and Stoughton, 1983.

Oquist, Paul. "The Epistemology of Action Research." *Acta Sociologica* 21(2):143 (1978).

Organization for Economic Cooperation and Development. *OECD Science and*

Technology Indicators. Organization for Economic Cooperation and Development, Paris, France, 1984.

Park, Peter. "Principles for Conducting Community Based Research." Amherst: Department of Sociology, University of Massachusetts, 1978a.

——. "Social Research and Radical Change." Paper presented at the Ninth World Congress of Sociology, Uppsala, Sweden, 1978b.

——. "From Universalism to Indigenization: Toward an Emancipatory Ssociology." Paper presented at the Tenth World Congress of Sociology, Mexico City, 1982.

——. "Toward an Emancipatory Sociology." *International Sociology* 3:161–170 (1988).

Participatory Research Group. "Class Forces and Urban Native Peoples in Ontario: Working Notes." Unpublished paper, Toronto.

Polyani, Michael. *Personal Knowledge: Towards a Post-Critical Philosophy.* Chicago: University of Chicago Press, 1958.

Ponting, J. R., and R. Gibbons. *Out of Irrelevance: A Socio-Political Introduction to Indian Affairs in Canada.* Toronto: Butterworths, 1980.

Popper, Karl R. *Objective Knowledge: An Evolutionary Approach.* London: Oxford University Press, 1972.

Price, J. A. *Native Studies, American and Canadian Indians.* Toronto: Butterworths, 1978.

Rader, Melvin. *Marx's Interpretation of History.* New York: Oxford University Press, 1980.

Rahman, Muhammad Anisur. "Participatory Action Research: Theory and Practice." *Mainstream,* September 18, 1982.

——. "The Theory and Practice of Participatory Action Research." In Orlando Fals Borda, ed., *The Challenge of Social Change.* Beverly Hills, California: Sage Publications, 1985.

——. "The Theoretical Standpoint of PAR." In O. Fals Borda and M. A. Rahman, eds., *Action and Knowledge: Breaking the Monopoly with Participatory Action Research.* New York: Apex Press, 1991.

Reason, Peter, and John Rowan, eds. *Human Inquiry. A Sourcebook of New Paradigm Research.* New York: John Wiley and Sons, 1981.

Reynolds, Larry T., and Janice M. Reynolds. *The Sociology of Sociology.* New York: David McKay Co., 1970.

Rose, Hilary, and Steven Rose. "The Myth of the Neutrality of Science." In Rita Arditti, Pat Brennan, and Steve Cavrak, eds., *Science and Liberation.* Boston: South End Press, 1980.

Roth, Lorna Frances. "The Role of Communication Projects and Inuit Participation in the Formation of a Communication Policy for the North." M. A. thesis, McGill University, Montreal, 1982.

Roy, Maria. *Battered Women: A Psychosociological Study of Domestic Violence.* New York: Van Nostrand Reinhold, 1977.

Sainnawap, B., N. Winter, and P. Eprile. *Aneshenéwe Machitawin: Human Centred Community Development.* Toronto: Participatory Research Group, 1984.

Schechter, Susan. *Women and Male Violence.* Boston: South End Press, 1982.

Schiller, Herbert I. *Who Knows: Information in the Age of the Fortune 500.* Norwood, New Jersey: ABLEX Publishing Co., 1981.

Schlesinger, Tom, with John Gaventa and Juliet Merrifield. *Our Own Worst Enemy: The Impact of Military Spending on the Upper South.* New Market, Tennessee: Highlander Center, 1983.

Schroyer, Trent. *The Critique of Domination.* Boston: Beacon Press, 1973.

Science. "The 'Lost' Mercury at Oak Ridge." Vol. 21, July 8, 1983.

Sieciechowicz, K. "The People and the Land Are One." *CASNP Bulletin* 18(2):16–20 (1977).

Singh, M. "Literacy to Development: The Growth of a Tribal Village." In W. Fernandes and R. Tandon, eds., *Participatory Research and Evaluation: Experiments in Research as a Process of Liberation.* New Delhi: Indian Social Institute, 1981, 162–171.

Smith, Anthony. *The Geopolitics of Information: How Western Culture Dominates the World.* London: Faber and Faber, 1980.

Smith, David N. *Who Rules the University: An Essay in Class Analysis.* New York: Monthly Review Press, 1974.

Smith, Dorothy. "A Sociology of Women." In J. Sherman and E. Bock, eds., *The Prism of Sex: Essays in the Sociology of Knowledge.* Madison: University of Wisconsin Press, 1979.

———. *The Everyday World as Problematic: A Feminist Sociology.* Boston: Northeastern University Press, 1987.

Society for Participatory Research in Asia. *Participatory Research: An Introduction.* Participatory Research Network Series No. 3. Toronto: International Council for Adult Education, 1982.

Society for Promotion of Area Resource Centers. *SPARK Annual Report, 1987.* Bombay: 1988.

Southern Exposure. "Who Owns Appalachia?" 10(1):32–52 (January/February, 1982).

Stavenhagen, Rodolfo. "Decolonializing Applied Social Sciences." *Human Organization* 30(4) (Winter 1971).

Swantz, Marja-Liisa. "Some Notes for the Participatory Research Approach." Paper distributed at PR seminar in Lempolampi, Finland, August 9–11, 1981.

———. "Research as Education for Development: A Tanzanian case." In B. Hall, A. Gillette, and R. Tandon, eds. *Creating Knowledge: A Monopoly.* New Delhi: Society for Participatory Research in Asia, 1982, 113–126.

Swantz, Marja-Liisa, and Arja Vainio-Mattila. "Participatory Inquiry as an Instrument of Grass-Roots Development." In Peter Reason, ed., *Human Inquiry in Action: Development in New Paradigm Research.* Beverly Hills, California: Sage Publications, 1988.

Tandon, Rajesh. "Participatory Research and Participatory Social Action." Presented at the International Forum on Participatory Research, Ljubljana, Yugoslavia, 1980.

———. "Dialogue as Inquiry and Intervention." In P. Reason and J. Rowan, eds., *Human Inquiry: A Sourcebook of New Paradigm Research.* Chichester, England: John Wiley and Sons, 1981a, 293–301.

———. "Participatory research in the Empowerment of People." *Convergence* 14(3):20–27 (1981b).

———. *Our Own Health; The Role of Adult Education in Community Involvement in Primary Health Care*. New Delhi: International Council for Adult Education, 1984.

———. "Conceptual Issues in Participatory Research." Lecture. Center for International Education, University of Massachusetts, Amherst, 1985.

———. "Social Transformation and Participatory Research." *Convergence* 21(2–3):5–18 (1988).

Tandon, Rajesh, and Walter Fernandes. *Participatory Evaluation: Theory and Practice*. New Delhi: Indian Institute for Social Research, 1984.

Taylor, Charles. "Interpretation and the Sciences of Man." In Paul Rabinow and M. Sullivan, eds., *Interpretive Social Science: A Reader*. Berkeley: University of California Press, 1987.

Television Northern Canada. "A Proposal for a Shared Television Distribution Service in Northern Canada." Unpublished manuscript, June 1987.

Theilheimer, I. "Native and Northern CED: Rethinking Individualism and Competition." *Transition*, June 1990, 8–9.

Thompson, E. P. *The Making of the English Working Class*. New York: Vintage Books, 1966.

Tobias, K. J. "An Exploration of the Political Economy of Native Women in Canada." Unpublished paper, Ontario Institute for Studies in Education, Toronto, 1980.

———. "Problems of Urban Native People: Producing A Collage." Unpublished paper, Ontario Institute for Studies in Education, Toronto, 1981.

———, ed. *Participatory Research: An Introduction*. Participatory Research Network Series No. 3. New Delhi: Society for Participatory Research in Asia, 1982.

Usher, P. "Indigenous Management Systems and the Conservation of Wildlife in the Canadian North." *Alternatives* 14 (1): 3–9 (1987).

Utopia Project Team. "On Training, Technology, and Products Viewed from the Quality of the Work Perspective." Pamphlet, Arbetslivscentrum, Stockholm, Sweden, n.d.

Vachon, R. "Political Self-Determination and Traditional Native Indian Political Culture." *Monchanin* 64: 39–55 (1979).

Vio Grossi, Francisco. "The Socio-political Implications of Participatory Research." Presented at the International Forum on Participatory Research, Ljubljana, Yugoslavia, 1980.

———. "Chile: Peasant Technology for Self-Defense." In Participatory Research Network, *Participatory Research: An Introduction*. New Delhi: Society for Participatory Research in Asia, 1982a, 33–35.

———. "Peasant Participation, Adult Education and Agrarian Reform in Chile." In B. Hall, A. Gillette, and R. Tandon, eds., *Creating Knowledge: A Monopoly. Participatory Research in Development*. New Delhi: Society for Participatory Research in Asia, 1982b, 153–174.

Vio Grossi, Francisco, Sergio Martinic, and Gonzalo Tapia. *Participatory Research: Theoretical Frameworks, Methods and Techniques*. Toronto: International Council for Adult Education, 1983.

Wainwright, Hilary, and Dave Elliott. *The Lucas Plan: A New Trade Unionism in the Making?* London: Allison and Busby, 1982.

Waldram, James. "Traditional Knowledge Systems: The Recognition of Indigenous

History and Science." *Saskatchewan Indian Federated College Journal* 2 (2): 115–124 (1986).

Warren, Roland L. *The Community in America*. Second edition. Chicago: Rand McNally and Co., 1972.

Weaver, S. *Making Canadian Indian Policy*. Toronto: University of Toronto Press, 1981.

Western North Carolina Alliance. *Over a Million Acres: Mineral Development Prospects in Western North Carolina*. Murphy, North Carolina: Western North Carolina Alliance, Fall 1984.

Winch, Peter. *The Idea of Social Science and Its Relation to Philosophy*. London: Routledge and Kegan Paul, 1958.

Wismer, S., and D. Pell. *Community Profit: Community-Based Economic Development in Canada*. Toronto: Is-Five Press, 1981.

Wright, E. O. *Class, Crisis and the State*. London: Verso Editions, 1979.

Zwerdling, D. *Workplace Democracy*. New York: Harper and Row, 1980.

Index

Aboriginal movement: capitalist ideology and, 59; class representation and, 55–57; complexity of, 48; current obstacles to, 63–64; current trends of, 60–61; economic research and, 50; economic strategies and, 54; fragmentation of, 48, 54; future of, 63–64; government dependence by, 63; government resistance to, 51–52, 53, 54, 61; health case and, 52–53; land use research and, 49–51; leadership of, 55–56; macrostructural change and, 146; methodological achievements of, 50–51, 53; 1980s characteristics of, 61–63; political achievements of, 51–52, 53; political culture of, 49; research control and, 55; research differences and, 50; sanitation case and, 52; social research and, 50, 52–53; state control and, 48; strategic shortcomings of, 54–55; sub-movements of, 48; violence and, 61; women and, 59, 63; working class and, 57–60. *See also* Inuit Broadcasting Corporation

Adorno, Theodor W., 106

Africa, 25

African Regional Workshop, 104

Alaska, 55

Alinsky, Saul, 130

American Association of University Women, 159

American Psychological Association, 141

American Sociological Association, 26, 141

Anderson County, Tennessee, 95

Antonio, Robert J., 105

Appalachian Alliance, 87, 91, 93, 96, 97, 98, 99

Appalachian Land Ownership Study: broad form deed and, 91, 92; control of information and, 89; failed attempt and, 96–97; findings of, 88; forest mineral development and, 93–94; foundation of, 85–86; goals of, 87–88, 89; Kentucky Fair Tax Coalition and, 90–93; legislative battles and, 91–92; mineral tax and, 90–91, 92; popular knowledge and, 39, 40, 86–87; property tax issues and, 95–96; publicity of findings and, 89–90; as research model, 97–99; Save Our Cumberland Mountains and, 85–96; stimulus for, 87; strip-mining and,

87; success of, 88–89, 101; Virginia
and, 96–97; Western North Carolina
Alliance and, 93–94; women's issue
and, 99–100
Appalachian Land Ownership Task
Force, 87–88
Appalachian Observer, 69
Appalachian Ohio Public Interest Cam-
paign (AOPIC), 98
Appalachian Regional Commission, 87,
89
Architectural Barriers Codes, 134
Asia, 25
Athens, Ohio, 98
atomic bomb production, 69–70

Barndt, Deborah, 109–10
Battered Families' Services (BFS), 159,
160–61, 164–65, 170, 171–72, 173,
174
Bell, Daniel, 23, 26, 27, 29
benzene, 75
Berea, Kentucky, 90
Big Trout Lake Band Council, 52
Bonneville Dam, 120
Brazil, 8, 43
Britain, 24–25, 38, 81
British Columbia, 50
Brown, David L., 60
Bryceson, Deborah, 105, 110, 111
Buchanan County, Virginia, 96
Bumpass Cove, Tennessee, 67–69, 79–
80
Bumpass Cove Environmental Control
and Mineral Company, 67
Bush administration, 36

Cain, Bonnie J., 110
Calgary, University of, 62
Campbell County, Tennessee, 95
Canada, 8, 145–46. *See also* Aborigi-
nal movement
Canada Lands Act, 51, 52
Canadian Broadcasting Corporation
(CBC), 147, 148, 149, 152
Canadian Journal of Native Studies, 62
Canadian Radio and Television Com-
mission (CRTC), 148, 151, 152, 153

cancer, 66, 75
capitalism, 17, 19, 56, 66
Cartagena Conference, 104
Cascade Mountain Range, 113
Chambers, Robert, 37
Charleston Gazette, 89
Cherokee Lake, 72, 74
Chicago Resource Center, 160
chromium, 77
Citizens' Education and Water Moni-
toring Project, 92
Clement, David, 81
Clinch River, 70
Colorado, Pam, 62
Columbia Gorge, 113, 120
Columbia River, 112, 113
Coming of Postindustrial Society, The,
23
Commission on Religion in Appalachia
(CORA), 97
Committee for Original Peoples' Enti-
tlement, 51
Committees on Occupational Safety
and Health (COSH), 82, 83
Communications Workers of America
(CWA), 82, 83
Community Accessibility Committee,
129–30, 133;
Community Accessibility Project, 126;
Community Accessibility Committee
and, 129–30, 133; conference plan
and, 127–28, 129; effectiveness of,
135–37; initial research and, 128–
29; objectives of, 127, 133–35; re-
searcher role and, 138–40; shopping
mall and, 129, 130–32
Conchelos, Greg, 108, 109, 110
Conference on Navajo Women, 169
conscientization, 8
Corp of Engineers, U.S. Army, 112,
113–14, 116, 117, 119, 120, 121
Council for Yukon Indians (CYI), 51,
52, 54
Council of Navajo Women, 160
Council of Southern Mountains, 89, 93
Couto, Dick, 78–79
critical theory, 4, 105–6, 107, 124,
141, 142
Cumberland River, 77

Daniels, D., 57–58
Darcy de Oliveira, Rosisca, 34, 111
Darcy de Oliveira, Miguel, 34, 111
de Vries, Jan, 110, 111, 122
Dene Indians, 50–51, 57–58
Denmark, 39
Department of Indian Affairs and
  Northern Development (DIAND),
  48, 52, 60
Department of Native Studies, 62
Developmental Disabilities Law Center,
  131
dialectical materialism, 104, 105–7
Dickson, Pollard, 118, 119–20, 121–
  22
disabled persons, 125, 126, 136. *See
  also* Community Accessibility Project

East Tennessee Research Corporation,
  75
Environmental Protection Agency
  (EPA), 72, 78
Environmental Protection Bureau, 70
epidemiology, 73, 76, 78–79
Evans, Daniel, 117
Evergreen State College, 114, 120

Fals Borda, Orlando, 29, 37, 107, 108
Federal Relocation Act, 113
Fern Lake, 76
Food and Drug Administration, 70
Former Battered Women's Support
  Group Project: accomplishments of,
  173–74; assessment of, 172–74; Battered Families' Services and, 164–65,
  170, 171–72, 173, 174; dissolution
  of, 172; goals of, 165; group action
  and, 169, 170–72; group discussions
  and, 168–70; group formation and,
  167–68; initial dialogue and, 165–
  67; knowledge production and, 173,
  174; participatory research and,
  157–58, 173–74
Fox, Russell, 114
Freedom of Information Act (FOIA),
  35–36
Freire, Paulo, 8, 43, 109, 142

Gallup, New Mexico, 157, 158–59.
  See also Former Battered Women's
  Support Group Project
Gaventa, John, 137, 141
General Motors, 26
Gough, Steven, 70–71
Gough, Larry, 70
Gramsci, Antonio, 38
Gramscian tradition, 37
Greenville, Tennessee, 67
guerrilla research, 36, 81

Habermas, Jurgen, 4, 17, 29, 141
Hall, Budd, 42, 103, 107, 135
Harper, Elijah, 61
Harvard University, 42, 43
health activism in United States: communications workers and, 82–83;
  empowerment and, 80–81, 82; experiential knowledge and, 68–69;
  guerrilla research and, 81; increase
  of, 65–66; labor education and, 81–
  82; mercury contamination case and,
  69–71; reasons for, 65–66; scientist-
  layperson cooperation and, 82–83;
  strip-mining case and, 75–76; toxic
  landfill case and, 67–69, 79–81; Yellow Creek pollution and, 76–79
Highlander Center, 36, 66, 79, 80, 81,
  99, 100
Holston River, 72, 74
Horkheimer, Max, 106
Horton, Billy D., 137, 141, 142
Horton, Miles, 142
House Appropriations and Revenue
  Committee, 91, 92

immanent critique, 105–6, 108, 110,
  120, 124
Independent Living Center(s), 126,
  127, 129, 132, 135
Independent Living Movement, 125–26
India, 8, 142
information society. *See* knowledge so-
  ciety
Institute for Community Living, 99
Institute for Southern Studies, 97–98

International Forum on Participatory
Research, 104
Inuit Broadcasting Corporation (IBC):
accomplishments of, 149; acculturating influences and, 146–47; funding
and, 150; internal community conditions and, 150; internal-external relationships and, 152–54; Inuit
Taparisat and, 147–48; socio-political context and, 150–52
Inuit Indians, 50
Inuit Taparisat of Canada (ITC), 51,
147–48
Inukshuk Project, 148
Inuktitut language, 146, 147, 148

Jackson, Ted, 108, 109, 110
Jackson, Henry, 117
James Bay and Northern Quebec
Agreement, 55
Jonesboro, Tennessee, 67

Kayahna Area Trappers Association,
63
Kayahna Tribal Area, 63
Kentucky Fair Tax Coalition (KFTC),
90–93, 98
Kentucky Revenue Cabinet, 92
Kerr, Mary Jane, 125
Kingsport, Tennessee, 71–73
Kingsport Study Group, 71
Kirby, Rich, 86
knowledge: academic versus experiential, 21–22; action and, 8; as commodity, 41; consumption of, 23–24,
25; critical, 4, 6–8, 16, 108, 111;
dialogue and, 12, 15; experiential,
21–22, 30, 36, 38–39, 67; historical
context of, 41–43; instrumental, 4–
6, 16, 106, 141; interactive, 4, 6,
16; monopolization of, 7; natural
sciences and, 4, 5, 16; objectivity
and, 16; official (scientific), 21, 29–
30, 36, 40; power and, 81, 120–21,
163; practice and, 15; public, commodification of, 24; reappropriation
of, 35–37; social sciences and, 5–6;
technical, 4; transmission of , 24–

25; universities and, 42. *See also*
popular knowledge; traditional research
knowledge production: battered wom-
en's project and, 173, 174; collective, 109; dialectical materialism
and, 107; industry of, 25; participatory research and, 3–4, 33, 34, 106,
141–42; popular control of, 39–40;
popular knowledge and, 108; power
and, 26–27; reform of, 31; scientists
and, 103; social action as, 142;
sources of, 25–27; university sponsored participatory research and, 46
knowledge society: computers and, 24;
corporate message-making and, 24–
25; democracy in, 39–40; elite and,
27–29; freedom of information and,
25; growth of, 22–23; ideology of,
29–30; imperfections in, 24–25; media control and, 24; reform of, 31–
34 (*see also* participatory research);
research and development and, 25–
27; universities and, 26, 27
Koppers Company, 95
Kuptana, Rosemarie, 147

Latin America, 25
Louisville Courier-Journal, 89
Love Canal, 38, 68, 69, 82
Lowe, Lewis, 75
Loxley, John, 56, 58
Lucas Aerospace workers, 38, 40

Machlup, Fritz, 22–23
Mackenzie Valley pipeline, 51
Magnuson, Warren, 117
Manitoba, 56, 58
Martin County, Kentucky, 90
Marx, Karl, 105
Marxism, 124
Massachusetts Architectural Barriers
Board, 130, 131, 132, 133, 135
Massachusetts. *See* Community Acces-
sibility Project
McKinley County, New Mexico, 158
Mduma, E. K., 109
mercury, 69–71, 72, 75

Middlesboro, Kentucky, 76–77
Middlesboro Tanning Company, 77
Minimata, Japan, 70
mining, 21–22, 75–76, 87
Mohawks, 61
Mondragon network, 60
Moser, Heinz, 111
Mountain Life and Work, 89, 93
multiculturalism, 145
Mustafa, Kemal, 105, 110, 111

Nader, Ralph, 35
Nahanni, P., 50, 51
Nashville Tennessean, 89
National Energy Program of Canada,
    51, 52
National Film Board, 148
Native Canadian Center, 53
natural sciences, 4, 5, 16
Navajo Nation, 157, 159, 160
Navajo Tribal Council, 160
Nazko-Kluskus, 51
Netherlands, 82
Nicaragua, 8
Nicholaus, Martin, 26–27
Nishnawbe-Aski, 51
Nolichucky River, 67, 68
Non-Status Indian Association, 59
Norfolk and Western Railroad, 90
North Bonneville case: city's character-
    istics and, 112–13; construction tax
    and, 119; effectiveness of participa-
    tory research and, 122–23; empow-
    erment and, 118–19; Evergreen team
    and, 114–17, 118, 122–23; ideology
    versus social reality and, 120–21;
    immanent critique and, 120; instru-
    mental knowledge and, 121–22; les-
    sons from, 123–24; objective(s) and,
    113, 114–15, 116; obstacles and,
    113–14; Phase I document of, 117–
    18; popular knowledge and, 116–17,
    118, 122–23; relocated town and,
    119; strategy and, 115
North Bonneville Life Effort (NOBLE),
    113, 120
North Carolina, 86, 97–98
North Carolina Committee on Occu-

pational Safety and Health
    (NCCOSH), 82
Northwest Territories, 50, 51
nuclear weapons, 69

Oak Ridge, Tennessee, 69–71, 73
Oak Ridge National Laboratories
    (ORNL), 70–71
Oak Ridge Operations, 69
Occupational Safety and Health Act,
    81
Office of Navajo Women, 160, 169
Ohio, 86, 97, 98
Old Crow community, 62
Olympia Washington, 114
Ontario, 50, 58
Ontario Metis, 59
Ontario Public Service Employees'
    Union (OPSEU), 59

Paigen, Beverly, 82
participatory research: battered wom-
    en's project and, 157–58, 173–74;
    characteristics of, 103; collective ac-
    tion via, 109; critical theory and,
    105–6, 107, 120, 124, 141, 142; di-
    alectical materialism and, 105–7;
    dissertation advice and, 175–76; ed-
    ucation via, 109; empowerment and,
    1, 2, 4, 11, 36–37, 38, 103, 111–12;
    environment for, 34–35; epidemiol-
    ogical studies and, 78–79; examples
    of utilization of, 8, 47; feminist
    movement and, 6; goals of, 2–3, 11,
    112; historical context of, 41–42;
    ideological power bases and, 109;
    increase of, 43, 103–4, 140–41; in-
    dividual contributions and, 45; in-
    dustrialized culture and, 18–19;
    knowledge production and, 3–4, 33,
    34, 39, 106, 141–42; male biases in,
    162–64; objectivity and, 15–17; pe-
    dagogic theory and, 3; popular
    knowledge and, 17–19, 37–39, 107–
    8; pragmatism and, 104–5, 107;
    reappropriation of knowledge and,
    35–37; researcher professionalization
    and, 46; researcher role and, 110–

11, 126, 127, 142–43, 161–62; research process and, 8–15; scientist-
layperson cooperation and, 83–84;
social macrostructure and, 145; social transformation and, 2, 19; sub-
ject-object relationship and, 34;
technical knowledge and, 4; term of,
creation of, 44; universities and, 43–
46; validity of, 16–17, 44–45, 111–
12. *See also* Appalachian Land
Ownership Study; Community Accessibility Project; health activism in
United States; North Bonneville case
Pennsylvania, 97
Philippines, 8
Pocahontas, Kentucky, 90
Pond Inlet, 148
Poplar Creek, 70, 71
popular knowledge: critical knowledge
and, 108; ideology and, 107; intellectual support for, 37; knowledge
production and, 108; North Bonneville case and, 116–17, 118, 122–23;
participatory research and, 83, 107–
8; recovery of, 17–19; validity of,
37–38, 76, 78, 81
positivism, 16, 29, 141
power: Aboriginal groups and, 48; to
define, 109; ideology of knowledge
society and, 30; industrial society
and, 27–28; knowledge and, 41, 81,
120–21, 163; knowledge elite and,
27–29; knowledge production and,
26–27; knowledge society and, 28;
official knowledge and, 21–22, 43;
participatory research and, 106, 109,
111–12; popular knowledge and,
37; pragmatic approach and, 107;
redistribution of, 176; science and,
66–67, 69, 71, 74–75, 81, 126; social evolution and, 23, 25; women
and, 99
Pyramid Company, 131, 132

Quebec, 61

Rahman, Muhammad Anisur, 31
Rayburn County, Georgia, 98

Reagan administration, 36, 72
Red Cross, 68
Rivers, Harbors, and Flood Control
Act, 119
Rocky Flats, Colorado, 38
Royal Commission on Aboriginal Peo-
ples, 60, 63
*Rural Development: Putting the Last
First*, 37

Saltville, Virginia, 72
Save Our Cumberland Mountains
(SOCM), 73, 95–96, 98
Scandinavia, 82
Scarbro, Tennessee, 69, 71
Schiller, Herb, 24
science/scientists: capitalism and, 66;
cooperation with laypersons by, 82–
84; experiential knowledge and, 67,
68–69; faith in, 29; "fake," 74, 81;
fallibility of, 36–37; Kingsport
chemical plant and, 72; knowledge
production and, 103; medical, 73;
mercury contamination case and, 69,
70–71; "new," 76; objectivity and,
29–30, 66, 73–74, 75–76; popular
knowledge and, 37; power and, 66–
67, 69, 71, 74–75, 81, 126
scientific research. *See* traditional research
Scott County, Virginia, 71
Settlement Act, 55
Skala, Ernie, 114, 119
Social, Economic, and Political Issues
Tax Force (SEPI), 97
social sciences, 5–6, 7, 137
Social Sciences and Humanities Re-
search Council of Canada, 61
South Carolina, 99
Southeastern Women's Employment
Coalition (SWEC), 99–100
Southern Appalachian Leadership
Training (SALT), 99
Spain, 60
Steinem, Gloria, 160
Storey, Hobart, 68
Supreme Judicial Court of the Com-
monwealth of Massachusetts, 132
Sweden, 39

Tandon, Rajesh, 60, 109, 142
Television Northern Canada, 149
Tennessee, 86, 95
Tennessee Department of Public
    Health, 67, 68, 72
Tennessee State Board of Equalization,
    95
Tennessee State Department of Public
    Health, 79
Tennessee State Tax Equalization
    Board, 95
Tennessee Valley Authority, 72
theory of communicative action, 17
Third World, 2, 18, 24, 35, 44, 141,
    145
Threshold Limit Value (TLV), 74–75,
    81
Tobias, K. J., 59
Toronto, Ontario, 53
Trades Union Congress (TUC), 81
traditional research: attachment to,
    140; critique of, 141; instrumental
    knowledge and, 14; language of, 73,
    80; popular knowledge and, 3–4;
    power and, 126; public access to,
    73–74, 76; study selection and, 69,
    71, 72–73; experimental control
    and, 138
Trent University, 62, 63
Tug Fork River, 87
Typographical Workers' Union, 39

Union of Ontario Indians, 52
United States, 8, 22, 24, 25–26, 35,
    159–60. See also Community Acces-
    sibility Project; Former Battered
    Women's Support Group Project;
    health activism in United States;
    North Bonneville case; names of spe-
    cific U.S. cities, towns, etc.
U.S. Attorney General's Task Force on
    Family Violence, 159
U.S. Geological Survey (USGS), 70

universities, 26, 27, 42, 43–46
University of Calgary, 62
University of New Mexico, 159
University of Washington, 113
Utopia Project, 39, 82

Vachon, R., 49
Vanderbilt University, 77, 78
Vigoda, Al, 108, 110
vinyl chloride, 75
Vio Grossi, Francisco, 105, 111
Virginia, 86, 96–97
Virginia Land Alliance, 96–97
Virginia Task Force, 97

War on Poverty program, 86
Washington County, Virginia, 96, 98
Washington state. See North Bonne-
    ville case
Washington state legislature, 119
Western North Carolina Alliance
    (WNCA), 93–94
West Virginia, 86, 99
Who Knows: Information in the Age
    of the Fortune 500, 24
Williamson, West Virginia, 87
Wing, Jerry, 70
Wise County, Virginia, 96
women, 78, 99, 159–60, 162–64. See
    also Former Battered Women's Sup-
    port Group Project
women's movement, 6
Women's Network, 99
World Watch Institute, 25
Wright, E. O., 56

Yellow Creek, Kentucky, 76–79
Yellow Creek Concerned Citizens
    (YCCC), 77, 78
Yukon, 51, 62
Yukon Indian People, 54

Zuni Pueblo Natives, 157, 159
Zwerdling, D., 60

About the Editors and Contributors

MARY BRYDON-MILLER is an associate professor of psychology at New England College in Henniker, New Hampshire. Her community-organizing experience includes working with physically disabled individuals in the Community Accessibility Project. She also was a founding member and convener of the Pioneer Valley Gray Panthers. Her current research is in the psychology of immigration and in the effects of various social models of assimilation on the immigrant experience.

MARLENE BRANT CASTELLANO, a member of the Mohawk Nation, Bay of Quinte Band, is a professor in the Department of Native Studies at Trent University, Peterborough, Ontario, where she served three terms as chair of the department, and associate professor in the Faculty of Education, Queen's University. Her teaching and research interests center around social development, participatory research methods, and contemporary applications of traditional knowledge. In 1992 she was granted leave from Trent University to assume the position of co-director of research for the Royal Commission on Aboriginal Peoples, an inquiry mandated by the government of Canada to develop recommendations to facilitate a new relationship between Aboriginal peoples and Canadian society.

DONALD E. COMSTOCK is currently a visiting member of the faculty of the Evergreen State College in Olympia, Washington, and a principal of the Phoenix Group, Inc., a community development firm in Seattle. Over the past decade, he has worked in community-based development in rural and urban areas founding and directing several housing and economic development organizations. He has recently helped with a participatory research project into bank lending practices in South Seattle neighborhoods.

RUSSELL FOX is a member of the faculty at the Evergreen State College in Olympia, Washington, where he teaches community development and environmental studies in a liberal arts curriculum. Currently he is involved in local participatory research projects addressing community ownership of neighborhood shops and affordable housing units. He is helping establish community-determined college programs in Native American communities, and he is part of an international network of participatory development activists and researchers in South Asia and North America.

JOHN GAVENTA is director of the Highlander Research and Education Center in New Market, Tennessee, and associate professor of sociology at the University of Tennessee. He has conducted participatory research projects in Appalachia and the South for more than a decade.

BUDD HALL teaches participatory research and adult education at the Ontario Institute for Studies in Education. He is the former secretary-general of the International Participatory Research Network. His ideas on participatory research were developed first during his years as head of the Research Department of the Institute of Adult Education in Tanzania. His work over the years has dealt with how the ideas of those experiencing oppression can legitimate their knowledge and make it accessible to others in similar situations.

THOMAS W. HEANEY is the cofounder and executive director of the Lindeman Center. Education, as conceived by the Center, supports local community goals for social, political, and economic change—with projects ranging from the struggles of residents of public housing to attain control over their homes to the efforts of low-income and minority groups to create alternatives to joblessness and poverty. Heaney has authored numerous articles and monographs both providing case studies of the Center's activities and also reflecting on the underlying theory and principles of popular education and participatory research. The Center, founded in 1984, is affiliated with Northern Illinois University, where Heaney is adjunct professor in the Department of Leadership and Educational Policy Studies.

BILLY D. HORTON spent six years teaching at Drew University and Davis and Elkins College before joining the Appalachian Land Ownership Study as researcher and co-coordinator (with John Gaventa). Upon its completion he spent two years as coordinator of the Appalachian Alliance, spending much of his time encouraging follow-up to the land study. In 1984, he became director of the Highlander Economics Education Project. He returned to teaching at Franklin Pierce College in New Hampshire in 1986.

TED JACKSON is adjunct research professor in the School of Public Administration at Carleton University in Ottawa, Canada, where he teaches development administration. A former staff member of the Participatory Research Group and the International Council for Adult Education in Toronto, he has taught participatory research and community economic development at Trent and Carleton universities and has served as an advisor to the Assembly of First Nations, the Canadian International Development Agency, the Canadian Labour Congress, the Dene Nation, and the Economic Council of Canada.

PATRICIA MAGUIRE is an educator and feminist activist. She is visiting assistant professor of education at Western New Mexico University, Gallup Graduate Studies Center. She is also on the board of the New Mexico Coalition of Sexual Assault Programs and works at the community level against violence toward women and children. Her participatory research work was awarded the 1986 National Women's Studies Association-Pergamon Press Feminist Research Award.

JULIET MERRIFIELD is currently director of the Center for Literacy Studies, an interdisciplinary research center at the University of Tennessee, Knoxville. Previously, she worked for ten years with the Highlander Research and Education Center, New Market, Tennessee, as codirector of research. At Highlander she was involved in participatory research with communities and workers facing occupational and environmental health problems.

PETER PARK is a professor of sociology at the University of Massachusetts, Amherst. He is the board president of the Center for Community Education and Action, an organization devoted to participatory research. He also is on the faculty of the Fielding Institute.